Dear, Molly and T,

Stay Connected + free

Lots of love,

Peter x

Our Story Called Life

A Personal Revolution

Peter Abrams

Peter Abrams has asserted his right under the Copyright, Designs and Patents Act 1988 to be identified as the author of this work.

The thoughts and opinions expressed here are those of the author alone and do not necessarily reflect the views of Lulu Publishers, its parents, subsidiaries or affiliates. The products, information, and other content provided by this seller are provided for informational purposes only.

Every effort has been made to contact any appropriate copyright holders. The publishers will be glad to correct any errors or omissions in future editions.

This book is a work of non-fiction based on life, experiences and recollections of the author. In some limited cases names of people, places, dates, sequences or the detail of events have been changed (solely) to protect the privacy of others. The author has stated to the publishers that, except in in such minor respects not affecting the substantial accuracy of the work, the contents are true and original, to the best of the author's knowledge.

This book is sold subject to the conditions that it shall not, by way of trade or otherwise, be lent, resold, hired out or otherwise circulated without the publisher's prior consent in any form of binding or cover other than that in which it is published and without a similar condition, including this condition, being imposed on the subsequent purchaser.

All rights reserved. No parts of this publication may be reproduced, stored in a retrieval system, or transmitted, in any form or by any means, electronic, mechanical, photocopying, recording or otherwise, without prior permission from the publishers.

© Peter Abrams – 2017

© Our Story Called Life – 2017

Yep, it's going to get controversial

Connect with me

Website: ourstorycalledlife.com

Email: Peterabramsofficial@gmail.com

Ourstorycalledlife@gmail.com

Facebook: Peter Abrams

Instagram: Peter.abrams

Snapchat: Peterabrams7

Twitter: Peter.Abrams

Youtube: Peter Abrams

Connect with me on any and all of these crazy social media platforms to get the latest news and updates on all events and projects I'm working on!

To the conscious spark of awesomeness within you

Acknowledgements

I suppose I should acknowledge some of the people without whom this book, or perhaps even myself as the transformed and content individual I am, could not be here today, I mean if I had tried to do this whole writing a book thing on my own, I would've fallen into the pit of mental insanity and be living in cloud cuckoo land permanently.

So, Russell Brand and Brett Moran, I thought I'd do you two together, the yin and yang of my spiritual enlightenment… or mental illness; I think having you two as my mentors is both equally delightful and dangerous! I appreciate your inspiration, belief and guidance and treasure your friendship, love and equally-terrible humour. Thank you for teaching me how to use my addictive nature, narcissistic tendencies and sarcastic tones as a force of good, seeing you both in the peaceful, tranquil space you now exist within reminds me every day to embody the first lesson you taught me; 'to embrace life', unconditional love to both of you.

Catherine, thank you for being the brightest light with the biggest smile and longest laugh, thank-you for teaching me unconditional love and how to survive as a spaced-out kid in a corporate world. The laughter, love and umbrella moments are forever, never stop smiling.

Charlie, thank you for blowing my reality apart, for scaring me on a daily basis and reminding me that there is always something new to discover, keep holding the beauty of the universe within your eyes.

Thank you, Shannon, for putting up with me for the whole of our lives, for being a beautiful, kind and an amazing mother to Elsie and most of all for being my best friend and always believing in me, you've restored my faith in humans countless times.

Auntie Gill, Margie, Nan and Oma thank you for the conversations, the Christmas memories and for teaching me that being a group of one is a privilege, not a curse.

Shaun Attwood and Selina, thank you for explaining to me how the process of publishing a book actually works. Without your guidance and support I would've given up before I'd even started if I'd discovered that words don't just appear on the page!

David Bowie, the Mozart of our time, you clearly don't need recognition, but thank you for teaching me to stay with the mad-men, instead of suffer with the sad-men roaming free.

Ian Hunter, for your words of wisdom, your lyrics of genius and for the song 'something to believe in', practically this book summarised into a more poetic form.

Tim, cheers for pulling me out of the gutter and into my own story, for embodying compassion and inspiring the start of my journey.

To all the guys at the Trew Era Café, thank you for providing a safe-haven in a crazy world, where creativity, freedom and love shines through… and for the amazing smoothies.

Thank you all the people that inspired and influenced my journey; positive and negative, in each and every way; forming this amazing life I now live in some way, there's too many of you to list... watch out for the sequel.

Thank you to all the people who didn't laugh when sixteen-year-old me decided to publish this book, all of you who gave me belief, I hope this does you proud.

Dave, thank you for constantly reminding me that life is one big party, for the laughter, arguments and love that is encompassed through brotherhood, thank you for being the best little brother that a big brother could ask for and for being my best friend.

Mum and Dad, well done for providing the genetic material required for my existence, also thanks for guiding me and teaching me life's true values, showing me love, guidance and expression... and for introducing me to Bowie, probably your crowning achievement.

Dad, for teaching me leadership, compassion and that there is always more to give, that tolerance is our greatest gift and that we all have a gift to give... also for showing me London is White and Blue.

Mum, for showing me unconditional love and support, for listening to my mad ramblings and believing in me beyond all doubt, also this book was published on your birthday and so is dedicated to you, so that's nice.

Finally to you, the reader... This path of personal revolution is a hero's journey which can at times be a lonely and treacherous one and takes both bravery and will-power to undertake. Know that I am with you; as are all the weird, freaky, kooks that decided to question the world around them, instead of settling for what they were given. Please know that your unique, funky quirks are your superpowers and that you are going to be *okay*... you are *NEVER* alone, we are all connected and no matter what; love will always win... thank you.

Contents

Prologue (1)

Chapter 1: The Revolution **(12)**

Chapter 2: The Author (that's me) **(19)**

Chapter 3: The Author II (that's you) **(40)**

Chapter 4: The History **(50)**

Chapter 5: The Illusion of choice **(71)**

Chapter 6: The Profit in Politics **(85)**

Chapter 7: The Click Illusion **(91)**

Chapter 8: The Wealthy **(111)**

Chapter 9: The 'Wholey' lie **(133)**

Chapter 10: The Brain **(146)**

Chapter 11: The Spiritually Scientific Conundrum **(158)**

Chapter 12: The Way Out **(182)**

Chapter 13: The Mind **(194)**

Chapter 14: The Dream **(214)**

Chapter 15: The Moment **(223)**

Chapter 16: The Miracle **(244)**

Chapter 17: The Under-lying Connectedness of a Connected Consciousness **(249)**

Chapter 18: The Revolution II **(278)**

Chapter 19: The Fantastic Voyage **(290)**

Chapter 20: Our Story Called Life **(297)**

Final Words: (312)

Foreword

Quite Simply; One Life. One Love. Live.

DON'T PANIC

We're going to be alright.

The Prologue

- Right now, 85 people have more wealth than *half* the world.

  85   These have more.

  3,500,000,000.   These have less.

  All Poverty, all over the world, could be solved by one of these 85 giving up HALF of their wealth. That's equivalent to giving 10p from £20 to end all suffering on earth... And it hasn't happened.

- A cleaner at a bank involved in the 2008 crash could work 6am-6pm at £7 an hour, every day from the day the American Revolution happened until right now... To make what the CEO of that bank makes in one year (The CEO's wage has risen 325% since that crash that screwed over everyone else).

- The number of slaves currently, today, is greater than in all the rest of recorded human history combined. (5.5 million of these are children).

  Slaves are also cheaper today than they have ever been. In 1860, a slave would cost up to $19,000 in today's money. Today a slave can be bought in some places for as little as $90 (that's if they're bought at all, thousands of people are simply kidnapped).

- 22,000 children die every day because they live in poverty. That's a life every four seconds, since you started reading this book...

45 children have just died.

- In 46 years, we've used up half of the worlds natural resources and will run out by 2050.
- Of the past 3,400 years, humans have been entirely at peace for 268 of them, or just 8 percent of recorded history, we are *currently* in the longest sustained period of peace ever, but is the world really at peace?
- At least 108 million people were killed in wars in the twentieth century. Estimates for the total number killed in wars throughout all human history range from 150 million to over a billion.

And last but not least...

You have one life and yet 87% of people in our society have said they wish for a 'better life'.

Fact, no matter what our leaders or media tells us; this current way of life is unsustainable for us as a species and for Planet Earth.

So why are we doing it? Our life, we've only got one. We're in control of it. We can do whatever we want with it. But most of us have forgotten that. Today we're working jobs we don't want to work, voting for politics we don't care about it, living lives we don't want to live, in a hyper-normalised state of emptiness and discontentment.

Things need to change, things have to change, our current political system doesn't serve us as a population and doesn't serve us as individuals, we're all living consumeristic, materialistic lives with no real value and we all have that feeling that we deserve more and guess what?

You do.

This story isn't fiction, this isn't a fairy-tale, this story is the hard, real truth of what's happening right now. As you read these words, as you turn these pages, what you're going to learn in this book is real, it exists, it's happening in this moment and it needs to change. This is the story of our society and how it's falling apart at the seams. This is the story that you've been living inside your head that will never give you any real fulfilment, this is the story of the story inside our heads, a tale we've been conditioned to live within, one that keeps us scared of the unknown, chasing empty dreams and disconnected from our true potential, working nine to five, obsessed with money, celebrities and addicted to external, material fulfilment, while totally over-looking the things that makes us human.

It needs to change; it needs to refresh and it needs a revolution. Our leaders no longer represent us; our society no longer serves us and we all know it's not quite right. If like me you want access to a different way of looking at things, a different way of living life, away from the fixed structure we're conditioned to follow from our births then know two things...

1. I've been in your shoes, and I'm not here to preach, but to simply show you facts and help you develop your opinions and thoughts. We can all achieve an inner peace; I'm no guru and I've been dedicating my life to how to show everyone

that all of us, everywhere can achieve an inner-peace, how I reached mine and how you can reach yours.

2. The information in this book will open both your eyes and your hearts, and will change the way you think and feel about everything around you. My opinions will be in there, I love a good debate, but all the facts that are so ridiculous you think I'd have to make them up, are one hundred percent true.

Most of us are so busy just existing, trying to break even, that we never even have time to look up and embrace life, to look up and realise that life is happening now, instead of tomorrow or that the best chance we had at happiness has just gone, that now, right now, lies the opportunity to embrace and enjoy life. We're all living consumeristic, materialistic lives with no real value and we all have that feeling that we deserve more.

Wait... Why should you listen to me? Well I'm a teenager from London, who's spent the last however many years travelling the world, researching and transforming my life from a boring, mundane one into one awesome adventure and I've done it with no money, no experience and no guidance, only my common sense and wanderlust to guide me.

I was a victim of society's narrative, I lived inside a story in my head that I didn't write for myself and where did that get me? It got me to the age of fifteen where I was an addict and 'lost kid' of western society, searching for life's answers and being provided with enough substance and material to numb the lack of answers being shown to me. That all changed when I had a **'personal revolution'**, an internal awakening that made me realise that we don't need to rely on others, on society, on our politics or TV screens to give our life direction and meaning, **we have all the answers that we're searching for**.

So, I set off on an adventure around the world, spoke to some of the most innovative minds alive today and to some of the people our society frowns upon, to find out how the hell did it get like this and what the hell can we do about it, when did we stop trusting ourselves and start following others blindly, in the hope they can provide the answers we need to discover ourselves?

On my journey I've delved head first into political parties, multiple religions, scientific theories and spiritual practices, encountered many different cultures and people and experienced happiness I didn't know was possible, unimaginable sadness that's shaken me to my core and through my journey, found a moment of peace, a connection something greater than just ourselves and now wake up every day content with my life, an 'inner-peace' that so many of us strive for, something some may view on the borderline of spiritual enlightenment... Or maybe mental illness, it's hard to tell from the inside looking out.

I'm no expert and I certainly don't claim to be, however I've met the experts, I've spoken to people who really know what they're on about and am going to try to translate their clever-talk into a digestible bulk of information.

I hope to be a gateway for you to enter this crazy world of realising your full potential and how incredible life really is when you choose to see it as exactly that; one epic journey.

I've decided to write it all down in this book, I'm going to expose the current stories and narratives we're born into, show you how and why you're being told the stories you hear and provide you with all the tools and knowledge you need to encourage and inspire you to stop living within the world that is presented to you and go and create your own one.

Your life is one awesome adventure that you'll only ever experience once, so you shouldn't spend any second of it doing anything that doesn't make you happy.

This book isn't for those of you that are happy living the life you're living right now, happy living in a system that is ripping us all off and confining us to live a life within certain perimeters, even though you're entitled to so much more. This book is for those of you who want change but don't know how to go about it, for those of you that know that something great, something epic is within you and you're just not sure how to get it out.

Don't panic if it seems like however nice what I'm saying might seem, you think that you can't change the world, that you're just one individual who won't be able to move the political systems, media narratives and cultural lynchpins into new, alternative ways that truly serve us, because you *CAN*.

The truth is; our life is a story inside our heads, a common-story we all tell ourselves, did you know it's proven that we have a conversation with ourselves every 20-30 seconds?

So, what happens when the voice talking to us is telling us somebody else's beliefs or serving somebody else's agendas? What happens when that voice has a negative, fearful and confused tone, instead of a positive, affirming message of love? AND what happens when that voice is what all of us hear, as a collective majority all having that same negative story, whizzing around our consciousness?

Well we wake up to find Donald Trump as President, Corporations more powerful then countries and corruption and poverty at an all-time high. No, I wasn't very happy either.

We live inside a story, **'Our Story Called Life'** and it's time for an internal awakening of your inherent awesomeness, a reconnection to love and a revolution in how to live our lives, it's time to learn how to become the author of your destiny and the story-teller of your reality, it's the time for YOUR personal revolution.

But don't panic, because this book won't teach you how to take down the government, overthrow a tyrant or destroy 'the system', that's not my style, however this book IS going to teach you how to look inside yourself, how to transform your life, your reality, your story from the inside out, to live without being dependent on the current external systems because they will never serve you and here's the plot-twist, you CAN create your own life, your own reality, your own destiny, all by learning how to break free of the story you've been born and conditioned into inside your head and by learning how to write your own story called life.

I'm not advocating an external revolution; I'm demanding a personal revolution.

A personal revolution is the realisation that our happiness, our buzz for life, our contentment, has never lay in the hands of the president, it's never lay in the adverts of huge corporations and it's never been in the decision of Kim Kardashian, because *we* experience our life, nobody else and so it is down to *us* to make it a positive experience, to change our perception and that is what a personal revolution is; it's realising that we are in control of our lives, it's about understanding that no matter who the powers that may be are, the people that you elect, the people that I elect, it's about *remembering* that we have the power; we are the leaders and that nobody can dictate our life unless we let it happen, a personal revolution is about taking control back.

The whole first part of this book is examining the story we've all been living in recent years and why this story needs to change; the second part of the book is looking at ways we can change the story, along with what we should rewrite as the new story.

Most of us have been living in a story that has played to the worst part of our nature, our selfishness, our ego, our reptilian mind (more on that later), basically most people have been searching their whole lives for external growth, whether that be economically, socially, materially, all these desires and fears lead to us being encouraged to be competitive with one another and of course, competition leads to conflict, which leads to a whole bunch of negative feelings; hatred, fear and jealously and so there is a whole other part of a personal revolution; firstly it's about taking power back and realising that we are in control of how we view life and then secondly realising that we have to decide *how* to view life once we realise we're the ones in control, the second part of the revolution is all about reconnecting to the best parts of our nature and elevating ourselves to be the best version of ourselves we can be, focusing on the beautiful parts that make us human; love, compassion and tolerance instead of the negative parts which we've been *encouraged* to display in the current story and narrative.

I know the fancy wording of 'personal revolution' may sound daunting but simplified, it means this; realise that you're in control of your life and then decide to live a good life that centres around living in the moment with love, now that's not too much to ask is it?

What I'm saying is, if the idea of changing the current system seems like it's never going to happen then check this out... the very system we need to change, the one we're conditioned into, the one we're maintaining, it really only exists inside our head.

What do I mean by that? Well I mean that the reason the current system is being kept in place is because we're all living within that system in our heads and we tell ourselves the story that it's the way things are. Put simply, if we all lived in a different system in our head, if we told ourselves a different story, one where we didn't serve the agendas we're currently serving, then eventually the system would change, because any system, any agenda can only be served if people serve it.

As simple as that sounds it's so true. If we don't comply with the current way things are done, then it would have to change, because what could they do? What could they actually do if everybody, tomorrow decided that it's going to be done differently, they would literally have to comply and do as we asked, that's proven every time we see masses of people protest and take a stand, the minority, however 'powerful' they are in a certain system, can never be as powerful as the majority if the majority choose to take a different path.

However how do we know that we as the majority will choose a better path? How do we know that we won't free-fall and go backwards and that actually what they say is right and that we should be happy with being controlled in a system because the alternatives are actually worse?

Well this is why the revolution comes from within, because once we revolutionise the way we see life, we no longer exist and comply within a system that doesn't serve us, we now serve ourselves and each-other. Once we serve each-other in the name of the beautiful parts of our humanity, then we will create a system, society, culture, narrative and story that gives us all real fulfilment, contentment and a truly beautiful life. Everyone should live the life they want to live, as long as it doesn't hurt anyone else or the planet; accept others and their way of doing it; and try to be compassionate and loving, all the while living in the moment, being an example to follow, with peace and unity at the centre of our intentions it really is that simple; we simply complicate it.

Now that's all on a global scale, there's a whole other type of revolution, the personal revolution I speak of, which can transform our reality in a moment and allow us to instantly learn how to write our own story. Which means that whether the current political, media or social narrative is running how it should be or not, you can actually exist and live a perfect life outside of all of that irrelevant nonsense. It becomes a 'shield' against all of those narratives, a personal revolution grants you an enlightened knowledge on life and places you above these systems, because that's another important point, we only exist inside and depress ourselves under the current narrative when we are working on a low frequency of consciousness.

A personal revolution elevates us to a higher frequency of consciousness and allows us to write a story of pure contentment. There's a reason why the monks in Thailand, the samurai's in Japan and the warriors of Guanabala don't feel like the world is going to end... Because their reality, the story in their head is on a higher frequency than that of the business men and women who work for the major banks in London, they exist outside and above that narrative. It's the same reason why children are so content, although they are geographically in the same place as us, people who live inside the narrative; they aren't living in that narrative inside their head.

We can learn to write our own story meaning no matter where we are, what we have or who we are, we can always be content. If we have a personal revolution we learn the most amazing truth about life; life is always perfect until we get distracted to see it in any other way, but more on that later!

So, if you're ready and dedicated to turn life from a boring, repetitive machine running out of gas and serving someone else into an awesome everyday adventure, if you're ready to awaken your mind and are crying out for change, then know that you're not alone and no matter how bad things seem right now, change can happen and change does happen. It all starts with you, so strap-in, get ready to focus, because this is all down to you...

And the revolution starts now.

Chapter 1

<u>The Revolution</u>

I don't want to start too heavy, or scare you off before we've even finished the first page, so to introduce you lightly and get you ready for what's coming, just for a moment, really think and answer to yourself the very basic question that is, 'what is the meaning of life'?

Whether you believe in atheism, science, religion, spirituality or anything else, all of said categories prove and testify in their own individual way that we have a connection to something.

That voice in our heads, whether we call that voice 'God', 'consciousness', 'the sub-conscious mind', or whatever other label you want to attach to it; it exists.

This story, this voice in our minds, in our consciousness, talks to us on an average of every 20-30 seconds, every half a minute you are talking to yourself, telling yourself a story, the story of your life, so what do you do when you find out the story you've been living is a lie?

That story inside your head is only one story; of an infinite number of stories you could be telling yourself and that actually the one you have been telling yourself, was written by somebody else, with other people's agenda in mind, all in the name of economic and financial growth, encouraging the worst parts of your nature, of your ego and your primal mind, depriving you of real connection and maintaining a low frequency of consciousness that can never give you true contentment.

*Yeah, I was p*ssed off too.*

Our life is a story in our minds and it turns out that the story we're conditioned into was written by a few economic elite to maintain a low frequency of consciousness, produce the worst parts of our nature and make us keep things the way they are because that way they keep getting money.

As I've stated; Donald Trump is president, Corporations are more powerful then countries, poverty is at an all-time-high; a child dies every *four* seconds, all because the majority are maintaining a common-story in our heads that doesn't serve us as individuals, or as a species.

So, what can we do? Can we really change the world? And how the hell can we 'write our own story' just by using our minds?

We need to have a personal revolution. What is that? I'm glad you asked…

A personal revolution is two things;

1. Putting down and breaking away from reading the story you've been handed.
2. Picking up a pen and writing your own story instead, one that will change the world.

A personal revolution is a disconnection from the narratives we're conditioned into, and then an elevation and reconnection to our own story, one that will allow us to live our own 'perfect' life and it only takes one moment.

Our lives change in one moment. Some people may say "It took me two years to stop that" or "It took me ten months to get there" but that's just not true. The truth is it took those people two years, ten months, however long, to have that moment when they decided to change, the moment for the seed they planted in their mind to grow, for the story they were telling themselves to be re-written.

The moment we say 'Never again', 'I quit', 'I'm doing it', 'I'm leaving', 'I'm going', 'I love you'... these are the moments in which we change our lives, and they only take one moment.

I hope to help you have one moment after you put this book down. Of course, let's not restrict ourselves to one, by all means, have as many moments as you want, there's no rule that after having one, you have to set this thing on fire for it to come true, you're not joining scientology (sorry Tom). You can have multiple breakthroughs and I hope you do. But how do we get to those 'moments', how are we going to connect to right now and live in this moment, how are we going to become the authors of our own story?

This book is going to make you think about your life. About the past, things in your life that have happened, the future, the things that can still happen and the right now, where you've clearly decided to spend it reading this book (I love you for that). This book is also going to make you self-evaluate, it's going to make you try some things you've probably never done before, ask you questions you've probably never thought before and possibly make you change things you thought were cemented in place, don't freak out, you're going to be okay.

In essence we're going to look at the force, the driving force that's responsible for every feeling and emotion of your life. Every thought, belief, decision, word, the rules you've set yourself, that's happened so far, that have controlled and shaped your life, then we're going to reflect on this, break it down and expose it, leaving us the opportunity to change, to shift, to revolutionise our lives.

You're not going to do it the way I tell you too, I mean who the hell am I? I'm not the one in charge here, let's not get confused straight away, just because you're reading words I've written on a page, doesn't make me the one in the driving seat. After all, it was you who chose to buy this book, it was you who chose to open the pages and start reading and it's also you that could simply close the book, put it down and walk away.

So, make no mistake, you're the one with the power here, what you're holding may look, feel, smell, (taste? I mean, why not, if you want to give this book a lick, you go for it, you little wonderful weirdo, own that sh*t) like a book, but it's actually more like a mirror, it's going to show you yourself, reflect on who you are, show you who you are. But the person looking back at you in the mirror, the version of you that you see, where you think all these little thoughts about yourself, they're only a reflection of you, they're not really you and they certainly can't go and live your life for you, as soon as you walk away from this mirror, that's still down to you. Who do you see when you look in the mirror? Is it someone you love, someone you hate? Someone you trust or someone you question? Are they beautiful or ugly, perfect or in need of improvement?

Whoever you see looking back at you, is just a reflection of the story inside of your head. If you live inside a story that views you as a consumer, a sales number, a person to profit off of, then your reflection will be untrustworthy, ugly and hateful, this is the self-image so many of us possess, insecure, unstable, vulnerable; if we are the authors of our story, then surely we have to make sure we live inside a story that we've written, one that views you as beautiful, loved, perfect, because if this is the reflection we see, we feel, we embrace, then our lives will be just that.

Well, that's exactly like this book, everything we discuss and talk about here, in the comfort of your private mind, is really only 10% of the work. Because everyone's got the million pound idea, everyone's got the life-long dream and desire, but to me, there's no point in having dreams unless we're going to work hard to make them a reality. You could read this book and do all the exercises and have a fun time, after all I don't take myself seriously and I love a laugh. However, if you want to see real change, the other 90% of work comes when you put the book down, when you take what you've learnt about yourself and decided to change and bring them into the real world, into your everyday life, into your story.

So how do we make sure this continues and doesn't end here? Because it's very easy isn't it, to live that perfect version of your life you wish you could have in your head, where everything is exactly how you want it to be, however it's not so easy to take these dreams and turn them into a reality, don't worry, I get that, like I've said, I've been there too. I'll tell you the secret; you can't read one book, attend one event and expect inner-tranquillity. You can't go to the gym once, do a sit-up and expect to be fit for life.

Ideally, you want to have a daily practice, whether it's 5 minutes or a few hours, practice is the key because the training never stops, think of it like trying to lose weight. You can go to the gym, run on a treadmill, do some sit-ups, get really into it, but then if on your way home, you go and get a kebab, you're probably not going to see results very quickly. The same applies for this: think of this book as the gym and the rest of your time as the walk home. What you do on your walk is equally, if not more important then what you do while at the place of progress.

But don't panic, this book isn't just me telling you to wake up and do better at whatever it is you do, far from it, I'm here to help you make that change, there are loads of techniques in this book to help you, (and not my ideas, this is the proper good stuff from experts in their fields), there are motivational stories from my life and others lives I've encountered to guide you, and there are also some nice words to comfort you (no-one said it was easy) but what I'm saying is that no matter what we hear, what we see, what we experience, at the end of the day, real change can only come from you, because you're the one living your life, so I'm going to help you, of course I am, I'm going to try and make it as easy as possible over the course of this book for you to shift your reality, to make the changes you want to make, but remember that when it comes down to it, after we've had our laughs and our moments of reflection, when you put this book down and return back to the world, it's your choice which version of you, which life you're going to live, what story you're going to be part of.

The good news is that the fact you're here, reading this book, suggests you're ready to make the change, we don't even have to shift the whole of your reality, you may just want help on how to quit smoking, or stop eating so much chocolate, which is perfectly fine too, but the reason I've decided to present my story this way is that I believe that instead of learning how to stop smoking, instead of learning how to resist that mars bar, if we learn why we think what we think, how we think what we think, we can change how we think.

I want to go deeper, instead of just solving a problem, I want you to discover and change the thing that's creating these problems so that going forward, because so often we decide to take small problems and turn them into big problems to shy away from the real problem, if we can face the big problem and be brave enough to make the difference, the possibilities for an amazing life are infinite. So as much as I could teach you how to not pick up a cigarette or tell you a stick of celery is better for you than a mars bar, by delving deeper, we can actually not just solve one problem, but solve the thing(s) that create that problem, maybe self-doubt, maybe lack of will-power, whatever it is, by changing the whole scene, we can learn that life can become an exciting journey, huge obstacles can become stepping-stones on your way to something greater and we can learn to appreciate the special moments in our lives, because the impossible now becomes possible.

But before we get into the main bulk of the narrative, like with any good story, we have to set up the story, so before we get you going on this long, windy road of having a personal revolution, I think it's only fair, after all the talking I've just done, that I explain how we got into this current mess and how I found a way out, how I had my personal revolution and why it's worth having one at all.

Chapter 2

The Author (that's me)

We looked at the beginning of the book at all the major problems we've got on our hands, no-one can argue that the issues facing us right now are anything short of sickening, so much so, at times it can be hard to comprehend what's really going on.

I think that this is an interesting time. I think that people are interested once more in formulating a different society, I think people are kind of bored of being exploited, they're bored of a cultural narrative that supports elitism and it exploits the people.

The planet is being destroyed, we are creating an underclass, we are exploiting poor people all over the world and the genuine legitimate problems of the people are not being addressed.

I suppose what's happened, and this is what I believe in, is that certain cultural narratives are promoted that are beneficial only to elites. These cultural narratives are not true.

I think the current contemporary bi-partisan political narrative is a meaningless spectacle designed to distract you from where power truthfully dwells.

I believe profoundly in the power of humanity. I believe that we are connected. I think there's inevitability to a successful revolution. I think this is a change in consciousness that we are experiencing.

I feel that we will survive, or at least will keep telling myself that until we don't, because there is bound to be radical changes. I think we need to be looking at the world as one inclusive entity; we need to look at how many people there are on the planet. We need to look at the resources that are available and what's the most sensible thing to do with those. I think there's going to be massive change for the power structures that currently exist.

You cannot define yourself by reference to other external co-ordinates. You must define yourself internally through your relationship with a higher entity. Think of yourself as a manifestation of some higher thing – some higher frequency.

This is the visible realisation and you know that because you can't see atoms can you? And you certainly can't see the forces that hold the atoms together. There, in the micro-quantum world, lies the answer... You can't understand it with our logical rational minds but we feel it intuitively. Get yourself in line with that stuff and you beam like the sun, you embrace life in every aspect and at that point, life becomes something more.

I suppose the ultimate truth is one that implies this is a temporary illusion that we all temporarily occupy these meat-covered skeletons made of stardust while we ride on a floating rock made of fire while spinning around a burning ball of energy in infinite space, all this knowledge and understanding all coming from the perception of a small squidgy thing in the middle of our skull which is able to do this by invisible energies and connections, for reasons that not a single one of us can confirm. How ridiculous is that? How crazy and totally impossible and yet that is the reality we live in, that is our actual life.

We believe so much in our own identities. We believe in our individualism. I talk as an egotistical man, I like my hair, I like my 'spiritual' beads and my bracelets, I'm a person that believes in the nature of my own individualism and my own identity, but that is on a very superficial level, on a deeper level, on a good day, when I wake up, meditate, pray to Jesus, Krishna, God, Allah and the rest of them, eat a vegan breakfast and sing 'Whistle while I work' as I skip around the room, going about my jobs, in those weird, spiritually enlightened (or borderline mental illness states) moments, I recognize that all these things are transient and what's important and what's defining me are the things that we all share: love, unity, togetherness and how much I embody these divine parts of my nature on a daily basis.

If we have cultural narratives that steer clear of these ideas, that suppress these ideas in favour of negative human traits: greed, selfishness, lust; and if these ideas are promoted, we will really only ever exist in opposition to one another and we will be exploitable by corporations that prey on these negative aspects of humanity.

There's going to be a revolution. It's totally going to happen. I don't have a flicker of doubt. Seeing Trump, seeing Brexit, seeing the news and the current state of things; this is a new world we're seeing, this is time to wake up. Like it says in Christianity's the Lord's Prayer: 'on Earth as it is in heaven.'

Now, I don't want to freak anybody out with super-sexy-spiritual talk too early on, but there are subtler dimensions, subtler frequencies where we can realise that we are already all that we need to be. If we could tune in to a different narrative, a different story, then the world would change automatically. It would just happen automatically. It doesn't matter how far down the rabbit hole we've been, think of it like a cave, it could be in darkness for ten thousand years, but as soon as the light is put on, as soon as the match is struck, the light is there and the whole dynamic of the cave changes (that's how Batman became Batman remember? I'm basically asking you to be Batman). So the light is coming.

My journey started after finding out those facts from the start at a young age. The fact that I was off at a nice, bubble-wrapped school for people a lot richer than me, while so many people were suffering and didn't have what I thought was a 'normal' lifestyle, it just didn't make sense to little, over-exposed to the riches of life, 13 year old me.

Why didn't they have what I had? Why shouldn't they have what I had? These thoughts crossed and pondered my mind for moments, and the high, twenty foot walls of Heath Mount 'protected' me from thinking that anything could be done about this 'natural' order of things.

However, the seed of these thoughts had been placed in my brain and no doubt it was these thoughts which were the reasoning as to why I decided against everyone's recommendation of graduating to the prestigious further education in the Haileybury grounds, opting instead to join the waiting list for a state school in Hertfordshire with the lowest rating at the time for the whole county.

Going to a rough state school showed me the contrast in lifestyles, I went from hanging out with David Beckham's kids to Dave the builder's (that's no lie either, The Beckham's went to my first school and my best mates' dad really was called Dave, crazy how many Dave's are all around, so many in fact, they overthrow the class system, maybe we need a 'Dave' revolution, bet my brother would like that).

I'd always played football in and around London and had always felt more comfortable around the people who didn't have a lot in Enfield than the 'have-everything-they-could-ever-want-with-a-Ferrari-on-top' of private school life.

I don't want to be coming across as a pompous dick, so don't get me wrong, I'm very appreciative for the grounding it gave me in education and if everybody could attend a school like that, then great, maybe that's where we'll end up, but the fact that places like Heath Mount can only exist because somewhere else, someone doesn't even have the opportunity to go to school, (after all, 70 million children don't get to go to any type of school) then I don't agree that it should be held in such high regard, let's start jazzing up all the schools once everyone can go in the first place.

Anyway we're not here to talk about me, so let's fast forward my time through the GCSE's, first girlfriends and first detentions (no-one could ever do anything wrong when you're paying to go to school) the parties, the alcohol, the whatever else I did to try and escape reality and I started to form my view of the world, not one which believed there was only the super-rich and then those in poverty, but one that realised that, while I was off getting well-educated and looking all smart in my blazer, like someone from the Eton Rifles, that the real world was like an enormous, over-worked machine, a machine whose sole function was to allow this super-rich lifestyle to be maintained with everyone else making sure it was running properly, but didn't encourage the 'have-mores' to give back or share with those who are holding the pedestal on which they stand.

My parents, from Hackney and Enfield, never really installed in me the 'typical' career path of doctor or surgeon, I always blagged an excuse for Latin lessons (which, to me, sounds weirdly like a herbal essence brand) all of this, water to the seed in my brain, that although the luxurious lifestyle was a suit that I wore, a face that I had on, a 'persona' I had adopted, that in fact my roots, where I felt relatively 'normal', was actually as far away from the imaginary utopian lifestyle as possible, because the reality was, it just wasn't real.

Seeing my mum rushed into hospital was horrible. Seeing my dad given the choice between going into work at the bank (where he'd been working tirelessly for 20 years) or looking after my bed-stricken mum along with me and my brother was even worse. My dad did the only thing any genuine human being would do, told his pig of a boss to take his job and shove it where the sun don't shine. My dad's story ends with him now coaching sports to hundreds of kids, doing something he loves every day, a lot less money and a lot better lifestyle.

Looking back, no wonder I have hatred for the major banks! However, this distrust is not unwarranted, all of us are not seeing the true colours of the banks in our major cities, did you know that the German philosopher Ludwick once stated that you can see what matters most to a society by its tallest buildings; well take a look around; in Thailand it's their temples, in England it's the banks!

My Dad has always had an eventful life, he lost his Dad very young and so quit school to go and get a job at his first bank, fast forward many years and he found himself second-in-command at a major bank that shall remain unnamed. The head of this bank, who we will call Seb, gave my dad the task of telling everyone who worked for him that sadly, due to cut-backs, their Christmas bonuses had to halved this year, there was simply no money around to be given out.

There was anger, there were explicit words thrown, even a punch was thrown, my dad tried to deal with the chaos while Seb sat in his grand office, disconnected to the blame and anarchy, with his own Christmas bonus... That had doubled that year... And tripled the next.

Did you know that in order for a cleaner at a major bank in London to earn what that bank's CEO will earn in a year, that cleaner would have to work every day, including weekends, from 7am-7pm at night, from the first day the American Revolution started, every single day, until now, just to make what the boss makes in a year, that's over double the life expectancy of an average person, about 250 years, to make what the main man will make in just 365 days?

Did you also know that in the 2008 crash, you know when there was no money around, when everybody's wages got cut, that since then, the CEO's of London's 5 most powerful banks have gone up 300%?

Regardless of what label we attach to the current way we do things, it's obvious that most of us are viewed as cogs in a machine, that can be easily replaced, like parts of a car, all of us serving the agendas of a few people who we haven't elected or voted into power, but who have all encompassing power because that's how this story is set up and that's why we need a new story, because this story will never give you any real fulfilment.

We need to be educated enough to maintain the system, to do the jobs, to operate the machinery, but too blind and distracted to question the reality of the world around us.

So, that was the next big lesson little old me learnt, I realised that the current way we do things doesn't benefit us as a majority and encourages the worst part of our human nature, the seed was starting to grow, water was pouring in, as I left school, the one-time private school, shy boy was now a louder, smarter-mouthed state school graduate, I just had no idea what I could do.

It was a confusing upbringing for sure, constant contrast, a lot of death (we lost family friends to suicide, cancer, you name it, my grandparents and aunties and uncles passed away every year for about 3 years straight) which was obviously hard for a young-mind. But inside me I had a real emptiness, I was lost. I didn't know my place, I never felt 'pain; or 'suffering' *but since I had everything; I couldn't see the point in anything.* Everyone was so worried about girlfriends and school while I was at home, in my imagination, wondering what the meaning of life was... when I was 13.

My head hurt, my brain hurt, my heart was in agony, I could feel the need for something greater, something beyond what was being offered, I just had no idea how to get this energy out, so I stumbled and crashed through my adolescent years, delving into numerous substances and activities, just trying to cope with reality and why I was having all these thoughts no-one else was having, I was having these dreams no-one else could relate too, I was wanting a life different from everyone else around me.

I was a really weird kid (in case you hadn't of worked that one out by now), I had this internal energy in abundance, I remember spending hours playing and staring at these little action figures, playing with animals and staring at the television too closely, I felt a great deal of solitude and spent many hours 'away with the fairies' and in my own head.

A lot of the other kids seemed to define themselves with things that were happening externally, while I always believed the person I am when I'm alone is the person I 'most' am, I felt a great deal of comfort within my own mind, my imagination a place where I spent the majority of my childhood.

That excess energy that I had inside of me, started seeping out into addictive and self-harming behaviours, never being able to grasp a hold on that energy became very taxing.

I had and still have an amazing mother who cares greatly about me, an equally loving father who guides me and an annoying little brother who is also my best friend. The older I get, the more I look back on my childhood and realise how lucky I was, I wouldn't want to blame my weirdness on anybody but myself, I would never want to disservice the amazing job my family did at raising me; I think it's cheap to blame my issues on a 'bad childhood' and I wouldn't want to belittle the suffering of others, there are millions of people who have had it a lot worse than me, don't get me wrong, I'm not saying I'm damaged or broken because I just couldn't fit in, I've had it a breeze compared to most, all my issues and problems are self-inflicted and I don't blame anybody else for those apart from me own consciousness.

Having everything I could ever want, adding in the crazy amount of energy I had inside of me, all led me to the point where I believed I was mentally insane.

As you would though, right? If your behaviour and normalities were completely different and bizarre to everyone else's around you, especially as a teenager, surely you'd think that you must be insane, I became lonely and angry at the world, frustrated by the fact there was no-one I could relate too, I hit a low point, where I would actually sit and bang my head against a wall, just to try to stop thinking, to try to get 'normal' thoughts.

I had always known from a young age that the story I was born into didn't serve me, but I didn't know what story to follow instead, so I broke down.

Like I stated earlier, to save you from that horrible mid-revolution crisis stage, this book will prove why the current narrative is a lie but then also provide you with how to create your own alternative.

Then something beautiful happened, arising from various reasons of my struggling to cope with my very existence, I found myself on a cold, Saturday night, sitting with a homeless man at a train station called Tiny Tim. Tiny Tim, as his name suggests was tiny. Standing only about 5'6", I was waiting to jump the train home and had 22 minutes to kill, he saw me and asked if I'd had a nice night and I decided against my judgemental persona to go and speak to him, surprised he hadn't asked for money.

We started speaking and Tim explained he was homeless because he decided to quit his job to travel but things went wrong, he got ill abroad and had to come back, he ended up coming back to find his partner had taken everything, done a runner, he'd lost all his possessions and had nothing left. But that wasn't what shocked me, what shocked me was what followed, the moment he'd found out all his stuff had been taken and that he was technically homeless, he had gone straight to the nearest arts shop and just bought 8 packs of crayons.

Since that day, Tim has spent every single day of his life, writing messages of love, unity and tolerance anywhere he could get away with; buildings, pavements, signs, walls, wherever he could find. He encouraged others to write messages too; around his, I saw his hat on the floor that was filled with about two pounds worth of one and two pennies, Tim explained that people offer him donations for his messages or will give some cash to write a poem for a loved one or friend, I was astounded, here was a homeless man who wanted to be homeless.

Here was a man that society destroyed and spat out and this betrayal had elevated Tim to a life of pure joy and happiness. No money, no possessions, just travelling the world writing messages of love to make enough money to travel somewhere else.

"You look lost" He asked me

"What do you mean?" I replied

"I can see it, in your eyes, you're lost and feel alone" he explained.

How? How did this random guy on this random encounter in this random location happen to be the first person in my life who saw it? Was it fate, destiny? I didn't know, but I was in awe.

"I know the feeling buddy" he continued, "I used to feel like it too, when I was working a job I hated in the city, living a life I didn't enjoy, heck I was borderline suicidal, but I met a man who showed me there was a different way, a better way to live, he inspired me to go travelling and sure I may be in hot water right now, but honestly brother, for all of life I experienced, it was worth every second, you're young alright, you got time, so go and enjoy life, you don't need to live to someone else's rules or expectations, create your own reality brother, it's the only way to be really happy".

We spoke for hours; I explained that it was so invigorating to hear what he was saying and that he was the first person who seemed to understand me. I ended up missing the train and we continued to speak, about the wrongs of the world, how things should be different, just two random people, from two completely different lives, completely connected on a conscious level through mutual suffering and then it hit me; our life is a story that we are in control of.

My whole life had been spent trying to be heard, to fulfil expectations or to become something; rich, famous, anything that was 'credible' as is the case for us all, but that night Tim proved it didn't have to be that way, it could be different.

I had a moment where it appeared through my eyes like the moments in the films when the camera moves from close up, panning out to the wide shot when the character realises what the audience have known for the last half an hour... I had a personal revolution.

Who was I living for? Whose story was I living inside of? Why shouldn't I write my own? I asked myself.

Here was Tim, a man who was everything society tells us not to be; homeless, poor, vulnerable, unstable, unemployed, with no money, no possessions, no anything; yet the calmest, most loving and most content person I'd ever met. This was the moment I realised that our lives are just stories and thoughts inside our mind; our pasts stories we tell ourselves, our futures; stories we tell ourselves, right now; the way we see ourselves, others, the world around us, it's all just a perception, a narrative, a story. I realised our world isn't an external place that we then perceive internally, but actually our world is an internal place that creates the perception of the world we see externally.

I'd known for a while that politics was corrupt and that the media lied to us, that generally the world wasn't great and that I was unique because I realised that society was broken and that nothing was right, but that night I realised that I was wrong; the world is great, I'd just been choosing to see it another way and that I was only half-correct, although I had understood that the story we're told while we grow up is like a 'cage' that makes us maintain the current system in the name of economic profit for a minority, I'd not realised until now, that story was only one of *many* possibilities that are available and that although it was important to break free from the caging story, it was equally important to then replace that story with something better, something I'd never previously done.

The way I like to say it is imagine we are watching television and as soon as we are born, as soon as we turn on the television, we are shown a programme that conditions us to hate, fear, lust and act as a primal animal, the channel we are watching keeps our consciousness on a low frequency. I worked this out from a young age and so decided to turn the TV off, thinking it would solve the problems, but it doesn't, because what do you get when you turn a TV off? You get an empty, dark, black screen, giving you the belief that there is no point in watching any story, any channel at all. Well that night I realised, that turning the TV off is not the answer, that just pulling the plug out doesn't solve anything, because you're still the same hateful, fearful, money-led person you were while the TV was on, you're just no longer watching the channel, instead staring at the darkness.

That night was the moment I realised that the real solution is to not stay on the conditioned channel, or to turn the TV off all together but instead to *change* the channel, to one that you want to watch, because we all need a story inside our head to live, to be happy, to be content and the only way to be watching a channel that makes you happy is to create your own one and that night I realised what my channel was: compassion.

Compassion was what was going to save me, it was my way out but even more so I realised, compassion was what was going to save anyone who needed saving. I'm not talking, roll-over, be pushed-around, taken advantage of compassion, where everyone uses you for their own agenda, I'm talking powerful yet kind, understanding with dignity, raw, untamed compassion, to not tolerate the farce anymore and to be compassionate dominantly in everything you do and how did I know this was the answer?

Because nothing else had worked, I'd exhausted all other options, material gain never worked, I'd had all I could ever ask for at birthdays and it didn't solve my issues. Alcohol, drugs, sex, all these things didn't work either, externally just numbing a sensation that was impossible to dispose of, they simply distracted me from facing the issues, whether it be for the length of a tequila or an orgasm, these things keeping me disillusioned and disenfranchised with life. I'd tried hate and I'd felt fear, I'd tried desire and felt vulnerability; nothing else had worked, it became obvious, power, status, the picturesque thought of being a politician who could save the world was a lie, the 'spiritual' community that sits on a bed of consumerism wasn't fulfilling despite looking edgy and unique, it was compassion, the answer was love; **a love for yourself, a love for others unconditionally, a love for life,** something I'd never felt and something that could never be fulfilled on a deeper level by the story we're born into. I don't believe that these 'moments' just happen, you can of course and I think some people do and call this a 'miracle' or 'destiny', however I do believe that we plant seeds in our mind that come to fruition in moments that change our lives and this was one for me, I realised that I felt most content, most alive, when in service of others, when helping somebody else, while being connected to the underlying connectedness which is a connected consciousness, call it God, call it Love, call it science, call it whatever you want but when I'm connected to the moment; I'm alive in life and I feel like everyone feels that way and I now had the urge for more! (Is that a vote for spiritual enlightenment or mental illness?)

Because in that moment, a feeling of compassion took over my body, took over my brain, it was the first impulse that reconnected me to something deeper and it was the spark that changed everything. It was the moment I picked up the pen and started to write my own story.

It gave me a raw desire and drive to make sure nobody else had to go through what I went through, because I knew what it felt like, through suffering and compassion I wanted to make sure anyone I could help would never have to suffer again, to make sure that when the inevitable breakdown of politics and media and everything else in our society happened (as it now has), that when everyone realises the channel they've been watching isn't right for them, that instead of turning off the television and feeling empty as I had, they could change to a new channel, their own channel, their own story.

I hugged Tim, I thanked him for all he'd done, I took out £20 and offered to buy him a ticket home. He broke down. He said it's the first time he can remember that someone had shown him compassion, he said he hadn't been hugged in so many years that he forgot what it was like and he couldn't believe I was willing to be so charitable, but he declined the £20. He told me that as much as he appreciated the gesture, there was something he wanted even more then my money, he wanted to have a line in my book, so that he could be remembered and that his message could be spread to a further reach than he could ever achieve, I hope he's happy with a chapter.

That night was a catalyst for me, a fixed moment in my life where everything changed, looking back, I class everything as either an event that happened before that night or after that night because it changed my whole life, it finally all made sense, for the first time in my life, I felt motivated, free and ready to make a difference. Sadly, I never saw Tim again. I got in contact with the local homeless shelter, and the surrounding areas, but none had ever heard of him, I visited the same spot but he was never there and I searched online everywhere. It was at this point where I debated whether I had just encountered a man who had spiritually awakened me to my consciousness, or if he was a figment of my imagination and I had now fallen off the deep end of mental insanity and was in fact still lying at the train station, dribbling from the side of my mouth.

I decided that it was the first one, but I hope that Tim gets hold of this book somehow, to see how far his message has gone. How far it's taken me and how far it may inspire others to go.

I don't know if I'm an addict that never really happened, maybe I just hit it lucky, because I know a lot of people have felt lost or alone, but ever since coming out the other side, I've become obsessed, addicted, to making sure if I can end someone else's suffering and help them change their course in anyway physically possible, then I have an obsession to do so, it's given my life meaning, it's what saved my life and makes me want to save anybody from suffering that I can during my time here, connected to someone on a deep level, helping them love their life.

Some people get that buzz, that energy through yoga, or religion, music, sports, comedy, art, painting, the list is pretty big and as to the point of the book, everyone's got their thing, I just get mine from helping others, being connected to them in the moment, seeing them have a moment, a change of heart, a shift in consciousness, a personal revolution. I've realised that for me, it's my purpose, my calling, my meaning of life, so thank you Tim.

So that's my story; I had everything that this society tells you that you need to have: A good family, lots of money, private education, friends, loads of material possessions and everything you could ever ask for and it still wasn't enough.

My emptiness never came from not having enough, but from having too much.

Having everything you could ever want externally makes you realise that it's all bullsh*t. When I had 'everything' you need to have a 'happy' life, as told by the current narrative we all live within, it made me realise that it wasn't me that was the problem… it was the current story of society I was living within.

The truth is that within this current narrative, political and culture system in the west, alongside our culture and society's mentality, the clear truth is that the majority are serving the few, you can call this capitalism, you can call this westernisation, maybe you could call it corruption, but it's all a great game; it's all a story, more accurately; it's a fairy-tale, we're told that if we can get all external things; family, money, material things and friends then we will be happy, *this is where we're all going wrong.*

The story is empty and the whole thing is one great big lie, an illusion, to keep the people at the top, on top; while keeping everybody else below them striving towards this 'picturesque' life. People who don't have everything obviously don't see this. People who had it worse than I didn't see this, people who live in great poverty right now don't see this, because they're still chasing the dream; the idea that if they get out of poverty and gain all the things I was born into, then they will be happy. If they can climb over the great wall then the grass on the other side will be a utopian green, but I was born in the utopian gardens and it's totally fake, because it doesn't give you any internal fulfilment.

If you're poor and moan; they call you bitter, if you're rich and moan; they call you a hypocrite… I think they don't like us talking about it.

I suppose what I'm trying to say is this: society tells us a story; the story that if we can get to the 'other side' of the life that we are currently living then we will be happy.

Well this is why you should listen to me; because I've seen the other side, I've come from the other side and call tell you for a fact it doesn't work, because I'm awake now.

Personally, it's through spiritual practice (meditation and all that malarkey) that I've found a reconnection to something deeper within myself, felt an 'inner-peace' inside my soul that we can all access.

I don't want that feeling in my stomach that people are being treated badly or exploited in the interest of some other human beings, since we're all the same when we remove all the bits we're told to label you know?

I'm also a human being and I think it's good to have access to the infinite consciousness that's available to all people, but through the five senses is delineated, keeping us trapped on a material plane.

We think reality is what we can understand through the limited instruments we call our 'senses', anything that we are describing through science, or with cold, hard fact, we're describing through the prism of our five limited senses; our eyes can only see between infrared and ultraviolet light, however there's more lights bouncing around your head, then your head could even understand.

Our ears can only hear a tiny decibel range, we can't hear the noise from a dog whistle, can't hear other high-pitched frequencies, isn't it likely then that other frequencies exist that we can't hear?

Other vibrations, energies and a consciousness that is within our own universe can easily exist without most of us even sensing it's there.

Our individual consciousness is prohibited by our senses, prescribed by our senses, living within the realm of these five tools to grasp life and reality; but reality is limitless, space is infinite, time eternal: it is us who put the limit on how 'big' space is, 'what' reality is and 'when' a time period ends; and it's all dependent on our perception on the situation.

Through spiritual practice, one can temporarily break these bonds, the chain to the mundane and if only for a moment; receive a taste of the infinite.

I don't want to get too cosmic or hippie about life too early on in this book, but we are just this sort of temporary blob of atoms, endowed with consciousness for the merest moments in infinite space.

I think it's difficult these days with religion getting such a rough ride, terrorism on every airway and 'life coaches' and 'gurus' selling enlightenment for a price, it's hard to access spirituality in a pure form, but we are, by nature, spiritual people. If we don't have access to the deeper part of our nature, we suffer as individuals and subsequently as a society.

We need to recognise at some point that within ourselves there is infinite capacity for connection with all things, a way to use that inherent energy that is damaging, to do some good; and we can all do that, all human beings.

We're basically alright, human beings, whenever there's a disaster, or an accident, people's impulse is to help one another. So I'm thinking anyone that galvanises people, helps people and unites people, points us towards our better aspects of our nature and help us to overcome our basic things like fear and desire, I think these are the people who are worthy heroes; rather than the heroes nominated by society, people who help maintain a low vibrational frequency that makes us concentrate on the dark parts and create the world full of the issues we currently see.

The human has fulfilled its potential. The 'human being' has not physically evolved for thousands of years. Look around you, this current world is the achievement of human's evolution. We must transform, become enlightened, so we can access the next realm of consciousness necessary for our evolution, because we've changed the world around us to the point where we're not going to physically evolve anymore, so the next stage is consciously.

This is why I'm now advocating a personal revolution, because if we consciously 'evolve' with our current social attitude and mentality, we're all f*cked, we need to sort our insides out so that when outside changes happen, we're all going to be alright and live a life of fulfilment.

That responsibility is totally down to you, however don't feel any pressure, you have all the answers you need, you have all the answers we need, it's inside of you, you're going to smash it, you are beautiful, you are capable, you are you.

Don't panic; we're going to be alright.

Chapter 3

The Author II (that's you)

So now here I am, a few years after all of that, having decided to go and travel to many parts of the world, meeting a bunch of crazy people, ranging from monks in Thailand, to a neo-Nazi murderer in America, to people I used to look up to such as Russell Brand, Brett Moran and Noam Chomsky, who I can now call friends, demanding that we all take that internal moment of reflection and really come to terms with what life's purpose is, what we're here to do. It's been a crazy ride and I've seen things I never believed I'd see, (both good and bad), that have made me question both whether after some of the disgusting things I've witnessed, if what I'm doing is worth it and things that have made me realise that life is incredible and that really everyone and everything has the potential to be amazing.

For the last few years, I've started my journey and have transformed my life from the routine rat-race I was joining after my education to now waking up every day content and amazed at how amazing life can be, just by realising we're in control of our lives, if we choose to be, if we reflect and revolutionise our way of enjoying our time here, but of course my journey is still progressing along, this book simply another turning point on my course, but it's amazing that because of that, we're now able to share this journey, if nothing more than a few chapters, who knows where it could take us?

So, while we travel on our journeys together, this book is going to look at loads of ways how people have connected to something deeper throughout history and still continue to do so in the present day. It's also going to present some shocking facts and truths that you won't see on Facebook. But before we continue, I just want to let you know that this isn't going to be me, telling you what to do or what to think, this is going to be me simply showing you tried and tested ways people have connected to consciousness, God, themselves, whatever way you want to word it, again, is up to you. I mean even Einstein couldn't work out what consciousness was!

I'm hoping to be a 'gate-way' of sorts, a more relatable kind of guy who understands your wish for something deeper than all those very serious old people you see talking about social structures on TED talks, because it's my *strong* belief that *you have all the answers you need.*

Nobody; no celebrity, politician, spiritual guru or 'Life coach' (what even is a life coach and how the heck do they know what life is meant to look like?) knows what you need, what your answers are… apart from you.

No politician telling you to go to university, or 'guru' selling you enlightenment for a monthly subscription of £300 can provide you any real solution, because you are the author of your story; there are no short-cuts, no easy-routes… if you want a revolution it comes from within and it comes from you.

So what's the point of me then? Well I'm going to be your mirror, to show you yourself, I'm here for those of you who have no idea about any of this crazy and amazing stuff. For those of you who want to get involved I will present this information to you in a digestible way and all I need from you in return is that you go out and create something positive in the world yourself, you don't have to write a book, you don't even need to do anything more advanced than being really nice to the cashier at the co-op you normally can't stand talking to (Because you know for a fact he's probably just a 17 year old pot-head from the local estate and you're sure he's the one who stole that bike you heard about off Facebook), but by going out into the world and making the smallest of changes, you do your bit, and you complete one of the three things you can do to change the world you live in, so be brave, be brilliant and do it with style!

So, it's time we delve into where exactly and what exactly YOU make of the world, your world, right now.

Below are 20 questions that were first asked to me by a Monk out in Thailand, at the very start of my journey, he told me these questions are markers, points that show where we are on our journey and where we are heading.

So, I thought we'd start you off with the same, to see where you are on yours. Answer the questions below with brutal honesty and let's see where your personal revolution can take you. Just think of it as the most intense game of '20 questions' ever, where instead of finding out about your crush's interests, you're searching for the meaning of life!

1. Why is there poverty and suffering in the world?

2. What is the difference between religion and science?

3. Why are so many people discontent with their lives?

4. What are we all afraid of?

5. When is conflict justifiable?

6. What is power and how should we use it?

7. What does it mean to live in the present moment?

8. What is our greatest distraction?

10. Is world peace possible, why?

11. What happens to you after you die?

12. Describe compassion and how we should use it.

13. What is wisdom and how do we achieve it?

14. What is the greatest quality humans possess?

15. How does one achieve peace?

16. If you could change one thing in the world, what would it be?

17. Describe your life in 3 words?

18. If you had 2 minutes to speak to the whole world, what would you say?

19. What is love?

20. What is the meaning of life?

(Bonus) Name a vegetable.)

You said carrot didn't you.

Also did you notice there wasn't a number nine? Did you just go back and check to see if I was lying? *More importantly*, did you realise that there are two number fourteens?

I bet you definitely went back and checked this time.

Do you see? Our life is purely what we see, what we choose to see, what we overlook, our life is a story we create for ourselves inside our heads, if I had never told you there was no number nine, you would've gone the rest of your life thinking this book had a number nine question, even though it doesn't exist, however do you also see that when you went and looked back for the two number Fourteen's, that you were expecting to see two questions both with the number fourteen by them? Because as much as we shape our reality; our story in our heads and our perception of the world, everything else shapes it as well. This is why a personal revolution requires a reconnection to consciousness, so that we can face everybody else's input and choose what to learn from and also what to ignore.

The funny little trick I just played on you serves an important point, everything in our lives, from politics and media, to religion and science, tells us a story to live inside of, creates a perception for how to see the world, the first half of this book is going to look at the perception these things create for us, ask 'do these things really serve us?' and then move into the second part of the book: how to write our own story.

But quickly before we do that, I'd just like to point out the fact that actually the word 'vegetable' was spelt wrong in the last bonus question!

Did I get you?

Anyway, welcome to the book, as you can see this will probably be the most bizarre and unprofessional piece of writing you ever read, but that's what's going to make it fun, who the hell agreed to let me write a book? (Don't panic, you're in good hands, although if we're talking literal, I'm in your hands, well, my words written on this book are in your hands, unless you're an online reader, in which case this last bracket-chat has been totally nonsense, although I like 'bracket-chat', I'm copyrighting that).

Anyway, bet the questions got you thinking didn't they! But that's good, it's good that we've gone beneath the surface, I can't stand living on the surface, I've never been able to, ever since I was a kid, just living on that superficial level of façade presentations of the suspected self we're meant to employ into a social surrounding, I always needed to learn more, to dive deeper, I'm glad you have too.

It's one of the reasons why I think so many people are so unhappy nowadays, we've been over-exposed to our surfaces, while everything below that has been locked away. Now when we talk, we text, instead of speaking directly into each-other's eyes and soul, we believe that our Facebook friends are our trusted allies, if we have a large enough following online, we have value... all these materialistic thoughts and patterns are covering our ability to go deep into each-other's lives and it's so false, when we're writing a paragraph about how much we love our partners, we're not transmitting it through our vocal chords to our soul, we're saying it over and over again in our heads, deleting and retyping errors, before finally sending that pristine message, so that we can present our story, our argument, our life; in a perfect, error-free model of our life…but that's not real life.

It's fake, it's like reality television and it serves no purpose. We've lost spontaneity, we've lost creation and expression, all so that we can fit into a mould that's been designed to pray off our primitive states, to manipulate ourselves into a state of depression. When was the last time you did something where someone showed you love where you didn't expect it? What I'm saying is that your family, your true friends, they will love you no matter what, but who and what happened the last time you felt love from an unexpected source?

Was it helping someone who'd fallen over? Was it celebrating with someone when your team goes one goal up (if you're an Arsenal fan, I'm assuming that wasn't very recently! How funny is that? I can sit here as a pretentious, 'spiritual' author and yet one quick thought about the old football and here we are, in another crazy bracket-chat, blabbering on about who really owns North London, which is of course, the lilywhites, we were there first).

But if you're not into the whole football scene, when was it? Was it joining a protest against something you feel is wrong? Was it being polite to a cashier when everyone else has been miserable?

Now think, why did that person show you that love? How did that love feel? I bet it was good, wasn't it? It's that natural love, from someone of a different background, culture, life, without any sort of agenda, just a moment of connection between two humans.

It's amazing how such a strong bond can be formed so quickly through doing one tiny little action. That one thing is universal, by the way, it's the same thing you're looking to do in your personal revolution, it's the same thing I'm trying to do by writing this book, it's also the only thing you can actually do to feel love from every kind of person, regardless of who they are, from people we don't even know: We do the right thing.

Because we know, don't we? Deep down, we know what the right thing is; none of us are little apes playing with our bums, flinging poo anymore. Even the most primitive humans on the planet know what's right and wrong, we know whether we should say those words, end that relationship, quit that job. It's inherent and present within all of us, as much as we have our animalistic drives like fear and desire, we all have that divine beauty as well, love, compassion, judgement to do what's right. The choice we have is to which side of ourselves do we want to act on behalf?

Do we want to cheat on our partner because of our desires for someone else, or do we want to go home to them because we know they give us honest compassion and love, are we going to choose that primitive desire, or play to that beautiful love, knowing it's the right thing to do?

Do we want to stay in our boring job through fear we may not find a replacement with as good pay, or do we want to quit our jobs and go in search for a job that we love and fulfils us with purpose, one which could see us making a difference to our community?

Do we want to go to University, through a fear that not going may result in a struggle through the rest of our lives, or do we want to travel and seek adventure, see things you could only dream of seeing, end up writing a book about the whole thing and change people's lives with the love and compassion that story entails?

It's these choices that make us who we are, that create the story we see as our life. The one on stage, or the one watching the guy on stage, the girl who travelled the world, or the girl who never left her home town, the ones who lived their dreams, compared to the ones who lived to society's expectations.

Our life is in our control, no matter the people that I elect, no matter the people you elect into power, remember, you have the power, these things are just so temporary, like a TV show going on in the background, these people have no real power, only power over people who let them have power, but if you wake up, you become the leader, you don't need to let anyone dictate your life or tell you what to do. Always fight for what you believe in, always believe in what you're doing and never settle for any less.

How do you do that? It's really simple; look within, look into your hearts and do what's right. Because people relate to authenticity, to genuinely good people, it's like a natural attraction of nature buried deep within all of us, it's not something that has to be taught, like to hate, or to fear, it's already there, you just have to reconnect to it and if we can do that, we will live the richest and most fulfilling lives possible, all by doing the right thing.

However, as simple as that is, how we get to learn to do the right thing can be a little harder to understand and to reach, but that's alright, if you act with compassion in your heart, trying to do what's right, you can't go that wrong.

But if only there was some sort of scripture, a sort of text, which entails numerous ways millions of people throughout history have found a way to connect to their consciousness, to learn to do the right thing, if only there was a kind of book that showed different sorts of 'guided techniques' people have used to find the easiest way for them to do the right thing... Oh look at what you're holding, you lucky little conscious being that you are... now let's begin!

Chapter 4

The History

So, now that we know what it is we've got to do to transform our life, I guess we should face the reality of the world and life we're living in right now, how screwed we all are in the system, so that we can learn to step outside this narrative; to allow ourselves to move to a platform to write our own story.

It's time we looked as to why and how it got like this, because societies have changed hundreds of times throughout history, the reason we no longer use a guillotine, or pray to the sun and moon gods for it to rain on our crops tomorrow is because over time we've evolved, it's a natural process of any functioning species.

But one thing that we've all seemed to dismiss is that maybe the 'evolution' process hasn't finished yet, we've just decided to put it on pause because we're no longer seeking to evolve or transcend to a deeper frequency, instead now simply existing to serve an agenda for someone else, working a 9-to-5 job filled with a Christmas bonus to keep us in our place and a huge load of emptiness to keep us stressed, desensitised and discontent.

To start our dissecting of our current narrative, we have to look at two of the largest pegs that hold the tent that is the current narrative in place; politics; our political policies, parties and politicians and the media narrative; the news we watch, the papers we read and the sources of information we shape our perception of reality around and so to start this analysis of the story of our politics and media, let's look at the recent history of both of these and how we've ended up in the current paradigm we find ourselves in.

So, here's a quick history lesson to get us back up to speed, on how we became the society we are today, I'm not about to run through the whole of human history so let's skip the part where we are all little cavemen, running around, worshipping fire and flinging faeces around.

Fast forward a whole lot of time, we get a little bit smarter, we learn to talk and gradually start building a 'society' and connecting to one another.

Now we're going to fast forward another whole lot of time, when we learn to read and write we create language and rules and political systems, go right up to Victoria and her lot and pause there. The social thinker John Ruskin states around this time, base pillars of our species at this point of evolution, things such as technology, health-care and understanding had now reached a point where we developed a society that resulted in the start of the things we now call 'corporations', (despite what some of them will have you try and believe, these all 'powerful', all 'over-seeing' corporations haven't always existed, they haven't always had loads of power and they don't always need to either!)

It was at this time Ruskin stated that this new 'industrialism' age (remember the industrial revolution lessons you were taught in history, all of that) would lead to an age of 'capitalism' which would lead to a breakdown in the western way of civilisation, predicting that at that point, we were either going to have a 'revolution' and live in a golden age... Or destroy ourselves. Whether you're a massive fan of Ruskin (don't worry, I hadn't heard of him either before getting into all this revolution jibe) you've got to admit that the guy's been pretty spot on and with everything going on now, it feels like we're fast approaching the 'make or break' decision he spoke of and I know which one I'd prefer.

So how did we get to become this army of technocrats, complacent radicals and Faustian internet entrepreneurs conspiring to create an unreal world; one who's familiar and often comforting details blind us to its total inauthenticity? Well a few major events played key roles in the formation of the society we now live in, obviously the first huge catalyst into how our culture and communities have formed is the World War, not the first one (I know, how many times until humans learn?) but the second World War and although the War was initially commenced by Great Britain and Germany, in order to understand how the War created the current dynamic, we have to focus on our big, scary brother, who until this point in time, was only on the cusp of being the global super-power that it now is.

In the United States before the war, policies implemented by Roosevelt's administration had proven to be moderately successful, but the US economy still faced serious constraints. In 1939, for instance, 15% of the American workforce was unemployed. The war effort quickly lifted the US labour force into full employment through high rates of output growth and investment (in other words, the economy was busy, with factories employing many workers, producing many products, which meant more income, which then re-enters the system creating an edge in productivity within the world system). This dynamic growth was driven initially by industrial production for the war, then by the expansion of production for export. The

American economy, thus hyper-charged with industrialisation, was ground zero for the ushering in of the Golden Age of post-WWII capitalism.

It is important to clarify that by "Golden Age" I mean only to the conditions of capital accumulation from the 1940s to the 1970s and to the rise of the "welfare state" in centralised economies within the capitalist sphere, primarily in Western Europe, Japan and the United States. These are also the countries that became related with the term "First World." It doesn't take into account the condition of complex social life around the world in an era that also brought forth other issues like the Cuban and Chinese revolutions, the Vietnam war, the de-colonisation in Africa and Asia, the Cold War, McCarthyism, and intense class conflict and political turbulence around the globe, but let's not get ahead of ourselves, baby steps people.

So, America realised how powerful it could be and started using the industrialisation of the war to set in place the foundations of a capitalist state, with politicians and the congress in the power seat determining how things got done and who had control over things, but then, in the late 1960s, the Golden Age had exhausted itself. There are many explanations for its decline and fall, but most of the theories agree that the end of the Golden Age was caused by a swift fall in the rate of profit towards the end of the 1960s, the beacon of this new system, the home of the new-age capitalism was of course New York, which up until this point, had been the capital of the capitalist world, representing the perfect example of how the system worked, a perfect blueprint for the capitalist utopia, however after the decline in the 1960s, with the new age thinking of the psychedelics who were less focused on politics and New York and more focused on mushrooms and free love, this resulted ilture that became disconnected to the rest of the capitalist state, this rash in how the financial currency systems ran and basically meant free-floating currencies immediately replaced the gold-based fixed exchange rate system, and inflation in the world economy shot up, with skyrocketing price increases, especially for oil (but more on that in a bit!)

So, we're now in the 70's and not looking great, the decade's crisis was marked by historically unprecedented, simultaneous, high inflation rates and high unemployment rates. This combination of high inflation and unemployment—and the corresponding recession it produced overtook the British economy in the 1960s and 1970s and the US economy in the mid- to late-1970s. Ideologies moved with the time, the harsh realisation that quality of life was plummeting, many 'hippies' jumped back into the cities to rescue some sort of 'life', however the people who had caused the mess, the politicians who had spent all their money, jumped ship and started backing themselves, leaving the rest of society to sink with the ship. This transfer of ideological leadership; within both economic orthodoxy and the political regimes in the US and Britain, sharply changed the way governments and central banks perceived the goals of fiscal and monetary policy.

So, to summarise, in the early 70's in New York, the centre of the ideology of capitalism, New York's politicians (politics being the go-to solution for us as a species at this point in time) ran out of money, they spent all their funding and then had nowhere to go, which, in 1975, meant the city, the hub of capitalist culture, was on the verge of collapse and bankruptcy. In a panic, the politicians were offered a helping hand from a group of people: the banks, people who until this point had only had the amount of power allowed to them by politicians now found themselves bailing out the politicians, for the first time in our history; politics was no longer the most powerful system to live by, now the banks had the power. Author of the time, Jonathan Mahler declared "The clinical term for it, fiscal crisis, didn't approach the raw reality. Spiritual crisis was more like it."

So, began the emergence of the idea that financial systems could run society, no longer were the men and women in government the people who held the cards, but instead the bankers; people we didn't vote for, faceless, money-led leeches who now held the whole deck in their hands, the politicians now bending to their every whim. Having power hungry, un-elected rulers, with a profit-at-all-costs mentality sounds like something out of a Hollywood dystopian blockbuster, probably starring Arnold Schwarzenegger as the non-American, white American guy who skydives in to save the day by shooting everyone while draped in an American flag, drinking a bottle of Budweiser and then riding off into the sunset with Kim Kardashian straddling the back seat. However the reality of the situation was even more of a disturbing image to imagine, because the scenario was real.

This was the start of the story inside our heads, this was the first misconception, this was the first time a veil was placed on the reality of the world we live in, politics still advocated that it had the power, the politicians were the leaders that shaped the world, however this was no longer the truth, now people from behind the scenes started taking charge of operations and influencing the direction of how politics was presented to us. This shaped the way of the future and similar situations started happening all over the capitalist world, capitalist cities and countries approached the verge of collapse, the banks bailed them out, more and more power being bestowed onto these faceless bankers. Now I'm not saying every banker is a banker with a 'w' in place of the 'b', but to be a CEO of a bank, to be the main man or women in charge; generally means one of two things; either they've inherited it from their families, in which case they are part of the super-rich elite that have only ever known wealth, will only ever know wealth and only ever think about economic gain, or, they've back-stabbed, lied and grafted their way to the top of the totem pole, mowing down anyone in their way, either way, probably not the people you want in power to make decisions for the whole of a population, yes the whole of a society, even the poor ones, potentially even ones from different backgrounds, maybe countries and, wait for it, maybe even people with a different ethnic background to them, how did they cope!

So now we reach the 1980s where political unrest is the fashion of the times, however at this point, we believe the issues are a result of bad politics, when in reality the issues stem from having a bad system. Since the sign of the times was an ideology of profit-at-all-costs the puppets, sorry, politicians who were in 'power' were in search for the new, favoured measurement of currency and wealth; oil and where did all this oil reside? In the Middle East of course.

Side-tracking briefly, remember earlier we said that oil was now the go to business to line your pockets? Well most of the oil lay in the Middle Eastern countries and so the next stage of the illusion was set into place, America, more specifically, then-US Secretary of State Henry Kissinger and Middle Eastern leaders in the Arab-Israeli dispute and the subsequent retreat by Hafez al-Assad of Syria; led to the same illusion being seen in the Soviet Union. An illusion Russia is still tranced in to this day under the direction of Putin. Basically, America went gung-ho chasing oil in the Middle-East, interfered with all the unstable politics of the area that were created thanks to America in the World War, starting to see a trend? So now the USA were dabbling their hands in other's serious agendas, to make some economic profit from the oil they snuck out. Obviously, this wound some people up, none more so than Syria and their leader at the time Al-Assad, who made an alliance with Ruhollah Khomeini of Iran.

They planned to force the US out of the Middle East by encouraging civilians to carry out suicide bombings on American targets in the region, thereby avoiding reprisals. In February 1984, the U withdrew all its troops from Lebanon because, in the words of then-US Secretary of State George P. Shultz, "we became paralysed by the complexity that we faced", basically they created a problem, which created another problem, which created another problem and then ran back behind their border, thinking everything would be forgotten, but this clearly wasn't the case, as the fuel for the fire had been lit and so was the creation of the idea that one man, one extremist, could be as effective at causing chaos in an ever-advancing world, quickly, thanks to the amount of different countries the US managed to wind up, the label of a 'country' became less prominent and instead the battle of ideologies (masked under the excuse of 'religion' was born).

Anyway, back in the 'thriving' and 'fruitful' first world, where the illusion of a 'perfect' world was cementing, the advancements in technology, contributing to the increase in globalisation all accumulated in corporations becoming stronger. It's like the world's worst Christmas cracker joke; what do you get when you mix the fabrication of politics and the power of the banks, under one banner in a system that is totally economically based and has a profit-at-all-cost mentality? Answer: Huge Corporations, with the same mentality, the same agenda and the same faceless leaders in the driving seat! How hilarious.

The method, called perception management, aimed to distract people from the complexities of the real world. The US Department of Defence (DOD) defines it as such, "Actions to convey and/or deny selected information and indicators to foreign audiences to influence their emotions, motives, and objective reasoning as well as to intelligence systems and leaders to influence official estimates, ultimately resulting in foreign behaviours and official actions favourable to the originator's objectives. In various ways, perception management combines truth projection, operations security, cover and deception, and psychological operations."

At the onset of the Iraq war in 2003, journalists were embedded with US troops as combat cameramen. The reason for this was not to show what was happening in the war, but to present the American view of it. Perception management was used to promote the belief that weapons of mass destruction were being manufactured in Iraq to promote its military intervention, even though the real purpose behind the war was regime change. You might think that the American public would begin to rebel against these messy entangling alliances with the 1984-like demonizing of one new "enemy" after another. Not only have these endless wars drained trillions of dollars from the US taxpayers, they have led to the deaths of thousands of US troops and to the tarnishing of America's image from the attendant evils of war, including a lengthy detour into the "dark side" of torture, assassinations and "collateral" killings of children and other innocents.

But that is where the history of "perception management" comes in, the need to keep the American people compliant and confused. In the 1980s, the Reagan administration was determined to "kick the Vietnam Syndrome," the revulsion that many Americans felt for warfare after all those years in the blood-soaked jungles of Vietnam and all the lies that clumsily justified the war.

So, the challenge for the US government became: how to present the actions of "enemies" always in the darkest light while bathing the behaviour of the US "side" in a rosy glow. You also had to stage this propaganda theatre in an ostensibly "free country" with a supposedly "independent press."

Perhaps not surprisingly much of the initiative came from the Central Intelligence Agency, which housed the expertise for manipulating target populations through propaganda and disinformation. The only difference this time would be that the American people would be the target population.

The ultimate success of Reagan's propaganda strategy was affirmed during the tenure of his successor, George H.W. Bush, when Bush ordered a 100-hour ground war on Feb. 23, 1991, to oust Iraqi troops from Kuwait, which had been invaded the previous August.

Though Iraqi dictator Saddam Hussein had long been signalling a readiness to withdraw and Soviet President Mikhail Gorbachev had negotiated a withdrawal arrangement that even had the blessings of top US commanders in the field President Bush insisted on pressing ahead with the ground attack. Bush's chief reason was that he and his Defence Secretary Dick Cheney saw the assault against Iraq's already decimated forces as an easy victory, one that would demonstrate America's new military capacity for high-tech warfare and would cap the process begun a decade earlier to erase the Vietnam Syndrome from the minds of average Americans.

Those strategic aspects of Bush's grand plan for a "new world order" began to emerge after the US-led coalition started pummelling Iraq with air strikes in mid-January 1991. The bombings inflicted severe damage on Iraq's military and civilian infrastructure and slaughtered a large number of non-combatants, including the incineration of some 400 women and children in a Baghdad bomb shelter on Feb. 13.

So as the banks maintained control, while politics maintained the illusion, corporations grew and started to form partnerships, friendships and all kinds of other 'ships' with the banks, using technology and subsequently media to join up the two together through computer networks to create a hidden system of power, this was also going on all over the globe, Margaret Thatcher in the UK, declaring 'there is no such thing as society' led to all us 'first world' places having a secret revolution for the 1% of people lucky or inherently rich enough to benefit from the ever expanding new way of doing things.

Most of society became 'technological utopians', people whose roots lay in the counterculture of the 1960s, saw the internet as an opportunity to make an alternative world that was free of political and legal restraints, a place where the majority could take the power back and although, thanks to corporations who ran the internet servers and shaped how the internet grew, this was a huge turning point into where we were going, the anti-establishment, the counter-culture of late 80's and early 90's managed to keep alive the hope of a truly free society, not solely focused on economic growth.

So, although this was all going on, people weren't blind, well, not everyone and the powers-that-be knew this, many conspiracy and obsessions of the 90's, everything from the UFO's and espionage tactics, became the craze, but in reality were the bankers and corporations way, along with the politics, of creating scenarios to cover-up the on-goings of weapon testing, data gathering and using technology as a means to control and predict the future trends.

You're probably wondering where the hell the media has been in all this. Well, without getting into all of the details, the media were doing okay, trying their best to not be too bias or controversial, but in a world where money made the planet rotate, it was a choice to decide to stand your ground and barely survive or join the gang and thrive. So, in a profit-based world, most media did just that and it was around the 80's and 90's where they really hit form in maintaining the illusion, with the new-age internet and media platforms, most mainstream media joined forces to help maintain the illusion, because there was a lot of money to be made by following suit, anyone who protested or stood their ground was disposed of.

On top of all of this, remember the problems that the USA were creating with the Middle East, (albeit the fifth consecutive problem caused solely by them), America did something so traditionally American it makes the super bowl look foreign; they created another problem.

The Reagan administration started using Muammar Gaddafi as a pawn in their public relations (PR) strategy of creating a simplified, morally unambiguous foreign policy by blaming him for the 1985 Rome and Vienna airport attacks and the 1986 Berlin discotheque bombing that killed US soldiers, both of which European security services attributed to Syrian intelligence agencies, basically America offered Gaddafi wealth and fame to take the blame for other's actions because America had now caused so many problems in the name of profit that they now had to lie about the lies that they lied about which all stemmed from the initial lies!

Gaddafi is described as playing along for the sake of increasing his profile in the Arab world as a revolutionary. The 1986 United States bombing of Libya, 10 days after the disco bombing, is described as an operation carried out mainly for PR reasons, because attacking Syria would have been too risky.

Confused yet? Good! That was the plan and what a fail-proof plan it was, create a world, totally run by money and power, which plays on the worst part of our human nature, which is stacked on top of so many lies and deceptions that everybody got so confused that they were happy to sit down and shut up, transforming into little consumers and cogs in the machine which had now become the robust, factory machinery of society. So, remember, now politics, banks, corporations and the media had created a little bubble world we'd shifted into existing inside of, manipulating other countries' affairs and political issues to shove the blame which was rightly theirs, onto other, unknown people, all the while taking what they could from these people on the way out.

This leads us to the turn of the millennium, the birth of yours truly and the start of where things get really crazy, yep, they've been relatively not-so-crazy so far, (if you want to grab a pen and paper to make sense of this, don't bother, I've been trying for two years and it turns out the whole thing is just diabolically mental).

So, Gaddafi was now the States' best friend, all of us first-world people were living in a bubble-world, kept 'safe' from the harsh reality of the world, when actually we were being kept from all the lies which created the society we lived in, concealing the harsh reality of what was going on. All of America's dabbling and concealing in the Middle East, led to a disturbance in peace-treaties across the region, importantly, the Israeli–Palestinian peace process. America was giving weapons away like it was going out of fashion in order to try and re-create the success they found with Gaddafi, however this time, the card didn't stick and they subsequently created the 'terrorist' groups we are now are so frightened of today.

The creation of these groups and the hatred instilled into these fighters of the bubble-world we lived in resulted in the 9/11 attacks, the destruction of the twin towers, however construction of these buildings caused the bankruptcy of New York that created the current narrative that created the terrorist group that destroyed the world trade centre! Now I'm not about to start dabbling in conspiracy theories, although I will state I find it amazing how a small group of untrained, unqualified and uneducated men with very little power bypassed the whole of the most powerful countries security systems in the world… twice.

But anyway, 9/11 obviously changed everything and the media and political narrative saw the perfect opportunity, by casting this new, fearsome terrorist threat into the lime-light, by making us so scared that some people might destroy our world that we didn't even think if the world we were standing in was worth standing in at all. This turn of events, the fear and hatred towards the Middle East, meant that Gaddafi's time in the spotlight was up, however instead of dealing with the lie on top of the lie on top... (You get the idea) and coming clean, the media and politics did the total opposite, Gaddafi came out and stated he was responsible for all the problems that he was credited for solving. Nobody bought it, but nobody dared talk about it, however this was a huge catalyst as people, some people, started to question if the trusted system that really shouldn't have been trusted for decades, was all it was cut out to be. The puppet politician that actually looked like a Toy Story puppet, Mr. Bush, spear-headed this continuation of illusion, however people had started to wake up.

So, quick catch up, the war happened, capitalism sky-rocketed, America became powerful, bestowed their fake-democracy on all the countries that didn't collapse after the war and then used all the countries that did collapse, along with the media, corporations and banks, to create an illusion, a story of a world where everything was fine, so long as you were willing to be a cog in the machine and hand over your money when asked. The advancements in technology led to Ulrich Beck (identified as a left-wing German political theorist), suggesting that "After the collapse of the Soviet Union, he saw the world as too complex to change, and Beck asserted that politicians should merely keep the West stable by predicting and avoiding risks. Aladdin, a computer that manages about 7% of the world's financial assets, now analysing the past to anticipate what may happen in the future; and how anti-depressant drugs and social media have come, to both stabilise the emotions of individuals".

So now we arrive in the late 2000's, where we see financial crashes in the western-world, 2008 was the year the neo-liberal economic orthodoxy that ran the world for 30 years suffered a heart attack of epic proportions. Not since 1929 had the financial community witnessed 12 months like it. Lehman Brothers went bankrupt. Merrill Lynch, AIG, Freddie Mac, Fannie Mae, HBOS, Royal Bank of Scotland, Bradford & Bingley, Fortis, Hypo and Alliance & Leicester all came within a whisker of doing so and had to be rescued.

Western leaders, who for years boasted about the self-evident benefits of light-touch regulation, had to sink trillions of dollars to prevent the World Banking system from collapsing. Of course, the money in politics which bailed the banks out was actually the money that banks and corporations had put in, and was it this fallout that led to a new-age revolution, where we realised that a financially-led system wasn't the solution? Well, no. Egypt had a revolution. Iceland had a revolution, so did Norway, Switzerland and a couple of other places, did you hear about it? Of course, you didn't, because it didn't happen here and so the media covered up the real explanations, yet another lie to cement our bubble-world in place because over here it didn't start a revolution, it diminished the hope for one. Over here, people became so disconnected and disenfranchised with the world they found themselves in, that many people retreated into the bubble, people were now happy to give up their freedom for security and to have the veil placed over their heads to the brutality of the world, choosing to exist inside the story they were given, in fear that any other option could result in devastating consequence, many people retreated into hyper-space and started to create a new life online, a new face in a new world where the harsh realities of the real world didn't exist; instead, online we could be whoever we wanted to be, we could lie to ourselves and create a new chapter within the same story, but that was never going to be a solution, the heightened interest in video-games, films and media all showed a desperation for us to escape from reality in small doses, there were despite this, people who started to use alternative ways of living to testify against the matrix-like scenario we found ourselves in, Occupy Wall Street emerged in an attempt to disrupt the system by imitating the leaderless system that the internet was once imagined to become. Occupy, although maybe not quite as successful as they had hoped to have been, lit a fire inside many and became the foundation for a new way of protesting and thinking, although not successful in completing what they set out do, Occupy subsequently created something even greater, the desire for change in a large number of people, in more recent years seeing many groups and activists emerge as a result of the work Occupy implemented, including the likes of Edward Snowden and Anonymous. So, although the majority slipped further and further into the bubble-world which had been created, a new wave of people from all generations; reminiscent of the counter-culture of the 60's and 70's started to realise just how bad the situation was.

    The reason it now seems that the world is getting scarier, that more and more tragedies are happening and the reason it seems like we are one day away from the apocalypse is because the atrocities and actions being carried out that we are now seeing in the spot-light, have been on-going for years, so many years, only now we are hearing and seeing about them on a mass scale.

The crash led to the unification of politics, banks, corporations and the media into one team of power-hungry, profit-at-all-cost mentality tyrants who, instead of previously being partners, were now all on the same team, wearing the same kit, under the same name; basically the result of decades of lies, fabrications and chase of economic wealth resulted in the merging together of all of our society's narratives, creating one big story which now existed in our universal heads, all of us now living in a story told by somebody else, with someone else's interest at stake, making us conditioned to play to the worst parts of our human nature to maintain a system that totally focused on economic growth for the people who were at the top of society… no wonder little old me, who had just celebrated his 10th birthday, was already on a crash-course for insanity, it had been over 50 years in the making!

There's been a secret plot twist brewing in this story for quite some time, but here it comes, while all of this has been going on, all the way back in the 70's, remember, when the banks first took control, there was one man who used the banks and the corporations for his own good, who used politics and media to get filthy rich and powerful, have you guessed who it is yet?

Well the reason I've kept this on the quiet up until now is because this simply proves that in 2008 and in subsequent recent years that all these different narratives, politics, the media, banks and corporations were now the same thing because a man who ran a corporation in the 70's, manipulated the banks in the 80's and used the media and political landscape in the 90's to grow more and more powerful so that in the 2000's he could establish himself as a mainstay power in all of these groups so that when they all joined forces in 2008, he could pounce at the opportunity to use his power amongst all the different sides to now place himself at the centre of the stories inside our heads, because the man who used all the different narratives coming together to get rich and gain economically, is a celebrity, is a friend of the banker's, is a corporation owner and is now the president of the United States because the man who used the corrupt system to gain money has now become the centre of its story, ladies and gentlemen I present to you, Donald Trump.

So now we've reached the world I grew up in, a world, a story created to maintain a lie, on top of a lie, on top a lie, which was lying about a whole bunch of lies, which were created to distract us from a lie within a lie, on top of a lie, with a few pointless lies added in for good measure.

Living in a society that prayed on our fears and desires, our fears to make us scared to question the obvious fabrication in the world around us and our desires to distract us with celebrities, consumerism and materialism to make us forget about the clear fabrication of a world around us, a story that was being told to us to maintain a system that didn't serve us. It gave my generation a choice, become part of the machine, part of the system and find a space to rotate like a cog, chasing external gain, totally disconnected from our divine nature, or the other, slightly less favourable option that I opted for (being the controversial type that I am),the 'off-the-deep-end-with-a-crash' option. This is where my personal story from the first chapter catches up and intertwines with this story, my meeting with Tiny Tim being my smack in the face, my 'lifting-of-the-veil' moment when I saw the world for how it was, not for how I had been told to view it. It was harsh, it was brutal, it was cruel and beaten and in need of help, but now I was out of the illusion, now I was no longer in the cage, I could be that help.

We as a society had spent so long just covering up our last mistake and so long chasing money and power that we now found ourselves in a situation where we would rather live in a 'fake' story we didn't write than take back control and although, being left vulnerable and potentially in a dangerous place, now also be granted the opportunity to rise, to revolutionise and to take a huge step forward, with our heads towards a bright future, instead of looking over our shoulder at the dark past.

This is what has happened in recent years, Brexit, Trump, distrust in politics and media, dislike of banks and huge corporations, because now with Trump getting elected and Britain being leaders as always (not the queen or the government, I mean the people, the revolutionaries) have ripped the veil off the illusion and so everyone has seen the ugly truth of what's been going on.

Let's not now act surprised at Brexit or Trump or the protests and marches, we've been creating this story for half a century! Did you know that in every single election in the US, ever, that the richest backed campaign has won? Every single time, not even one outlier or dark horse, is that not enough to prove that the whole thing is an economically ran stage-show? The person with most money wins, we might as well not even bother holding elections and just wait to see who has the better funding and then give them the presidency.

I'm not saying that we should be like another country or operate in the same way as somewhere else, I'm saying that we should realise that the narrative we're conditioned into doesn't serve us and that it is only one of many different ways in which we can live and that it's down to us to figure out which alternative works for us and centre our lives, realities and stories around that, because change can happen and change does happen, we have one life and shouldn't spend any time not living to the fullest, all of this stems from realising our life is a story and that we can write it for ourselves, we should take all the best from all the alternatives and then create our own way that best serves us and the beautiful parts of our humanity.

But now we're here, now we've had a political, media (sort of) revolution and revelation in how we view banks and corporations the most important question still remains: If we can't trust the story we're told, what story do we replace it with?

Think of it like being injected with poison, dripped into our consciousness by the powers that were and that still exist today, now we've managed to pull the needle injecting the poison out, we still need to flush the poison out of our systems so that we can heal and become healthy again. We were conditioned people in cages, now the cage has been opened; we have to recondition ourselves so we don't walk right back into another cage with a different captor at the door. How do we do that?

Quite simply; we have to write our own story.

Chapter 5

<u>The Illusion of choice</u>

So, what's all that history resulted in? Well let's look at the fact I chose to open the book with, the fact that made me sit up and pay attention, the fact that 85 people have more wealth than half the world, we need to consider this more, because if you're like me, that ratio is so ridiculous that it's actually hard to comprehend.

So just think about that, 85 people (that's 0.00000121428 of the world's population) have *the same* 'wealth' as 3.5 billion (50% of the population). What's crazier is, *just one* of the richest 85's incomes would be enough to end extreme poverty *four times* over, not once, but *four* times and yet no action has been taken. That works out that out of £20, you'd need to give up 20p of that to end poverty 4 times over... has anyone stepped up and done that? Nope, not one.

It's not even like money is a resource that's running out, we make it ourselves! Not like food for example, where we choose to throw away one third of all food (1.3 billion tonnes a year) and then ask why 80% of the world live off less than $10 per day, why more people have access to a phone worldwide than they do a toilet?

We are so blind today that in the three decades since Reagan's propaganda machine was launched, the American press corps have also fallen more and more into line with an aggressive U.S. government's foreign policy strategies. Those in the mainstream media who resisted the propaganda pressures mostly saw their careers suffer while those who played along moved steadily up the ranks into positions of more money and more status.

Even after the Iraq War debacle when nearly the entire mainstream media went with the pro-invasion flow, there was almost no accountability for that historic journalistic failure. Indeed, the influence at major newspapers, such as the Washington Post and the New York Times, has only solidified since.

Today's coverage of the Syrian civil war or the Ukraine crisis is so firmly in line with the State Department's propaganda "themes" that it would put smiles on the faces of William Casey and Walter Raymond if they were around today to see how seamlessly the "perception management" now works. There's no need any more to send out "public diplomacy" teams to bully editors and news executives. Everyone is already on-board.

Rupert Murdoch's media empire is bigger than ever, but his messaging barely stands out as distinctive, given how he has also gained control of the editorial and foreign-reporting sections of the Washington Post, the New York Times and virtually every other major news outlet. For instance, the demonizing of Russian President Putin is now so comprehensive that no honest person could look at those articles and see anything approaching objective or even-handed journalism. Yet, no one loses a job over this lack of professionalism.

The Reagan administration's dreams of harnessing private foundations and non-governmental organizations have also come true. The Orwellian circle has been completed with many American "anti-war" groups advocating for "humanitarian" wars in Syria and other countries targeted by U.S. propaganda.

As you can see, some of us are waking up, but for those of us still caught in the old story, or old perception, more and more of us have been funnelled into a smaller and smaller margin of options when looking at our media, we now truly exist inside an illusion of choice.

If someone could control the production of the entire media, that would make them immensely powerful. They would literally be able to tell people what to think. Well, what if I told you that there are just six enormous media conglomerates that combine to produce about 90 percent of all the media that we consume?

Would that alarm you? It should alarm you. The truth is that our attitudes, opinions and beliefs are greatly shaped by what we allow into our minds. After all, they don't call it "programming" for no reason. Even those of us that realise that we are connected to "the matrix" probably greatly underestimate the tremendous influence that the media has over us. We live in a time when it is absolutely imperative to think for ourselves, but most people are absolutely overwhelmed with information and seem more than content to let others do their thinking for them. Sadly, this is greatly contributing to the downfall of our society.

And of course, the mainstream media desperately does not want you to look at "the man behind the curtain". They just want you to stay plugged in to the "programming" that they are feeding you without asking any questions.

Fortunately, a growing minority of people are waking up and are starting to reject the mainstream media. An increasing number of people are beginning to recognise that the mainstream media is the mouthpiece of the establishment and that it is promoting the agenda of the establishment.

George Carlin made it so clear and so simple. That was his genius. With humour that we could all relate to, he told us the truth about how our world works and how most of us are cattle for the super-rich. How we are conned into believing in the very people who enslave us, how we are conned into believing in the illusion of freedom. He knew and he told us. We laughed, but did we really listen?

Carlin passed away in 2008. At the time, I thought it was sad – just like it's sad when any beloved entertainer dies. But looking back on it, we lost something unique and irreplaceable when Carlin left us. We lost one of the few people capable of telling us the truth in a way that we were willing to hear it.

The following routine, from his 2005 video 'Life is Worth Losing', explains the illusions we're talking about here in a more poetic and emotional way than I ever could, so I'll let him do it instead:

"Politicians have traditionally hidden behind three things: the flag, the bible, and children. No child left behind, no child left behind. Really? Not long ago you were talking about giving kids a head start. Head start, left behind... Someone's losing ground here.

But there's a reason. There's a reason. There's a reason for this, there's a reason education SUCKS, and it's the same reason it will never ever, ever, be fixed. It's never going to get any better. Don't look for it; be happy with what you've got...BECAUSE THE OWNERS OF THIS COUNTRY DON'T WANT THAT. I'm talking about the real owners now...the REAL owners. The big wealthy business interests that control things and make all the important decisions.

Forget the politicians. The politicians are put there to give you the idea that you have freedom of choice – you don't. You have no choice. You have OWNERS. They OWN you. They own everything. They own all the important land. They own and control the corporations. They've long since bought and paid for the Senate, the Congress, the state houses, the city halls, they got the judges in their back pockets and they own all the big media companies, so they control just about all of the news and information you get to hear.

They've got you by the throat. They spend billions of dollars every year lobbying . . . lobbying, to get what they want . . . Well, we know what they want. They want more for themselves and less for everybody else, but I'll tell you what they don't want . . . they don't want a population of citizens capable of critical thinking. They don't want well informed, well educated people capable of critical thinking. They're not interested in that . . . that doesn't help them. That's against their interests. That's right.

They don't want people who are smart enough to sit around a kitchen table and think about how badly they're getting screwed by a system that threw them overboard 30 years ago. They don't want that. You know what they want? They want obedient workers ... obedient workers, people who are just smart enough to run the machines and do the paperwork, and just dumb enough to passively accept all these increasingly worse jobs with the lower pay, the longer hours, the reduced benefits, the end of overtime and vanishing pension that disappears the minute you go to collect it, and now they're coming for your Social Security money. They want your retirement money. They want it back so they can give it to their criminal friends on Wall Street. And you know something? They'll get it . . . they'll get it all from you sooner or later cause they own this fucking place.

It's a big club, and you aren't in it. You and I are not in THE BIG CLUB. By the way, it's the same big club they use to beat you over the head with all day long when they tell you what to believe. All day long beating you over the head with their media telling you what to believe, what to think and what to buy. The table has tilted folks. The game is rigged and nobody seems to notice. Nobody seems to care.

Good honest hard-working people . . . white collar, blue collar it doesn't matter what colour shirt you have on. Good honest hard-working people continue, these are people of modest means . . . continue to elect these rich people who don't give a damn about you. They don't give a damn about you . . . they don't give a damn about you. They don't care about you at all . . . at all . . . at all. And nobody seems to notice, nobody seems to care. That's what the owners count on. The fact is that Americans will probably remain wilfully ignorant of the big red, white and blue pole that's being jammed up their back-side every day, because the owners of this country know the truth. It's called the American Dream, because you have to be asleep to believe it . . ."

Does anyone else want to start a revolution after hearing that? I don't see how anyone can read it and go back into the daily rat-race without at least questioning the daily ration of lies that emerges from their televisions daily.

It is worth repeating again and again that the bulk of America's mainline media is owned and controlled by a mere six corporations. This, of course, means that unless you're already consciously avoiding these mainline media sources, then most of the news and entertainment that makes it onto your screen and into your mind comes from a small pool of corporate sources, all of which play important roles in delivering propaganda, social programming and perpetual crisis narratives to the public.

Anyone who relies on mainstream newspapers, television or radio for news to get an honest opinion will have a very superficial and one sided view of what is going on, honestly. What masquerades as news is simply a mixture of lies, half-truths, spin, counter spin and propaganda. The aim of the media today is to misinform, to manipulate and to make you afraid.

Quite rightly, distrust of the press is becoming widespread. A major recent survey in the USA showed that 45% of Americans believe little or nothing that they read in newspapers. Twenty years ago, only 16% of readers expressed such profound scepticism.

Apart from newsletters and small publishers there is no free press in America and except for newsletters and small publishers in England there is no free press in England either.

In most countries where there is no free press it is because the government has used brute force to censor the media. Tyrants from the dusty depths of history right up to the Nazis and the communists knew the importance of controlling the press.

But things are different now.

The difference with the 20th century despots is that they know how to manipulate the media and, instead of just dipping journalists in boiling tar they hire tame journalists to spread their message. Labour's spin doctors were, in a spiritual sense, fathered by Hitler and Goebbels.

Today, politicians may not own the media and they may no longer need to chop off the arms and heads of troublesome scribes, but they can control the media with ever increasing subtlety. News used to be defined as things someone didn't want to see in print - these days it's the opposite; it's stuff someone in power wants you to read.

The result is that although we may seem to have a free press, we don't. And that's worse than having a despot who boils disobedient journalists in oil. What you read in your newspaper and what you see on television and what you hear on the radio are, by and large, the accepted messages. People believe what they see and what they hear and what they read.

But today's journalists are muzzled not by the threat of violence but by the promise of wealth and fame and success. The statist elite of the EU and Labour don't kill journalists - they buy them.

Today's journalists have given up their spirit in return for money, fame and honours. Journalists used to pride themselves on their freedom and independence. Today's journalists are servile, weak and greedy. They are also easily bribed.

The people who should be protecting our freedom are helping our tyrannical rulers take it from us. The rulers tell the journalists that what they are doing is `inevitable' and `necessary' and they talk of threats from terrorism and the need for progress.

Today's journalists have no sense of history, no ability to think for themselves; they have become part of show business. They are not in the slightest bit interested in truth. They will blow whichever way the wind takes them.

Journalists and editors have chosen popularity with their bosses, gold and fame, above principle. They want to be 'in' with the 'in crowd', they want to be liked. They are sycophantic quislings not journalists. They grovel at the feet of third rate politicians and businessmen and they suppress the truth for an invitation to Chequers and a company car (preferably with chauffeur).

It is the role of journalists to harass, criticise and question politicians. Always. Whoever is in power, journalists should never have friends among politicians and should never accept favours. It is as bad for a journalist to accept hospitality from a politician as it would be to accept a bribe from an industrialist.

Among the 300 guests officially entertained, at taxpayers' expense, by the Blair's during Labour's first term in power between 1997 and 2001 were (in addition to an Italian nobleman and his wife and two daughters, who had loaned Tony Blair his Tuscan villa for a holiday) a clutch of well-known journalists.

Now, if any of those journalists had been writing a story, say, on the oil industry and had spent a weekend dining and wining at the expense of an oil company chief do you not think there might have been raised eyebrows?

The conglomerates are: General Electric, News Corp., Disney, Viacom, Time Warner and CBS. (So don't expect to see this book on any of the major news stories anytime soon).

Did you know that the president of CBS and the president of ABC both have brothers that are top officials in the current administration?

The big news networks have developed an almost incestuous relationship with the federal government in recent years. But of course, the same could be said of the relationship that the media has with the big corporations that own stock in their parent companies and that advertise on their networks.

This is one of the reasons why we very rarely ever see any hard-hitting stories on the big networks anymore. The flow of information through the corporate-dominated media is very tightly controlled, and there are a lot of gatekeepers that make sure that the "wrong stories" don't get put out to the public. As a result, many of the "big stories" that have come out in recent years were originally broken by the alternative media.

One hundred and eighteen people comprise the membership on the boards of directors of the ten big media giants. These one hundred and eighteen individuals in turn sit on the corporate boards of two-hundred and eighty-eight national and international corporations.

The power that these companies have is so vast that it is hard to put into words... so let's do it in this funky bit of book writing instead, seriously, look how many of these companies are on here!

Time Warner
CNN, Home Box Office (HBO), Time Inc., Turner Broadcasting System, Inc., Warner Bros. Entertainment Inc., CW Network (partial ownership), TMZ, New Line Cinema, Time Warner Cable, Cinemax, Cartoon Network, TBS, TNT, America

Online, MapQuest, Moviefone, Castle Rock, Sports Illustrated, Fortune, Marie Claire, DC Comics and People Magazine.

Walt Disney

ABC Television Network, Disney Publishing, ESPN Inc., Disney Channel, The History Channel, SOAPnet, A&E, Lifetime, Buena Vista Home Entertainment, Buena Vista Theatrical Productions, Buena Vista Records, Disney Records, Hollywood Records, Miramax Films, Marvel, Star Wars (partial), Touchstone Pictures, Walt Disney Pictures, Pixar Animation Studios, 277 Radio Stations, Buena Vista Games and Hyperion Books.

Viacom

Paramount Pictures, Paramount Home Entertainment, Black Entertainment Television (BET), Comedy Central, Country Music Television (CMT), Logo, MTV, MTV Canada, MTV2, Nick Magazine, Nick at Nite, Nick Jr., Nickelodeon, Noggin, Spike TV, The Movie Channel, TV Land and VH1.

News Corporation

Dow Jones & Company, Inc., Fox Television Stations, The New York Post, TV Guide, Fox Searchlight Pictures, Beliefnet, Fox Business Network, Fox Kids Europe, Fox News Channel, Fox Sports Net, Fox Television Network, FX, My Network TV, MySpace, News Limited News, Phoenix InfoNews Channel, Phoenix Movies Channel, Sky PerfecTV, Speed Channel, STAR TV India, STAR TV Taiwan, STAR World, Times Higher Education Supplement Magazine, Times Literary Supplement Magazine, Times of London, 20th Century Fox Home Entertainment, 20th Century Fox International, 20th Century Fox Studios, 20th Century Fox Television, BskyB,

DIRECTV, The Wall Street Journal, Fox Broadcasting Company, Fox Interactive Media, FOXTEL, HarperCollins Publishers, The National Geographic Channel, National Rugby League, News Interactive, News Outdoor, Radio Veronica, ReganBooks, Sky Italia, Sky Radio Denmark, Sky Radio Germany, Sky Radio Netherlands and STAR.

CBS Corporation

CBS News, CBS Sports, CBS Television Network, CNET, Showtime, TV.com, CBS Radio Inc. (130 stations), CBS Consumer Products, CBS Outdoor, CW Network (50% ownership), Infinity Broadcasting, Simon & Schuster (Pocket Books, Scribner) and Westwood One Radio Network.

Comcast

NBC, Bravo, CNBC, NBC News, MSNBC, NBC Sports, NBC Television Network, Oxygen, SciFi Magazine, Syfy (Sci Fi Channel), Telemundo, USA Network, Weather Channel, Focus Features, NBC Universal Television Distribution, NBC Universal Television Studio, Paxson Communications (partial ownership), Hulu, Universal Parks & Resorts, Universal Pictures, Universal Studio Home Video.

Can you believe that? There's literally not one name I can think of that isn't on that list! (There goes my chance of a movie adaptation anytime soon and with it, any serious coverage on the news, but the price of freedom is high!)

All of these corporations have their own shady histories, dealings and suspicious characters, even Disney which is widely regarded by many of the people in media that I've interviewed as an occult enterprise aimed at warping the minds of children with disturbing subliminal imagery. Now I know hearing the fact that Mickey Mouse and Peter Pan might be maintaining and creating a frequency of consciousness from an early age that encourages consumerism, materialism and subliminal messages that condition us into a perceived reality is something that is always going to hit home hard, we all love Disney, but that's the point, there's a REASON we all love Disney, there's a reason you've thought what I've said so far has resonated with you, but as soon as I expose your dear Disney you now think I'm saying far-fetched and ridiculous proposals, there is no way that Disney could be doing that, there is no way that 9/11 was an inside job, these things are facts, but facts according to whom? Such a large part of this personal revolution is about questioning the whole of your reality, because as scary as it is to face, all our reality has been constructed by other people, people who probably don't want the best for you, people who really, just want you to buy the Mickey Mouse ears and then come back next year to do the same again, it isn't Mickey's fault, it's the whole damn system.

Young people watching Disney, older people watching one of the other ones, regardless, we are all spending more than 240 hours a month connected to the media.

But we are only awake for about 480 hours a month, about half of our time awake is being spent consuming media, consuming a story into our subconscious of the world we're living in, one being shaped in the name of profit.

When it comes to influencing the American people, nobody has more power than the big media companies do and until we can break this sick addiction to the mainstream media and get people to start thinking for themselves, we will never see widespread changes in our society. If people are being "programmed" by the mainstream media, they will continue to express the opinions, attitudes and beliefs that have been downloaded into their minds, it's only when we take a step back and intuitively question the information being told to us from all angles, that we will be able to turn the current media theatre show into a reality we want to be part of.

Chapter 6

THE PROFIT IN POLITICS

By surveying what is available for consumption in the mass media, it is easy to see how they are creating the narrative in society these six corporations are helping to maintain. They have the power to warp reality by calling staged shows 'reality' shows. Ideas which don't support mainstream narratives and the consumer agenda are omitted, and stories about independent people over-coming strife without dependence on government are seldom if ever elevated.

The promotion of shallow, materialistic, ego-centric values on our screens and the obvious dumbing down of the American population is coming from these six corporations. Think about that. These are the companies that glorify consumption, obedience, ignorance, the hyper-sexualisation of youth, the glorification of war and government surveillance, and so on. The advertisers that support these media companies have tremendous sway over what makes it onto the airwaves. They help to control public perception; they create the story we're born into.

The bottom line is that corporate media is a gigantic collection of special interests and economic profit. So much of the human story is omitted in this capitalistic, for-profit environment scheme like this, which is why, now more than ever, the independent, alternative media is such a gem for human kind.

However, it's not just the media that are maintaining this, as we know, they are joined at the hip with politics and so now it's time to look at politics and how politics as well, has become the Disneyland version of itself inside all our heads.

For a long time we have seen recurrent struggles between those who seek an alliance between business and government, against those who seek to extend democracy to all the people through our representative form of government.

This began with the early Federalists. Alexander Hamilton did not believe that a society could succeed "which did not unite the interest and credit of rich individuals with those of the state." As Secretary of the Treasury, he helped to found the Bank of the United States. This succeeded in giving the business interests of America a stake in government.

So, began the struggle to prevent that power from leaving the wealthy. They fought to prevent the extension of the vote to any others.

We witnessed this fight over power from the beginning. The importance of Andrew Jackson is that he fought successfully to not only extend the vote to others but to give the power of governance to the people. He also put an end to the Bank of the United States. Our history has seen repeated examples of this continuing struggle and we see that today. Some call what we have today a plutocracy. A plutocracy is defined by Wikipedia as being a society ruled and dominated by a small minority of its wealthiest citizens.

Although we may not have a conspiracy to deprive the people of their rights, we are seeing a concerted effort by the top 1% of our population to dominate and influence our present-day politics. Money is used to influence our elected officials, through lobbying at the state and federal level and through campaign contributions. The growth in the expenditures of money in our elections has grown to epidemic proportions.

Whether you are talking about the early Federalist days, the Gilded Age, the years that preceded the Great Depression or now where we have seen a return to the recurrent pattern in our history, where the wealthy seek to dominate and the rest of us fight to maintain our rights and to gain new rights.

The use of the word conservative is a joke. What are they conserving? Today's modern day so-called conservatives, like their predecessors, have fought against all progress for us the people. Conservatives were against the extension of the vote to all white males, they were against the 13th Amendment to end slavery, they were against women having the right to vote and they fought against the Civil Rights legislation of the 1960's. They were against Social Security and Medicare and now they are against the Affordable Care Act. The question that should be asked is, what do Conservatives want to conserve other than their financial self-interest?

Republicans now use the very human goals of social stability and religious salvation as a means of sustaining their power and money against the interests of the people, just like they did 200 years ago.

So, what do we see in the politics of today? We see the same recurrent themes and patterns of the past. It is still a struggle for the many to have an equal opportunity for a better life against those who would seek to maintain their power and influence.

Throughout these years we have witnessed the struggle between the Jeffersonian ideal of individual liberty and equality against the forces of moneyed interests and power.

Today, we have the frustrated and angry minions of the wealthy being conned into believing the sales pitch that they too can become millionaires. The danger in today's politics is that we have a segment of our population that are not willing to accept the outcome of elections and the will of the majority.

Montesquieu, once said, "Men are born equal and then society makes them lose It.", **well, it is up to us, as a united majority to come together as one and love everybody**. We must reject the tyranny of the minority that we are now experiencing. We only have one choice and that is to re-affirm the majority rule and to provide a different alternative, a locally-based operation. I'm not going to spend the whole of this book talking about what we as a society should replace the current system with (that's the sequel), because before we start worrying about building a new system, we have to make sure we're internally ready to build one that isn't going to look identical to the one we just tore down, however what I will say is that regardless of personal opinion and thought, universally it is obvious now that the current political story we've been told doesn't work and that we need a revolution.

We need to take a page out of the past as a guide for our future. We need to recognise that no class distinctions exist nor should they. We are all working men and women and we are all on the same team. Within a purely political sense, we must admit that we are all mutually dependent on each other for each person's success. Let us declare not just our independence but our mutual interdependence and understand that;

> **We are the solution, we are the revolution, we are the leaders that can change the direction of our politics.**

If politics has done anything over the last 100 years it has proven that a financially-led, profit-at-all-costs based society run by a small minority doesn't work for the majority; psychically, emotionally, financially or spiritually; regardless of what 'party' or 'wing' their specific details and plans relate to, the whole thing is corrupted and needs to go, needs to change.

Noam Chomsky (this guy is a big deal on this whole revolution deal, so remember him) reminds us that "the head of the serpent that must be severed is the United States as defined by the Monroe Doctrine and 'Manifest Destiny'." Basically, Noam wants us to make decisions for ourselves.

Trans-pacific and transatlantic pacts are being negotiated in secret with the collusion of corporate lawyers. These pacts, like the ones drawn up in the past, are not free-trade agreements, they are investors' rights agreements, insurance for corporations that conditions being created will guarantee profit. Why is this all secret? Because the conditions that would benefit us would totally destroy the foundations they're set up on.

They spy, lie and control us with violence and fear, they sell us McDonald's and destroy the planet, all for a little bit of paper (you know that money we all so desperately crave) that we've all agreed is worth something. I wish they *were* lizards, at least that way we'd know why they are like they are. They certainly are playing to that reptilian consciousness, but we're coming back to that later.

When looking at modern politics, one thing is obvious about this current landscape; we're screwed unless we collectively organise ourselves and disobey. They've got us caged, they own both the teams we're playing for, the stadium we're playing in, the grass we're playing on and we're the ball they're kicking around. They have spent the last century removing the possibility for reform or redirection within the system; the change must come from us.

Our only hope of a new system is to overthrow their structures and take our politics back.

Chapter 7

The Click Illusion

Over the last few years, I've been fortunate to speak to some front-line forward thinkers in how we could use technology to better our society and in this chapter, we're going to get all technical and look at how technology can be a tool for change.

We can now act as a network that can provide autonomous solutions, a system that has organised itself through the feedback of information around the network created. People organising each-other without the exercise of power, labels or judgement, but a collective of people using each-other to help create an existence that allows each individual to live a life they wish to live, without the tyranny of imposing their views onto others, simply accepting everybody else's life and helping maintain the plane which allows the individual to maintain theirs using tools such as technology to further advance everybody's physical well-being, allowing a more open and equal platform to elevate consciousness, allowing more opportunity to end poverty, austerity and cruelty, now using the inner-beauty as the go to morale to live by, instead of the worst parts of our primal nature; allowing a revolution of the mind, a revolution of the soul, a revolution of the political, media and social narrative, leaderless, everybody equal, everybody content, everybody lives the life they want to live.

This alone advocates the call for an alternative, that uses neither politics nor profit as the main mentality on which a society sits, the poverty so many people find themselves in today and the lack of fulfilment for so many people who find themselves not in poverty prove that neither of these two structures can truly give us as self-aware conscious beings contentedness in our lives, we need a re-shift in how we view our lives, we need a revolution. I appreciate that it may appear a bit 'doom and gloom' and that on this path to a personal revolution you're fighting pretty much the whole world, however while this mainstream shift in how society was running occurred, alternative solutions were also being born, developed and calculated and unlike the current narrative which has come to a crashing full-stop, these calculations are still going on, and because things are changing it doesn't have to be that way. The other cyber-space, universe, eternal realm or whatever else you want to call it has also seen a change; ideas such as Occupy and Anonymous have grown and are now disrupting what used to be a rigid, pre-recorded message, with countries like Turkey, Egypt and Iceland all revolutionising their economic, political and social landscape to one of a fairer mould; social media is seeing a rise of alternative messages; the corporations and criminals who had created the ideal world for themselves to thrive in, the very system that has created and maintained itself, oppressing and distracting us as a species from our true potential has now reached breaking point and created its own demise. The fear, lust and hatred that the very system has to operate and run with are now being replaced and we're at a turning point where we can evolve, we can revolutionise our lives and the world we're living in. Technology for sure is one of these tools which can help provide an alternative and can play a huge part in bringing about that change.

So how can we use technology in a positive manner, without the possibility of corruption or greed taking over to pervert the original purpose?

Well like with anything, it's dependent on how we use it. I love my Nan's saying 'you are what you eat', short and simple, also astoundingly true. (Sure it may not be the most philosophical statement ever said, but now watch me and try and make it just that!).

I think we can apply my Nan's advice on choosing a banana over a burger when looking at technology, (not like my nan would've been able to grasp the concept mind you, the fact Golden Balls was on her TV was a miracle enough, bless her), because technology and how we can use it, both positively or negatively is dependent on the individual. Like we spoke about earlier, think of your phone, chances are you have an IPhone. Today, in 2017, eighty seven percent of the western culture owns an apple product, but even if you have the android or the whatever else you're using to socialise on, just think, on that device, you hold the key to accessing the whole of human history. Every picture ever posted, every video ever recorded (no, not in that way, we're trying to start a revolution here!), every article, event, story ever told, all at the tips of your fingers. Now re-wind to the previous brackets and think, what do you use the Internet, your social media, your online connection to do?

Now obviously, I don't know your search history, I'm not the American government after all, (controversial maybe, but Ed Snowden sure had a point) but the chances are, you like myself and the rest of society aren't using technology to the maximum benefit it could be, we as a society are certainly not using technology to the positive extent we could be and because of this, technology can be used to maintain a story in our head that perhaps doesn't serve us.

What I see as the common enemy of all movements is the power structure that empowers groups to be able to oppress. It does get confusing as different groups have different opposing opinions, but hypothetically let's say for a minute that we could temporarily put some of those differences aside and the movement shifts to a multiple layered movement with the primary objective of equality and the secondary objective of gay rights, black lives matters or whatever the specific movement may be. Then we have a group which includes every movement towards equality all fighting for the same cause against all those who deny that this world should be equal. The problem I see now is we have many separate movements which are all fighting the same common enemy, but also fighting among themselves, which is the perfect divide and conquer strategy for those doing the oppressing. Let's say we all unite and I know this is far more complex than my oversimplification I have given here, but should we do that we then have a true global movement that cannot be stopped, but in which differences would need to be worked out along the way, technology, the online world and the new inventions being invented every day could be a fantastic way to unite the world.

So, remember, technology itself isn't a positive or negative tool, really it's just a 'thing'. What determines whether we use advancements in technology to elevate our species into a brand new age of freedom Snowden-style or turn into a corporate illusion Matrix-style is down to us; how are we going to use technology, what and who are we going to support or boycott, do we crave freedom or security, how far are we willing to take technology before we lose our humanity? Well, I hope you're close to having a personal revolution because personally, I have no idea.

Every movement is a metaphor for the same thing, and when we realize that deep down that all (most) people want is love, happiness and to not feel threatened in life, we can work out the rest of our differences. There is a very small group of people who want everything, the rest of us are happy to share and get along, and the sooner those in the latter group can unify and work together the better, but it needs the leaders of separate movements to set aside some differences and communicate towards the better cause for the collective. A shift is coming, let's embrace it and unify.

We've now worked out that politics just needs to be the administration of certain spiritual and universal principles. For me the spiritual (or universal) principles that are important are that we are all one, we're all together and every individual's rights need to be respected, principles that the current system doesn't represent.

I think that we need to see that politics is the implementation of spiritual principles of oneness, togetherness, tolerance of one another and making sure the people are taken care of. This is why I think we need a personal revolution more than a political one, quite simply; we as individuals all together make the majority of a society, who then all decide to make our political laws and vote for our political leaders and so if there is a problem with our political narrative, it has to be because there is an internal problem with us which is creating the political problems we see.

The last 20 years have been witness to some truly amazing innovations thanks to the internet. The introduction of the world-wide web has had more lasting effects than any other invention in history. This, of course, is something you know very well.

However, there are some huge implications that are much less obvious than our new-found ability to Google anything or 'poke' our friends online. The internet is revered as a source of endless entertainment, but that is barely scratching the surface.

Despite being separated by borders, cultures, languages, politics and idealisms, we can all come together on the internet. Grassroots movements are now as common as, well, grass. Facebook groups, Support-This-Cause websites, PayPal donation buttons and other internet tools make it easy for any cause to attain massive support.

The best example of this is how Twitter has been breaking news stories faster than reporters. Most recently a single tweet from protesters who were fired upon by police in Libya spread like wildfire, rallying international support for their cause. All news is now international news. This puts an incredible burden of accountability on world leaders and organizations: no longer is it so easy to cover up the mistakes that would've previously been swept under the carpet, now if you screw up; the world will know within a matter of minutes.

Apple spoke true when they preached about the magic of seeing someone's face while talking to them. That addition changes the dynamic of the conversation in a profound way. When someone laughs, you can see the smile evolve into audible glee. It's almost like you're there with them. (Which will do until teleportation comes around, unless you've realised that teleportation isn't physical but conscious, but more on that another time.)

Technology can create the platform for creative, local direct action (which is the answer), an answer and solution to the idea that we shouldn't be looking for sort of glamorous new figures to lead us. We shouldn't be looking to conventional politics. Because, you know, it's difficult to get any political purchase. There are no political figures that are interested in representing ordinary people and so we 'ordinary' people must represent ourselves. It's happening too, a one million people's women march against Trump, just organised off Facebook and the online petition tool Change.org, which prides itself on empowering individuals by enabling them to start petitions against politicians, corporations or others. Founded in 2007, the site now has 45 million users in 196 countries.

The opportunities technology presents are paramount as we head towards a new way of doing things, the 'cyber-space' web's whole creation was a protest to the delusion previous generations felt, it's a way to over-ride the rules and restrictions that politics, a controlled media and fixed agendas have, it's a whole new world where the rules haven't been set yet.

Did you know that the 'known' web, the web that you can access with your average browser is only around 10-15% of the internet, the rest is known as the

"Deep Web" or "Dark Web", think of it like an iceberg, the servers we all use, Google, Microsoft and all of that lot are only 10% of the whole web that we see and use, so surely somewhere in the other 90% of the web, there must be room to provide an alternative?

Because the web we do use, is getting smaller, albeit more popular. As more and more people start creating profiles (sometimes multiple profiles), the number of people in the online world is around forty percent of the world's population, in 1995, it was less than one percent. Since the year I was born, the number of people on the internet has gone up by 3 billion people.

Now, nearly seventy-five percent (greater than two billion) of all internet users in the world (about three billion) live in the top twenty countries. The remaining twenty-five percent (about seven-hundred million) is distributed among the other one hundred and seventy-eight countries, each representing less than one percent of total users.

So, the whole world isn't online, despite its prominent presence in most of our lives, the internet isn't everywhere, in fact less than half the world are on the internet, doesn't feel like it though does it?

In our current story, our current narrative, the internet and social media play a huge part in maintaining the frequency of consciousness that we are living on.

THE first internet boom, a decade and a half ago, resembled a religious movement. Omnipresent cyber-gurus, often framed by colourful PowerPoint presentations reminiscent of stained glass, prophesied a digital paradise in which not only would commerce be frictionless and growth exponential, but democracy would be direct and the nation-state would no longer exist. One, John-Perry Barlow, even penned "A Declaration of the Independence of Cyberspace".

Even though all this sounded Utopian when it was preached, it reflected online reality pretty accurately. The internet was a wide-open space, a new frontier. For the first time, anyone could communicate electronically with anyone else—globally and essentially free of charge. Anyone could create a website or an online shop, which could be reached from anywhere in the world using a simple piece of software called a browser, without asking anyone else for permission. The control of information, opinion and commerce by governments—or big companies, for that matter—indeed appeared to be a thing of the past. "You have no sovereignty where we gather," Mr Barlow wrote.

The lofty discourse on "cyberspace" has long changed. Even the term now sounds passé. Today another overused celestial metaphor holds sway: the "cloud" is code for all kinds of digital services generated in warehouses packed with computers, called data centres, and distributed over the internet. Most of the talk, though, concerns more earthly matters: privacy, antitrust, Google's woes in China, mobile applications, green information technology (IT). Only Apple's latest iSomethings seem to inspire religious fervour, as they did again this week.

Again, this is a fair reflection of what is happening on the internet. Fifteen years after its first manifestation as a global, unifying network, it has entered its second phase: it appears to be balkanising, torn apart by three separate, but related forces.

It is still too early to say that the internet has fragmented into "internets", but there is a danger that it may splinter along geographical and commercial boundaries.

The role of social media in protests and revolutions has garnered considerable media attention in recent years. Current conventional wisdom has it that social networks have made regime change easier to organize and execute. An underlying assumption is that social media is making it more difficult to sustain an authoritarian regime — even for hardened autocracies like Iran and Myanmar — which could usher in a new wave of democratisation around the globe.

The situations in Tunisia and Egypt have both seen an increased use of social networking media such as Facebook and Twitter to help organise, communicate and ultimately initiate civil-disobedience campaigns and street actions. The Iranian "Green Revolution" in 2009 was closely followed by the Western media via YouTube and Twitter, and the latter even gave Moldova's 2009 revolution its moniker, the "Twitter Revolution."

The key for any protest movement is to inspire and motivate individuals to go from the comfort of their homes to the chaos of the streets and face off against the government. Social media allows organisers to involve like-minded people in a movement at a very low cost, but they do not necessarily make these people move. Instead of attending meetings, workshops and rallies, un-committed individuals can join a Facebook group or follow a Twitter feed at home, which gives them some measure of anonymity (though authorities can easily track IP addresses) but does not necessarily motivate them to physically hit the streets and provide fuel for a revolution. At the end of the day, for a social media-driven protest movement to be successful, it has to translate social media membership into street action.

The Internet allows a revolutionary core to widely spread not just its ideological message but also its training program and operational plan. YouTube videos explaining a movement's core principles and tactics allow cadres to transmit important information to dispersed followers without having to travel.

Social media can also allow a movement to be far more nimble about choosing its day of action and, when that day comes, to spread the action order like wildfire. Instead of organising campaigns around fixed dates, protest movements can reach hundreds of thousands of adherents with a single Facebook post or Twitter feed, launching a massive call to action in seconds.

With lower organisational and communication costs, a movement can depend less on outside funding, which also allows it to create the perception of being a purely indigenous movement (without foreign supporters) and one with wide appeal.

Eventually, a successful revolutionary movement has to appeal to the middle class, the working class, retirees and rural segments of the population, groups that are unlikely to have Internet access in most developing countries. Otherwise, a movement could quickly find itself unable to control the revolutionary forces it unleashed or being accused by the regime of being an unrepresentative fringe movement.

Not only must protest organisers expand their base beyond Internet users, they must also be able to work around government disruption. Following the Internet shutdown in Egypt, protesters were able to distribute hard-copy tactical pamphlets and use faxes and landline telephones for communications. Ingenuity and leadership quickly become more important than social media when the government begins to use counter-protest tactics, which are well developed even in the most closed countries.

In using social media, the trade-off for protest leaders is that they must expose themselves to disseminate their message to the masses.

Keeping track of every individual who visits a protest organisation's website page may be beyond the capabilities of many security services, depending on a site's popularity, but a medium designed to reach the masses is open to everyone. In Egypt, almost 40 leaders of the April 6 Movement were arrested early in the protests and this may have been possible by identifying and locating them through their Internet activities, particularly through their various Facebook pages.

Beyond monitoring movement websites, governments can also shut them down. This has been common in Iran and China during times of social unrest. But blocking access to a particular website cannot stop tech-savvy Internet users employing virtual private networks or other technologies to access unbanned IP addresses outside the country in order to access banned sites. In response to this problem, China shut down Internet access to all of Xinjiang Autonomous Region, the location of ethnic Uighur riots in July 2009. More recently, Egypt followed the same tactic for the entire country. Like many countries, Egypt has contracts with Internet service providers that allow the government to turn the Internet off or, when service providers are state-owned, to make life difficult for Internet-based organisers.

This new age of technology can also be used to directly engage people into the current narratives; Donald Trump credits social media as having a huge influence on his victory and Dr. Laeeq Khan, who is the head of department for a university that studies Social Media, was a man I was lucky enough to speak to about all this impact and he had this to say…

"Donald Trump won social media. Simply put, Trump's campaign was more engaged with voters. He mastered Twitter by embracing immediacy (right now), transparency (unvarnished expression), and risk (rather than caution).

To be clear, I am not claiming causation that Trump won because he was better at social media. Twitter skill alone does not determine political outcomes. But understanding social media certainly is helpful, if not essential, in assessing the 2016 presidential election.

I am director of the social media analytics lab at the Scripps College of Communication at Ohio University. As scientists, we looked at trends and metrics: Overall, online interest in candidate Trump was three times higher than Clinton, according to Google trends analysis. Trump was the most Googled candidate, and also most mentioned on Twitter and Facebook. Trump had 4 million more Twitter followers than Clinton.

Clinton's social media engagement increased somewhat by the third debate, but by then many voters had made up their minds.

Meanwhile, the public's trust in mass media dropped to its lowest level in Gallup polling history. Less than one in three Americans has confidence in the media to "report the news fully, accurately, and fairly." Among Republicans, trust of media is lower than the norm.

Nearly half of television viewers — 42 percent — do not bother to watch campaign commercials, according to research done by the University of California at Los Angeles (UCLA) and Stanford University.

Only one of four younger voters said they used TV ads as a source of political news, said a survey commissioned by a group allied with Republicans.

In the context of widespread distrust of mass media while many voters tune out political TV advertising, social media engagement by candidates and campaigns rises to new prominence in politics.

I specialize in metrics, not psychology, so I defer to others to discern P.T. Barnum's premise as it relates to the 2016 presidential election.

However, based on what I know about metrics, I suggest a behavioural change in social media habits that I believe would benefit our Republic. As social media consumers, we should resist limiting ourselves to an echo chamber of like-minded voices.

Four of 10 social media users blocked or minimized content due to politics, according to Pew research. More than eight of 10 say they ignore political posts they disagreed with.

What this means is that in a pluralistic society, healthy social media engagement should be unafraid of competing views, even welcome them."

Good stuff right? Dr.Khan makes a lot of sense and agrees with us that people have become disconnected to the world around them, he's also expertly pointed out that government and politics is getting smart at how to use this tool to keep things the same way.

The most effective way for the government to use social media is to monitor what protest organisers are telling their adherents either directly over the Internet or by inserting an informant into the group, counteracting the protesters wherever and whenever they assemble. Authorities monitoring protests at World Trade Organisation and G-8 meetings as well as the Republican and Democratic national conventions in the United States have used this successfully. Over the past two years in Egypt, the April 6 Movement has found the police ready and waiting at every protest location. Only in recent weeks has popular support grown to the point where the movement has presented a serious challenge to the security services.

If social media is presenting a demonstrable threat to governments, it could become vital for security services to continually refine and update plans for disrupting new Internet technology.

There is no denying that social media represents an important tool for protest movements to effectively mobilise their adherents and communicate their message. As noted above, however, the effectiveness of the tool depends on its user, and an overreliance can become a serious detriment.

Moreover, a leadership grounded in physical reality is one that constructs and sticks to a concerted plan of action. The problem with social media is that it subverts the leadership of a movement while opening it to a broader membership. This means that a call for action may spread like wildfire before a movement is sufficiently prepared, which can put its survival in danger. In many ways, the Iranian

Green Revolution is a perfect example of this. The call for action brought a self-selected group of largely educated urban youth to protest in the streets, where the regime cracked down harshly on a movement it believed was not broad enough to constitute a real threat.

If the right conditions exist, a revolution can occur, and social media does not seem to change that. Just because an Internet-based group exists does not make it popular or a threat. There are Facebook groups, YouTube videos and Twitter posts about everything, but that does not make them popular. A neo-Nazi skinhead posting from his mother's basement in Illinois is not going to start a revolution in the United States, no matter how many Internet posts he makes or what he says. The climate must be ripe for revolution, not restricted due to problems like inflation, deflation; food shortages, corruption and oppression, and the population must be motivated to mobilise. Representing a new medium with dangers as well as benefits, social media does not create protest movements; it only allows members of such movements to communicate more easily.

Social media represents only one tool among many for an opposition group to employ. Protest movements are rarely successful if led from somebody's basement in a virtual arena. Their leaders must have charisma and street smarts, just like leaders of any organisation. A revolutionary group cannot rely on its most tech-savvy leaders to ultimately launch a successful revolution any more than a business can depend on the IT department to sell its product.

Sure, US banks did lower their debit card fees; but could a more powerful and engaging activist campaign have evolved if the activists were vocally and physically present? Are people just becoming lazy, thinking that they are involved in a social cause just by starting at a screen and making a click?

The trend to more closed systems is undeniable. Take Facebook, the web's biggest social network. The site is a fast-growing, semi-open platform with more than 500m registered users. Its American contingent spends on average more than six hours a month on the site and less than two on Google. Users have identities specific to Facebook and communicate mostly via internal messages. The firm has its own rules, covering, for instance, which third-party applications may run and how personal data is dealt with.

Apple is even more of a world apart. From its iPhone and iPad, people mostly get access to online services not through a conventional browser but via specialised applications available only from the company's "App Store". Granted, the store has lots of apps—about 250,000—but Apple nonetheless controls which ones make it onto its platform. It has used that power to keep out products it does not like, including things that can be construed as pornographic or that might interfere with its business, such as an app for Google's telephone service. Apple's press conference to show off its new wares on September 1st was streamed live over the internet but could be seen only on its own devices.

Even Google can be seen as a platform unto itself, if a very open one. The world's biggest search engine now offers dozens of services, from news aggregation to word processing, all of which are tied together and run on a global network of dozens of huge data-centres. Yet Google's most important service is its online advertising platform, which serves most text-based ads on the web. Being the company's main source of revenue, critics say, it is hardly a model of openness and transparency.

According to Malcolm Gladwell, online petitions carried out on platforms such as Change.org are classic cases of 'slacktivism' whereby young people today do not feel the need or urge to physically participate in a cause and feel content just by checking a box on a petition sent to them by one of their Facebook friends. Comparing slacktivism to real activism, such as the violent protests in the 1960s civil-rights movement in the American South, he claims that many people today have forgotten the real purpose and value of activism.

Gladwell also argues that whereas political activism of the past was carried out by people with strong personal involvement who were willing to risk their lives for a cause, people today do not need to risk anything, personal or financial. Further, he asserts that as no personal sacrifices needs to be involved in online activism, the weaker ties between participants are likely to produce weaker results.

In a nutshell, even though online activists may be able to shame a company and force transparency on one specific issue, the causes are often arbitrary and do not necessarily illuminate the bigger picture. There is clearly a trend towards increased scrutiny and demand for transparency of companies. People could easily raise awareness of bad practices: even if they are not always too involved in a cause.

Conclusively, the slacktivism movement should not be entirely dismissed. Even if much of it lacks capacity to instigate fundamental change, it has growing power as more people learn to organise themselves online through tools like change.org, and join the dots with previously disconnected networks.

At the heart of this is individual empowerment. The slacktivism movement is enabling the masses to act in spaces that have traditionally been the preserve of organisations like NGOs, trade unions, and consumer advocacy groups. Slowly, but surely, this mobilisation is paving the way towards the creation of a cyber civil society which, for good and bad, will have potentially far-reaching implications for all of us.

I think all of this is pointing towards the obvious realisation that for as long as we stay conditioned into this frequency of consciousness, as long as all continue to have the current perspective on life and the same internal story inside our heads that we've been conditioned into, the closer we come to seeing an Apple, or Google sponsored Matrix-like dystopian reality. The answer has to be, to make sure we use the internet and technology in the right way; we must make sure we address it in the right way, that we have the right mentality to use it, before we sit down and open up Facebook.

It is part of the overall strategy, but it cannot be the sole strategy. For years, the financially-led narrative spent years dividing and separating everybody, the internet has created the opportunity to bring us all back together and so remember…

Technology is a terrific tool for uniting the world and providing a platform to write our own story, away from the one presented to us, however it is only a tool; and despite being one of the most accessible and powerful tools we can possess, the result of how much impact it will have on our lives is still down to us, anyone can open a Microsoft word document, but unless we sit down and type the words, it will remain blank.

Technology is a tool for change, if used in the right way, but if we have a personal revolution then we will be in the right mentality to use technology to help us *revolutionise everything else and turn the click-illusion; into revolution.*

Chapter 8

The Wealthy

We're all searching for some sort of connection, to live, to each other, to ourselves and so in this chapter we're going to be looking at something that is a huge pillar, cage and tool for change in our current story: Wealth.

What is wealth? To the people in the upper classes of society, the super-rich elite, 'wealth' is obviously a financial scenario, however this is obviously not the only form of wealth, but we can't be mad at them, because they don't know any better yet, all they know is how to be selfish, they've never been given the poverty to realise the wealth they stand in is false (remember we're all compassionate and caring now!).

At this point in the book, we've realised that the world governments don't tend to have your best interests in mind and that generally, any enemies of 'the State' could more aptly be called 'enemies of the globe's corporate and banking elite, wealth' and power comes sharply into focus. Those who actually hold the power control the world's economies, and it's clear the fates of over 7.4 billion souls now inhabiting the planet are, at best, the least of their concern.

Of those at the top of the food chain, so to speak, a small collection of families dictates both domestic and foreign policy — mainly through fuelling war and conflict for the good of the military and pharmaceutical industries, and to a greater extent, corporate and central banks.

"The real rulers in Washington are invisible, and exercise power from behind the scenes." – Felix Frankfurter, Supreme Court of Justice, 1952

Some people have started realising that there are large financial groups that dominate the world. Forget the political intrigues, conflicts, revolutions and wars. It is not pure chance. Everything that has happened has happened with an agenda in mind and has done so for a long time.

Some call it "conspiracy theories" and many people are quick to jump on the 'illuminati' tag-line, I'm not really into discussing conspiracy, as that's where work starts to lose credibility and turns into the dramatisation of valid points; what I'm saying is for the purpose of this book, we're just going to be looking at cold, hard, facts.

Anyway, the key to understanding the current political and economic events is a restricted core of families who have accumulated more wealth and power then everyone else, but who aren't included on Forbes wealthiest lists, for reasons 'officially' unknown.

We are speaking of six, eight or maybe 12 families who truly dominate the world. Know that it is a mystery difficult to unravel to identify all the individuals who own what share of the wealth, after all these people aren't exactly on your television screens, but what are the names of the families who run the world and have control of states and international organisations like the UN, NATO or the IMF?

To try to answer this question, we can start with the easiest inventory, the world's largest banks, and see who the shareholders are and who make the decisions.

The world's largest companies are now: Bank of America, JP Morgan, Citigroup, Wells Fargo, Goldman Sachs and Morgan Stanley.

Let's look at who their shareholders are...

Bank of America

State Street Corporation, Vanguard Group, BlackRock, FMR (Fidelity), Paulson, JP Morgan, T. Rowe, Capital World Investors, AXA, Bank of NY, Mellon.

JP Morgan

State Street Corp., Vanguard Group, FMR, BlackRock, T. Rowe, AXA, Capital World Investor, Capital Research Global, Investor, Northern Trust Corp. and Bank of Mellon.

Citigroup:

State Street Corporation, Vanguard Group, BlackRock, Paulson, FMR, Capital World Investor, JP Morgan, Northern Trust Corporation, Fairhome Capital Mgmt and Bank of NY Mellon.

Wells Fargo:

Berkshire Hathaway, FMR, State Street, Vanguard Group, Capital World Investors, BlackRock, Wellington Mgmt, AXA, T. Rowe and Davis Selected Advisers.

We can see that now there appears to be a nucleus present in all banks: State Street Corporation, Vanguard Group, BlackRock and FMR (Fidelity). To avoid repeating them, we will now call them the "big four" (also it makes it sound a lot more dramatic) and we could go on for hours, talking of the 'passing by tax havens' in the Cayman Islands, Monaco or the legal domicile of Shell companies in Liechtenstein.

Throughout the world, in the corporate and political centre, there is a network where companies are always the same, but never a name of a family.

In short, the eight largest U.S. financial companies (JP Morgan, Wells Fargo, Bank of America, Citigroup, Goldman Sachs, U.S. Bancorp, Bank of New York Mellon and Morgan Stanley) are 100% controlled by ten shareholders and we have four companies always present in all decisions: BlackRock, State Street, Vanguard and Fidelity.

In addition, the Federal Reserve is comprised of 12 banks, represented by a board of seven people, which comprises representatives of the "big four," which in turn are present in all other entities.

In short, the Federal Reserve is controlled by four large private companies: BlackRock, State Street, Vanguard and Fidelity. These companies control U.S. monetary policy (and subsequently, most of the world) without any control or "democratic" choice. We don't vote for these guys. These companies launched and participated in the current worldwide economic crisis and since that crash, all companies have managed to become even more enriched.

So, just looking at facts, it's obvious that very 'wealthy' people have a say in what they'd like to see go on, they have this power over everyone, not because they are evil or brain-washing the politicians, but simply, because they have the most money and anybody who is high enough up the food-chain in media and politics can be trusted to be willing to take a different direction, if the cash is right.

However, if we want to look at who to blame, it's initially quite hard to get hold of names of people who want to remain nameless, however if we skim through the thousands of conspiracy posts, look at released government records, interview people high enough up the food chain (who wish to remain anonymous), then we would start to see a trend, a group of names that keep popping up, luckily for you, I did!

The families that keep popping up, who attain this vast wealth are; Goldman Sachs, Rockefellers, Loebs Kuh and Lehmans in New York, the Rothschilds of Paris and London, the Warburgs of Hamburg and Paris and the Lazards Israel Moses Seifs of Rome.

Perhaps the most well-known among those five are the Rothschilds, whose dominance of central banks, nefarious insider trading, and a nearly invisible hand in world governance, without consideration for the greater good, cite them as one of the main players in this game.

Mayer Amschel Rothschild's dealing in rare coins and antiques in Frankfurt, Germany, in the 1760s earned a rich patronage, allowing him to broaden his focus to include banking by the 1790s. In its 2005 list of 20 of "The Most Influential Businessmen" of all time, Forbes describes Rothschild as "a founding father of international finance," who "helped invent modern banking by introducing concepts such as diversification, rapid communication, confidentiality and high volume."

Carrying on the various aspects of the family businesses, Rothschild's five sons "effectively formed a multinational bank." During the Napoleonic Wars, they facilitated "loans to warring regimes and traded in cotton, arms, and wheat in defiance of Napoleon's ban on British exports" — cementing the family's prominence in political circles as well as influence over governmental affairs. Nathan Mayer Rothschild formed the eponymous bank in London and financed the Duke of Wellington's interests during those wars.

Estimates of the Rothschild family's net worth vary greatly, in part because Mayer Amschel dictated a male-only inheritance structure in his will, forcing female descendants into family marriages to maintain their grasp on wealth. Additionally, the sheer number of family members and locations of Rothschild financial and business dealings make assessing the totality of family wealth virtually impossible — though it's believed to be in the hundreds of billions.

Cloaked in secrecy for centuries, rumours concerning the Rothschild family run the gamut, including the widely-held suspicion it maintains a degree of control over the U.S. Federal Reserve. One defining fact about the Rothschilds; noted by both establishment historians and so-called conspiracy theorists, alike; has been its astonishing abilities to not only maintain such a high degree of wealth and influence, but to keep numerous businesses under family control over such a long period of time.

Mergers and partnerships aid have absolutely assisted the Rothschilds' rise to power, such as the 2012 purchase by the Rothschild Investment Trust of a 37 percent stake in Rockefeller Financial Services, which cemented the family's financial ties to the second dynasty we're looking at.

Son of a conman, John Davidson Rockefeller effectively began to solidify his American empire after buying out several partners who owned Cleveland's largest oil refinery in 1865; which became the foundation for the formation of the Standard Oil Company of Ohio in 1870. By then purchasing rival refineries and distributing its oil around the world, Standard and Rockefeller, established a staggering monopoly on the industry, cornering some 90 percent of America's refineries and pipelines.

Rockefeller's pursuit of the market extended to every facet of Standard's business, and "In order to exploit economies of scale, Standard Oil did everything from build its own oil barrels to employ its own scientists to figure out new uses for petroleum by-products," according to History.com. Simply labelling Standard Oil a monopoly not only undercuts the company's breadth, but downplays the savage and covert tactics Rockefeller employed to maintain its control over American oil.

Thanks, in part to a series of 19 articles by Ida Tarbell, published in 1902 by McClure's Magazine; the U.S. attorney under Pres. Theodore Roosevelt sued Standard Oil of New Jersey under the Sherman Antitrust Act of 1890. Over the course of the 1908 trial, Standard Oil's dubious practices came to light — including secret deals with railroads, corporate spies, and bribes of elected officials, among other things.

Rockefeller "was accused of crushing out competition, getting rich on rebates from railroads, bribing men to spy on competing companies, of making secret agreements, of coercing rivals to join the Standard Oil Company under threat of being forced out of business, building up enormous fortunes on the ruins of other men, and so on," the New York Times summarised in 1937.

Though the trial resulted in the fractioning of Standard Oil into 34 companies, the government permitted the original stockholders, including Rockefeller, to keep their ownership stakes while putatively acting as competitors. Thus, the monopoly effectively continued for at least another decade afterward, though it arguably lives on in the exertion of power by companies like ExxonMobil, Chevron, and BP — just a few of those resulting from the official destruction of the Standard Oil empire.

Called "history's richest man" by Forbes in 2014, at the time of John D. Rockefeller's death in 1937, "his assets equalled 1.5% of America's total economic output. To control an equivalent share today would require a net worth of about $340 billion, more than four times that of Bill Gates," whom the publication listed as the world's richest man at the time of the article.

Other estimates imagine Rockefeller's worth closer to $400 billion, and considering his habit of shady business practices, it wouldn't be difficult to believe some of his fortune remained secreted away from the public spotlight.

All notoriety aside, Rockefeller stands as a testament to self-education, with his only formal training being a ten-week course in accounting — though it remains a matter of conjecture what good could have been accomplished had he focused his craftiness on other pursuits.

In 2015, the approximately 200 descendants comprising the Rockefeller family were conservatively estimated to have a combined net worth of $11 billion — placing the dynasty well below the top of the list of America's richest, at number twenty-two.

Grandson David Rockefeller was, in 1954, among the founding members of the Bilderberg Group — whose highly secretive annual meetings have long been fodder for theories that ultra-elite families seek to gain or maintain control of world governments, what isn't up for debate is that both the Rockefellars and Rothschilds are two very rich groups of people, with ties in the corporate world and leaks in the past which show dabbling in politics.

A very rich family, whose interests lie in politics, leads us to our next group. A panic overwhelmed the U.S. in 1893, partly resulting from fear about the flow of the country's surplus gold to foreign nations. A man called John Pierpont Morgan seized the opportunity to 'save' the economy and restore confidence in the dollar. Morgan had followed in his father's footsteps in the banking industry, and formed J.P. Morgan & Company in 1895 — which, in effect, rescued the gold standard.

In an agreement with then-President Grover Cleveland, Morgan "led a syndicate of bankers" which, incidentally (coincidentally?), included Rothschild, "to sell U.S. bonds to buy back gold from foreign investors. The firm sold out the entire issue in New York within 22 minutes," according to J.P.Morgan.com.

With that gold and bond exchange, Morgan now controlled the U.S.' gold supply — allowing him the flexibility to then finance the creation of U.S. Steel, after an offer to buyout Andrew Carnegie for a price in excess of the U.S. government's entire budget. After threatening Westinghouse, which had employed Nikola Tesla's electricity using alternating current, with a patent infringement lawsuit, Morgan gained control of the emerging electric light industry and formed General Electric.

Morgan's unethical, cutthroat business practices saw the creation of monopolies by eliminating competition, maximizing profits by slashing jobs and reducing wages, and lack of workplace safety, became the blue-print for the society we now live in, also dabbed 'morganization.'

In fact, figures like Morgan became known as 'robber barons' for such tactics, their uninhibited greed fuelled a severe stratification of wealth and became a popular target for muckraking journalists. (Now you know where Assassins creed stole their plots from, that's a point, if any of this starts to sound like a film plot, or a television series and so you start to doubt the reality of the situation, remember although you've learned these facts after you've watched the programmes which have similar plots, remember that the events took place before the films were made and ask yourself, who's really taking what from who!)

Many theorists claim that Morgan's attempts to profit while exerting influence didn't stop there. They say that in an unofficial investigation afterward, it was revealed America had entered World War I, not for political and policy concerns, but for the profits of the banking and munitions industries. I personally don't want to start making such bold claims, however what we do know as fact is world war one, wasn't that far from world war two, which as we know from the previous chapters, was the catalyst for the hyper-normalised society we now live within. (Don't you find it ridiculous out of all the countries in the world, the same two started both wars!).

Senator Gerald P. Nye, who headed the eponymous Nye Committee, vowed at the outset, "when the Senate investigation is over, we shall see that war and preparation for war is not a matter of national honour and national defence, but a matter of profit for the few."

What is fact though, it that as it turned out, U.S. banks, including Morgan's, lent over 100 times as much money to allied countries than it had to adversaries, naturally, and in order to protect those loans, the financiers urged the Wilson Administration to come to the aid of their allies by joining the war. Dubbed the "merchants of death," arms manufacturers were again rumoured to ally with the Morgans in the build-up to the Second World War could this be the prologue to the story in the second chapter?

Recent reports have suggested a more than comfortable relationship than the public would prefer, between what is now JP Morgan Chase and the Federal Reserve. Despite the U.S. abandoning the gold standard, the New York Fed still houses the country's precious metals in a fifth sub-basement, across the street from JPM's own fifth sub-basement-situated gold vault.

Considering the sheer number of military conflicts Americans would rather their government not have been part of over the last century, the old allegations of Morgan family war profiteering become quite relevant, how can a majority who keep wanting to not go to war, end up being at war?

But it's not just Americans (who really haven't even been around that long) who factually have vast amounts of wealth, Pierre Samuel, Sieur du Pont de Nemours was a French economist whose protean political views both led him to be imprisoned during the French Revolution, when his views were found to be too moderate, and later to play an instrumental role in negotiating French side of the Louisiana Purchase.

After being held as a prisoner of war during the French Revolution, Éleuthère Irénée du Pont de Nemours fled to the United States, where he founded the empire responsible for such ubiquitous inventions as nylon, Teflon, and Kevlar, beginning with a gunpowder mill in Delaware.

After becoming the largest supplier of gunpowder to the U.S. military in the early 1800s, DuPont began manufacturing dynamite, growing to such incredible proportions — through collusion with its competition in the "Powder Trust" to fix prices — its monopoly on the industry was broken up under the Sherman Antitrust Act. However, similar to J.P. Morgan, DuPont's supposed breakup allowed the family to maintain dominance over the munitions industry; and during the First World War, it supplied nearly 40 percent of all munitions used by allied forces.

Its ventures as military munitions supplier expanded from that point, and the company played a key role in the Manhattan Project's development and production of the first atomic bomb — which the U.S. readily used to decimate Hiroshima and Nagasaki during World War II. DuPont reportedly produced 4.5 billion pounds of military explosives used over the course of that war.

Reports still circulate about DuPont's possible role in the prohibition of hemp and cannabis, due to its breakthrough patent of nylon and a process for using wood pulp to manufacture paper in 1937. While both products could facilely be replaced by hemp, which arguably would have severely limited DuPont's massive profits, those rumours have yet to be either summarily proven... or thoroughly debunked.

DuPont also claims infamy as the second largest producer of genetically-modified corn and soy in the world and has seeds in cold storage inside Norway's Svalbard Global Seed Vault, itself the subject of countless theories, one which states has been designed to be able to replant the earth should an apocalyptic event come to pass (which we should all hope is not true, if someone who is in the inner-circle don't fancy our chances, we should all start 'preppin' now!).

Documents declassified in 2003 revealed George W.'s grandfather, could have been prosecuted for providing aid and comfort to the enemy for nefarious business dealings during the build up to, during, and after World War II. As the Guardian reported in 2004, the National Archives documents "show that even after America had entered the war and when there was already significant information about the Nazis' plans and policies, Bush worked for and profited from companies closely involved with the very German businesses that financed Hitler's rise to power."

That description only vaguely scratches the surface of both the Bush family's and U.S.' apparent involvement in possible criminal activity surrounding the Second World War. Though entire books are devoted to the subject, a lawsuit brought against the U.S. government and Bush family in 2004, claimed both materially benefited from slave labour at Auschwitz and because the government knew what was taking place, it should have bombed the camp, the Guardian reported.

Whether Bush had actually been a Nazi sympathizer or had just grossly capitalized on the Nazis extreme human rights abuses will probably never be known with certainty, though both the Bush family and U.S. government deny all allegations in the matter.

One stunning conspiracy Bush did, in fact, take part in that did prove true, involving the same Bush-led companies as in the Nazi matter, as well as those of other families on this list, has been so lost to history; it's often discussed as rumour.

There was, indeed, a plot to overthrow the U.S. government and install a fascist dictatorship by most of the magnates on this list and others and were it not for the suspicions of renowned Marine General Smedley Butler, the coup would have succeeded.

Feeling threatened by Roosevelt's New Deal, wealthy businessmen organized The American Liberty League and in 1934, approached Butler with what they felt to be a tantalizing offer, $3 million up front and $300 million after the success of the coup, which would involve 500,000 veterans of the first world war.

"The League was headed by the DuPont and JP Morgan cartels and had major support from Andrew Mellon Associates, Pew (Sun Oil), Rockefeller

Associates, EF Hutton Associates, US Steel, General Motors, Chase, Standard Oil, and Goodyear Tires," CounterPunch explained.

Funding for the coup would be secreted away by Prescott Bush's Union Banking Corporation and Harriman Brothers Brown — the same companies with strikingly apparent ties to the Nazis. As revealed later, Bush's connections to Hitler had been a draw for those plotting the fascist coup, and they later claimed the Nazi-headed German government had offered to assist materially in the plan.

Though the plotters' brazen plan would almost certainly have failed on its own, Butler's secret testimony before the McCormack-Dickstein Committee revealed the group's intent to install a fascist dictatorship of a similar vein to Germany's, complete with concentration camps.

A clique of U.S. industrialists is hell-bent to bring a fascist state to supplant our democratic government and is working closely with the fascist regime in Germany and Italy," wrote U.S. Ambassador to Germany, William Dodd, in a 1936 letter to Roosevelt. "I have had plenty of opportunity in my post in Berlin to witness how close some of our American ruling families are to the Nazi regime ... A prominent executive of one of the largest corporations, told me point blank that he would be ready to take definite action to bring fascism into America if President Roosevelt continued his progressive policies. Certain American industrialists had a great deal to do with bringing fascist regimes into being in both Germany and Italy. They extended aid to help fascism occupy the seat of power, and they are helping to keep it there. Propagandists for fascist groups try to dismiss the fascist scare. We should be aware of the symptoms. When industrialists ignore laws designed for social and economic progress they will seek recourse to a fascist state when the institutions of our government compel them to comply with the provisions.

Over 4,300 pages of testimony were collected by the McCormack-Dickstein Committee — part of the House Un-American Activities Committee — until its disbanding at the end of 1934. Butler, who pretended to accept the plot in order to gather as much information as possible, provided key evidence in the investigation.

"In the last few weeks of the committee's official life it received evidence that certain persons had made an attempt to establish a fascist organization in this country … There is no question that these attempts were discussed, were planned, and might have been placed in execution when and if financial backers deemed it expedient," the Committee's report stated.

Indeed, propaganda had so readily touted the League for its, albeit hollow and obviously false, claims it would help the common worker and restore so-called American ideals, researching the plot has been difficult even for historians. TIME Magazine, the New York Times, and other publications have so whitewashed the plotted coup as to make it appear theory instead of proven fact.

In what might be the most revealing aspect of the planned coup, no one, not a single business or businessman involved, was ever prosecuted over the matter. No criminal charges were levied; no repercussions handed down … nothing.

Most telling of all is the same families — for all their dirty deeds to an actual, planned coup d'état — remain thoroughly entrenched as the American economic aristocracy today.

"War is a racket," Butler famously wrote. "It always has been. It is possibly the oldest, easily the most profitable, surely the most vicious. It is the only one international in scope. It is the only one in which the profits are reckoned in dollars and the losses in lives."

Regardless, it's important to remember that these people, these dynasties and families, whether they be lizards wearing human suits; ruling the world, or just a bunch of nice-guys that have had bad-press, factually, it's unarguable to see that regardless of their agenda, they are richer than everybody else. In a system whose manifest is 'become rich', whether we're going to believe the theories or not, we've got to admit that they must have some sort of influence, however, apart from the facts stated, everything else about these families are just opinions and it's important to remember that in order to have a personal revolution, we have to form our own unbiased opinions, without an influence, however if we look inside ourselves, truly connect to consciousness and then take a second glance, regardless of who they are, it shouldn't sit right with anybody that so very few people can have so much.

Regardless of personal opinion, the people we've spoken about are the foundations of the society we live in, they are the prologue to the story we told earlier and they are incredibly powerful when we are all acting on a low level of consciousness.

What is worth noting is that if we work on a higher-level of consciousness, with a different agenda in mind, these people would become *powerless.*

People, whose total influence comes from money, will become un-influential if we stop all wanting money. This is why the revolution takes place inside first. If we change what we're looking for from life, then we will stop looking to the people we used to look to for salvation, people who are only looking to save themselves.

But enough about global syndicates and cabals, I saw something much scarier, in the shape of a man and woman, who were in a monogamous coupling, a shared partnership based on love, by very superficial judgement, you could tell they were 'wealthy' and yet on a closer look, they had no wealth at all.

This experience took place while I sat at a train station the other day, in the little sweaty indoor seating area, where everyone's coughing and sneezing and generally trying to create the next worlds epidemic, because well, British weather, that's why. It was raining, but not like a really heavy downpour, not that kind of rain that says "step into me, get soaked, I dare you", more that kind of annoying drizzle, that rain that says "step in if you want, or don't, I don't really care either way mate" and it made me realise something. Everyone in this little disease den was like the rain outside, not one conversation was taking place, not one. Not even the couple standing with each other, or the work colleagues, nobody was talking, everyone was texting, or tweeting, so busy consumed by what they could see looking down, that virtual world of data and status', of faraway plans and places that no-one dare look up into the harsh reality and the flimsy rain, in the now, in the moment.

If, on the odd occasion, one or two of them would, at the moment where the awkwardness reaches its peak, as their two eyes gaze into each other, it would turn into a race of who could withdraw their glance quickest, like a western shootout, in reverse. But how shocking is that, how did it get this bad, that one moment of connectivity, of real connectivity, where one man's reality, soul, life, stares directly into another's, that moment where anything is possible, love, friendship, hatred, jealously, a moment of endless possibilities, endless realities we could create between one another is replaced with a quick retreat, back down to our structured and pre-determined connectivity, our internet connection.

Bob Marley once said "The greatness of a man is not how much wealth he acquires, but in his ability to affect those around him positively", he was also the man who said (rather appropriately to my story), "Some people feel the rain, others just get wet".

Because they're trapped as well you know, the rich, the celebs, as hard as it is to believe, there's a reason why we're seeing more and more celebrities come out as depressed and mentally ill, even Lady Gaga has her own insecurities, her own issues, we just don't know about them, well not all of us, because if these people that some of us worship like 'gods' appear to us as human, as flimsy, scared, insecure little people, like we all are deep down, then we start realising that this reality we get conditioned to believe, may not be as legitimate and real as it first seems. If Queen Kardashian and King Kanye start to worry about their spiritual connection then they lose the god-like regard they're held in, we realise we're all just people in a society that plays on our fears and desires, they become human and the industry can't sell 'human'.

But believe me, the rich aren't happy either, they'll say they are of course, but they're not, not really, they hide behind the fancy cars and big houses to try to fill up the void that is present in all of us, that desperate need to have 'more' in a system where there is always more stuff. More money, more stuff, more friends. Because you don't become rich and then all get along you know. Once you're rich it becomes even worse, you've now got to be richer than him, more well off than her, if someone finds themselves in their personal prison of luxury, all the same problems occur, because financially wealthy is not a state that can truly satisfy the human condition.

Russell has a great quote where he says, "The poor are trapped in their poverty, the rich trapped in their luxury."

The quote's true, most celebrities openly admit to hating being famous. Now I'm not defending or supporting them, ideally in our little utopian realities, we wouldn't have celebrities or people who are worshipped like gods, ideally celebrities wouldn't even exist, so I'm certainly not saying we should feel sorry for them, I'm saying that this system screws us all over and while it's much better to be screwed over as a celebrity than as a refugee, we have to see the bigger picture and act with compassion towards all of us if we want to see a real, authentic change.

So, we really are all screwed, apart from the super elite of course, richer than posh school kids, richer than the celebrities, I mean the super-rich, the bankers, the fraudsters, those dodgy ones that you haven't even heard of. These are the people that keep the system the same way, because these are the ones that are really benefitting from it being this way, of course celebrities and rich people wouldn't mind it staying the same, they're doing alright in this one, but even them deep are yearning for something greater, something within.

Why is it all these super-elite can have all this money and choose not to act on it, choose not to end poverty or stop wars? Because of course the system has conditioned them to act that way, the thought doesn't even cross their minds. All these super rich guys with their psychopathic tendencies, with all their riches and power, don't even think to do what seems so obvious to us, they believe they are wealthy, but due to the nature of their wealth and the conditioning that brings, never allows for them to think of any other sort of wealth, but what are the other types of wealth?

When we're with one another, friends, families, lovers, enemies, mutual associates, whoever; the possibilities in that moment are endless, it's the beauty of human interaction. In those moments when we're connected, anything can happen, any words can be said, any stares can be absorbed, enemies can become friends, associates can become trusted allies and friends can become lovers. ***Because we're meant to love one another you know? It's not something that may or may not happen for you, it's made for all of us*.** Noam Chomsky, an activist, philosopher and all round good guy (in all this talk for change, he's a pretty big fish to remember so you're going to need to remember his name) said "life's empty without love" and I'd have to say I agree.

However, it's not just Noam or I advocating that compassion for others is so important in fulfilling our true potential, it's a timeless message, scattered throughout our existence and the message is always the same. Whether it be from Jesus telling you to love thy neighbour in the bible, the Buddha telling us to connect to love, icons like Luther King or Ghandi telling us love will defeat tyrants, or our nans telling us to stop throwing potatoes at our little brothers heads because 'it's not the right thing to do' (or was that just me?), because that message, it isn't my opinion or my belief, it's an inherent universal truth. No matter who is saying the message, the message is the same, maybe presented or worded differently, but anybody who is on a high enough level of consciousness will be of the understanding that love is key, love, or if love is too hippie a word for you, compassion, tolerance, understanding, whatever label you want to attach to it, that undeniable feeling when you're around family and friends, the moment you fall for someone, moments of connectedness and unity, that feeling we feel is love and *love is what should be guiding us when we need guidance.*

Chapter 9

The 'Wholey' Lie

Over my lifetime, I've found it surprising how little we're taught about religions mainly followed in the eastern part of the world, both in education and in our media.

Not because these religions are any better than the main ones followed here in the west. I do however think that if we were given an equal, unbiased pack of information on all religions from all around the world (much like how we spoke about equal information in our media earlier) then not only would we be given a fair choice as to which religion to worship if we wanted, (potentially leading us to find a religion which we really connect to, which in turn could possibly lead us to find our inner peace) but we would then also be less fearful of others religions and have a better understanding of each other and everyone's beliefs, therefore making it more likely for us to all understand each other.

This in turn would both make conflicts fuelled by misunderstanding about each other's faiths occur less frequently and also allow us to all understand each other in greater depth. We shouldn't be encouraged to follow a specific religion, but to follow any religion that we can resonate with. However, what we're looking at in this chapter is how religion, ideologies and the clever manipulation of pure values can be twisted to serve not so pure agendas.

One of the most important things to over-turn in this revolution is the halting of using the language of religion or spirituality to assert an economic or materialistic agenda, something which has created a sour-taste in our mouth when we hear the world 'religion'.

Now we're going to look at the key factors people use when tailoring languages and stories to fit to their agenda.

One myth that any empire, regime or leadership, especially America is built upon, is the idea that it has a sublime, even divine reason to exist. If it didn't have this, it would be obvious that it's just a hashed together system put in place for the benefit for elites.

Nobody, not even the bigots of Trump's corner would want to be part of a nation that states, "This mass of land that we've called America is controlled by financial elites that will harvest the planet of both material and human resources so shut up and salute to a remix of the union jack".

It's not very patriotic and not something you'd expect Captain America to say, better to tell people that 'God' likes your land mass above others land masses and that the leaders and people in charge have been gifted that power to maintain this 'perfect' system you should feel privileged to be a part of.

Many regions were put together as one country for the colonial commercialism of the British. The British could do it only on the line of a nation as the nation-state was the in-thing in the emerging capitalistic form of governance. Later Japan and Hitler used nationalism for outgrowing their nations. Fascism developed unhindered. People loved it and citizens welcomed it.

But how ridiculous is the notion of nation? (And how much of a tongue-twister is that!), Britain is only Britain by our universal consent as a majority, the only thing that makes money a valid 'thing' is the fact we all believe in 'money'.

My mate Jacob once told me this fact and at this point in writing this book, I don't really want to do anymore research so either this is true and astounding, or it's totally wrong, but that's fine, because it still works as a nice metaphor if not.

He told me once that the whole of the global economy was denominated in colonial times, largely by the value of tulips, then, one day everybody decided that tulips were no longer valuable and that actually they were just an ugly, irrelevant flower and the whole market fell apart.

Half way through the nineteenth century, America had this idea that they could use their belief that they had some God-given right to be there to take over and impose their laws on whatever they wanted. Turn on your TV and you'll see this is an ideology that they still attach themselves too.

The people of Thailand don't get into their fishing boats, sail over to Norway and tell them they're taking over because they are Thai; they just get on with all their Thai-activities.

This ideology has been branded by the idea to 'Manifest Destiny' as Chomsky calls it, regardless of whether this is religion being manipulated, an ideology pushed or a dictatorship being inflicted, all these 'manifests of destinies' have some similar trends.

The first of which, is they literally think they are better. Let's take America as our example, even though there was no such things as 'Americans' a couple of hundred years ago, their leaders think that by moving to a new bit of rock which is part of the same rock floating in infinite space, they somehow acquired supremacy above everyone else; the last people to do that were the Nazis.

The second thing all these forced beliefs have in common is the desire to impose their self-image onto everything else. Again, America show us perfectly how this is done, more and more frequently we're seeing the merging of our culture to mirror the one of America, now even celebrating their own made-up holidays such as Black Friday. We must be so careful going forward that we don't merge into one, mirroring the culture of our repressors, just as our politics and media have done so.

The third thing all these organised belief systems have installed in them is this idea that they have a destiny to complete. I like this one, the word 'Destiny' really disproves the argument that their agenda is just an idea that's convenient for them, it's an external divine force, that even if you disagree with it, will make you a cog in the machine, because you are part of this destiny that is bound to happen. This is great because it makes the scenario unquestionable, America bombing Syria is as unquestionable as the obviousness that a chair is a chair, you can't argue it, don't even question it, it is, as stated, simply destiny.

These points that hold the whole idea of 'manifesting destiny' can be seen throughout history, in Rome, in Nazi-Germany, in America. I once taught a boy called Tommy who at 10 years old could recite every single empire from 1066, from anywhere across the world, at 10!

This wasn't the most amazing thing about Tommy, the thing that astounded me the most about this young kid was despite knowing all the finite details and facts of all these reigns, his answers to what should've been done to sort out these issues, were so simple.

"Why don't they just share? Why don't they make sure the people who will end up revolting are happy, they'd sort out their problems" As simplistic as Tommy's answer is (he is 10 people), it's so true, as idealistic as his solutions are, they only seem so far-fetched because we complicate matters with all of our adult-nonsense.

The point that I'm making here is like what we've said about fear tactics in our media, this relates hugely to religion, if we're all worried about the extremists of each other's religions, we won't take time to realise that really, no matter what religion, we're all trying to get to the same place and although we're doing it differently, we can all still get along, something we're more than aware of as children.

Because there are always extremists in every religion, people who have taken some words a bit too literally, or are using 'religion' as their reason to enact selfish actions, whether it's the 'Britain First' twisted Christianity belief that the whole of the United Kingdom is for a supreme race of Christians, which coincides nicely with the extremists we're all bored of hearing about who have twisted the Islamic religion, but for all of them, there are also children who have the potential to restore the faith to its purest roots.

It's one of the reasons I love working with children, the purity and simplicity to the world's problems never ceases to amaze me. How do we make sure everyone has enough food? Share the food. How do we make sure everyone has a house? Have a sleep-over! The answers are so simple and it's painful how much **we've forgotten how simple it can be**.

The greatest weapon we have as a society is to *change ourselves* and realise that Isis, Britain First, all these people, are only distractions as to who's really to blame... the support everyone has shown against the attacks that have happened recently in places such as France and Belgium is incredible, it shows that people are waking up and realising that things aren't working like this, now we need everyone to become as passionate about doing something about the system and people who make these attacks happen, then none of this would happen in the first place.

When I speak to groups of kids, it's sometimes shocking what I hear. I was once doing a talk to a group of about 150 kids, and as I was talking a huge, loud, army helicopter flew over our heads, (the unthoughtful bastards, could they not see I was talking?!) and as soon as they saw the huge machine in the sky, a few of the children turned around to each other and said "that's ISIS you know, mummy was telling me how they fly helicopters and go and do bad things to people like us" and a tiny panic broke out, these children were no older than 10 and they were already worried about being under attack from these scary men they hear about from their parents, on the telly.

It made me really think about both how much responsibility parents have in developing their kids' perception of the world and how much responsibility the media have in developing our perception of the world, and how a lot the time, a lot of people are being conditioned and not thinking about what they're listening to and what they're telling people and the impact that information can have.

What these extremists are doing is obviously wrong, obviously inhuman, we don't need to clarify that, however terrorism exists on both sides, both sides think that the other-side are the evil tyrants, everyone thinks they're doing the right thing, that the cost of the conflict is worth the victory, worth the bloodshed, but as my first ever history teacher taught me, "There are no winners in war, only some lose more than others".

One of the most astounding things I ever learnt at school was about the truce on Christmas Day during WW2. How despite all the hatred and blood-shed, both sides humanity burst through because the day was one of love and celebration.

Christmas may have lost its religious practices to a lot of people in Western culture and been re-painted red as the pinnacle of consumerism, but seeing children wake up full of joy on Christmas morning, seeing whole families laughing and living in the moment at the big lunch, or seeing soldiers on two opposite sides lay down their arms and give up the fight for a day, shows that deep down the meaning of Christmas is still there somewhere, the meaning of why we choose to be religious and part of something bigger than ourselves is still there and that deep-down that beautiful, humane side of all of us is still there, waiting to be awoken.

One of the worst things I learnt in school was how after that day, they went back to slaughtering and murdering each other, all in the name of fear, hatred and for a geographical location that separates us by an invisible line.

Rich elites with unprecedented money and power have different views or end-games and so send little boy soldiers to fight battles on tops of hills in the 'name of religion', throw in some money and the cocktail you end up with is one where corruption of a religion is twisted as one side is fighting another, letting the poverty-stricken and diseased act as pawns in a game that has nothing to do with religion, or God, but everything to do with money, profit and power.

So as much as these extremists' actions are wrong, to fight them in a compassionate way, is to truly defeat them, we have to remember that a lot of the time, these are young or disillusioned individuals desperate for change both politically and individually and so Islam, Christianity, whatever religion these people are 'using' as an excuse for their actions is a product of a bigger problem and we have to fight the issue with love in order for real change.

Ghandi himself said, "When I despair, I remember that all through history, the ways of truth and love, have always won. There have been tyrants, and murderers, and for the time they can seem like they're invincible, but in the end they always fall. Think of it, always."

And old master Ghandi is right, the only power we have on a personal level is *loving tolerance*, and a continued suspicion of the media and our politicians who have their own agendas to meet. As we spoke about earlier, the media want to create stories for the sake of corporations that benefit from wars in foreign countries. Our politicians are always looking for ways to make capital and augment their own power, so next time you see our PM and all his or her little elite mates holding hands, condemning the action of 'terrorists', remember, if they cover their own backs, we're all too busy saying 'oh look at the humanity', 'oh the horrors' and so while of course terrorism is bad, that doesn't need saying, we all know violence is always wrong, I'm not questioning that! What I'm questioning, asking you to question, is why do these people exist?

They don't just spawn out of countries being stripped of their oil, there has to be a catalyst as to why it's happening. This is the perfect time to start questioning why do these things keep happening? And what can we do, as a society of one species, only here on earth for a very small amount of time, all connected by our biological make-up and spiritual divinity, what can we do to change this?

There are violent people on all sides of these ideologies and they are exacerbating it; so it's down to us, not the extremists or the leaders, the people in the middle to stop supporting it; we have to love more, love harder and fight for equality with everything we have and that starts with questioning who screwed up this 'society of equality' we're told we have.

"Give a man a gun, he can kill a terrorist; give a man an education and he can kill terrorism". Terrorism won't be defeated by firing back or hating and creating prejudice with other groups of society, terrorism will be defeated by all of us realising that the terrorists are not the ones with the bombs; these are simply the reaction and product. The real terrorists aren't the ones who we're told they are in our media, the real terrorists are the ones telling us who to look at and to hate because they need us to look everywhere else because these are the real people to blame, it's time we all forgive.

Just because a couple of drops of water are dirty, the whole ocean doesn't become clouded and polluted; we have to have faith in each-other in order to create new waves.

Chomsky explains that America has always seen themselves as 'Christian soldiers' marching into war to protect its divinely chosen population (who are all immigrants, remember, apart from the people who aren't, who now only have Standing Rock to stand by) from 'evil'. He also states, in his life-long message, which could quite easily be seen as a running audition for assassination, that any excuse, using religious or divine language, using the phrase 'for the people', should be more appropriately named 'from the people', 'Top-secret' can also be translated to 'Don't let them find this stuff out, they'll go nuts'.

Hence why Edward Snowden was so quick to be branded a traitor; once the love child of Harry Potter and the Milky Bar kid had exposed to the people the fact that their government was hiding secrets from them, the government quickly added in, "only to protect you from terrorism", which is something they'd created in the first place!

On that note, while we're here, the 'war on terror' hasn't really gone according to plan has it? Did you know that since the war on terror started, (since 9/11), the federal Homeland Security and Intelligence budget has increased by $65 billion per year?

If local and state, private sector, and opportunity costs are included, the cost goes up to $132 billion per year. Additionally, U.S. military expenditures rose sharply every year from 2001 until 2010, resulting in the U.S. military budget being over $200 billion more per year than it was in 2001.

When we add it all up, the total increase in spending justified by terrorism is approximately $350 billion per year. Of that, at least $275 billion comes from the U.S. federal budget.

On top of all of that, taking into account a wide range of costs, the total cost of anti-terrorism efforts is over $3 trillion since 9/11; that's enough money to give the terrorists a whole new utopia to live in.

Did you know that terrorist attacks around the globe, have gone up eight times the amount? How crazy is that? We've created more terrorism from trying to stop it; on top of that, almost 10,000 Americans have been killed in the "war on terror," outside of terror attacks themselves.

The Iraq Body Count reports there were at least 115,000 civilian Iraqi deaths in the Iraq War, based only on documented events.

What Chomsky has explained to us, as if we were 10 year old Tommy, is that we're being told, "A whole bunch of lies by hell-bent swine's, living in virtual slavery.''

Noam is reaching the end of his lengthy contribution; however, Chomsky is too intelligent and reserved to be running around, writing colloquial books, screaming 'Revolution!' but his final contribution gives clarity to his message: "As we are all surely aware, we now face the most ominous decisions in human history. There are many problems that must be addressed, but two overwhelming issues have significance: environmental destruction and nuclear war. For the first time in history, we face the possibility of totally destroying the prospects for decent existence, for the near and distant future. For this reason alone, it is imperative to sweep away the ideological clouds and face honestly and realistically how policy decisions are made, and what we can do to alter them before it's too late."

Finally, Chomsky points out that "the architects of power in the United States must create a force that can be felt but not seen. Power remains strong when it remains in the dark; once you shine light on the problem, it can evaporate," very philosophical from old Noam, but really all he means is that instead of living in darkness, we accept responsibility as sentient adults; with fearless desire to shift the current narrative and question the imposing agendas of the people in charge who use belief, faith and a religion to channel their economic agenda through, although they have used organised belief systems to manipulate the system to stay the same, to keep us in darkness, it only takes one 'Harry Potter' hacker, one political commentator, one genius kid, one idealistic author or one reader of one book to become a flame and shine light to the whole world.

If one autonomous collective wants to live as the most extreme and fundamentalist version of Islam as possible, then that is fine, as long as they don't hurt or impose their belief on anybody else, if they do that, it's nobody's business but their own. We can believe whatever we want to believe in, so long as it doesn't hurt the people or the planet, Tommy really had got it simplistically right. All that terrorism, jihadi, extremist, and murderous stuff is expedient materialism.

Remember, when people get all worked up about which religion is 'superior', that is *not* religion, (we've got a whole chapter on real religion later), no what that is, is an individualistic, materialistic, territorial agenda asserted through the language of religion, to keep us disillusioned and scared.

As Joseph Campbell says "all religions are true, in that the metaphor is true' and regardless of what belief we follow, they all have a little bit that says, in some form "Don't kill one another, love instead."

Religion is there to remind us that we are a temporary expression of a subtler and connected electromagnetic realm, unknowable on our narrow frequency of consciousness. The defining principle in any religion should be oneness; not division; not conflict.

At this point in our evolution, we are reconfiguring into infinite oneness, so let's all individually harmonise to that message and in doing so, totally dissolve the power organised religion and belief systems have had over us, *while we revolutionise everything else.*

Chapter 10

The Brain

If we dare to use our brains for a moment to talk about our brains, (there's a paradox, but more on them later!) we can actually come to terms with why we encompass the capacity to be inherently good and righteous, as much as we have the capability to be the greedy little selfish humans we so excel at portraying at the moment.

Although we think and believe that we are in control, just one day of observing yourself will prove to you that most of your life is run on auto-pilot and in a subconscious way, especially your emotional and habitual life.

Unless you have training, when your emotions hit you have little control. Your brain is an amazing bit of kit; however, the control centres for survival and reproduction are based in a very early part of your physiology. The parts of you that decide whether you live or die are very old; in fact you are run by a brain similar to a T-Rex.

Only a small part of your subconscious mind is similar to your inner child. The rest is a 'lizard'. Herpetology (the study of reptiles) was popular in society for many years and recently it has come in use again as you look deeper in to the human mind.

Our brain at its core has a lizard-like thought-process that controls all our survival instincts and emotions (remember that conspiracy that the world's leaders are actually all just lizards in human suits? Well they're not technically wrong, only the difference being is that we're lizards in a metaphorical way and we've got the rest of our brains, while the leaders of the world have only got that lizard part, which is why they're so selfish and manipulative, doesn't seem so crazy now, does it?)

It has been around a few million years longer than man and served the dinosaurs well for millions of years.

So, the reptilian brain (this isn't the scientific word for it, but did you really want the embarrassment of reading a word you didn't understand and having to google it for the sentence to make sense? No, you didn't, so we're going with reptilian), is the part of our brain which creates our primal, animalistic side; its behaviours are comparable to wolves and hyenas (we all know they're bad, they were the baddies in The Lion King!). This part of our brain is responsible for controlling the body's vital functions such as heart rate, breathing, body temperature and balance, all the stuff you do without even thinking about it.

Our reptilian brain is the oldest of the three parts of our brain; it also includes the main structures found in a reptile's brain: the brainstem and the cerebellum, hence the name. The reptilian brain is reliable but tends to be somewhat rigid and compulsive.

So basically, you have three brains in your skull. Each built one on top of the other, stacked, almost like a new level has been placed on top of the old one, like levels of a video-game. Interconnected with different functions, programs and memories, a bit like three computers joined together. They all have different functions and distinct abilities; if you're not a computer-nerd, think of it like a Russian doll, or layers of an onion.

Guess what gets activated when you are afraid? Yep, that inner-reptile inside your head.

This part controls rigid, obsessive, compulsive, ritualistic and paranoid frenzies and is still very active even in deep sleep. This part is still similar and driven by the same basic survival programs as T-Rex's, (You sweet little dinosaur in a human's body). It is responsible for your basic survival and it focuses on fighting, running away, playing dead and being responsible for looking for food, sex and to act all territoriality and tribe-like.

You can see how this works when you go into a stress response and have all those amazing chemicals in your body activated; you lose your higher brain functions and many of your later programming and social habits. This part looks after you and includes your brain stem and your cerebellum.

The second brain in you is the mammalian brain. This is your Limbic Brain; this comes off the first brain and looks a bit like a limb (the guys who named this stuff must've been on the big salaries). This part of you controls your more complex emotions such as memory, love, compassion and other emotions. If you have a mammal pet then you know that your dog shares some of the emotions that you have, and often when you feel higher emotions it is this part of your early brain that is being fired off.

Just like your old survival brain, a skilled hypnotist or neuro-linguistic programmer, can fire this area of your brain off for desired results. So can that bitch at work.

Your third brain in that little head of yours is the neocortex. This is the part of your head that you share with the higher apes. Ours is just a little bit bigger and has more wiring in it. It sits above your limbic brain that sits on your reptile. All stacked one on top of the other. This part of the brain deals with the higher functions such as logic and time, words and symbols.

This is why when you have a subconscious incongruence, your 'older' brains will win and take over and with it comes all those painful emotions. One of the tricks is to get your limbic and your reptile part working together. If they agree with your neocortex you win, if not they will take over and run the show.

This is why when stress hits us or we feel fear of losing something, our prestige and ego create an imaginary threat to our life; your subconscious mind will generate some very old and primitive resources. We can learn to control most of these, but it does take practice and knowledge.

But the fact that our beautiful human nature is resting upon a lizard and a drama-queen doesn't mean that humans are 'bad'. We are, after all, just a species of animals who have developed further along the road than those we share the planet with, to the point where we can now write books about how we are, after all, just a species of animals who have developed further along the road than those we share the planet with (and stick in cages to stare at, unless we're talking about SeaWorld, where they obviously do more than just stare...).

Mastering these parts of our brain doesn't stem from avoiding the fact all three parts exist, but by learning how to understand and utilise all three.

It's important to remember that one of the biggest steps towards changing ourselves is to be compassionate and look for each other's similarities, the things that bond us together, instead of pointing out the differences.

Now, if we reflect on what we've just learnt, it's that in our head, (scientifically speaking), there are three parts to our brain which create the conditioning that makes us human. The lizard, mammal and neocortex parts, all three responsible for different parts of our existence.

However, that is just the scientific way of labelling these things, but it's not the only way.

In some religious and spiritual teachings, our lizard-brain is embodying the 'devil'; our mammal brain is embodying 'us' and our neocortex is the embodiment of 'God'. Makes sense, though right? That well-known eternal battle, between God and The Devil, in a constant conflict trying to get you on their side, to go to heaven or to bite the apple; what if that battle wasn't thought about by the two omnipresent beings that exist outside the universe, but is actually just another way of conceptualising that internal struggle we all face inside the universe in our heads?

It's certainly food for thought, and to me I like to think the lizard brain is our *ego*, the part of our brain that is responsible for all of our primal urges and desires, also accountable for our tribal tendencies and 'worst' traits; selfishness, individualism, short-sightedness.

The mammal brain acts as our sub-conscious mind, the part of us that inherently feels, observes and separates us from total primal animals.

Finally, I see our neocortex as our 'consciousness', the part of us that makes us human, that makes us divine and beautiful, the reason why we have the capacity to see the bigger picture, understand deeper concepts of reality and connect to something greater.

But now you're probably wondering where does this ego come from, he seems to be causing problems doesn't he?

Where does our higher-self come from, how do we choose one over the other and why the heck hasn't your brain gone into meltdown yet?

Well the answers lie in the fact that we, as humans, are half primal animals, with fundamental physical requirements; we need to eat food to survive, we need to consume water to survive, we need shelter and the right environment, all so that we can survive, all of these physical musts need to be met if we're going to be around for any amount of time.

However, we are also sophisticated creatures that have psychological and emotional needs, we as a species have the ability and capacity to understand the deeper meanings of the universe.

Tony Robbins suggests we have six emotional requirements we all need to satisfy, the first of which states "at a basic level, each of us has a need to satisfy a core sense of stability in the world. At a very primal level, satisfying the need for certainty helps guarantee the continuation of our DNA. We do what we need to claim certainty by covering the basics; doing the work that is needed, paying our bills, securing the roof above our head, staying safe in our endeavours and relationships.

We all have a need to satisfy a core sense of stability in the world, we need structure to live by, to give us some sort of purpose.

The challenge of satisfying this need is that the world and lives of those around us are constantly changing and so sometimes our need for certainty causes us to put a fence of controls around our life and/or to stay in our comfort zone and resist change (even healthy change).

In the positive, fulfilling the human need for certainty means finding and creating a sense of centeredness and stability within. As the world moves, we claim power in taking the time to know who we are, in having faith in the currents of life and trusting that one of the certainties of life is change."

Okay, so we need to have a structure and stability to live by, so far so good, but I'm certainly someone who needs to not be caged in, so what do you say to that Tony?

"Just as we each need to experience a sense of Certainty in the world, there are times when we must also break from that which is known, defined and predictable in order to allow ourselves to evolve and become more of who we came here to be. The need for uncertainty, diversity and movement interrupts patterns of predictability and stagnation, allowing us to expand who we are and experience ourselves in motion. Of course there is risk in letting go of that which is certain and known, but when we let go of 'needing to know,' we enter a realm of possibility that is not bound by past experience."

So, these first two 'Human Needs' (Certainty and Variety) work in polarity with each other – seemingly opposing forces that together make a whole. When we are out of balance with one (i.e. so certain that we are bored) it is often the other (i.e. a dose of something new) that brings us back into balance.

Tony describes the third basic need as something I certainly lacked before discovering my path: meaning.

"As we balance the forces of Certainty and Variety in our life and step out into the world, the next Human Need is to be seen and validated for whom we are and what we do. The need for 'Significance' tells us that we do not exist in isolation but as part of a greater whole, and to be an effective part of that whole we need to know that we are playing our part – and being honoured for that expression. Satisfying our need for 'Significance' is part of creating our sense of identity in the world and for those who follow the Chakra system; this need can be aligned with our Solar Plexus and the experience/expression of the Self."

Love how Tony is jumping on the old Chakra craze, the chakras are great and seriously worth checking out if you don't feel like you're balanced or good enough, but more to the point, I think we can all agree that we need validation, however what's important to remember is that the validation we seek can come from ourselves.

"We each have a need to love and be loved by others. We each have a need to belong. Central to our experience of fulfilment in life is to authentically love and make deep connections with other living beings. While fulfilling our need for 'Significance' may temporarily fill our own cup, exchanging genuine Love and

Connection with others allows that cup to overflow and pour into the hearts and lives of those we are with. The shift to this Human Need is much like a shift from the Solar Plexus up into the Heart as it takes our energy and focus beyond self-concern into the discovery of power in our depth of communion with others.

As with the previous Human Needs, there are different ways to experience and express our Love and Connection with others – some more healthy and balanced than others. In most cases the most balanced place to ignite the fulfilment of this Human Need is by taking time to genuinely connect with and love the many aspects of our own being. When we are connected to our Self in the truest sense, this connection naturally aligns with and permeates out to genuine Connection and Love for others."

This is a biggie, I think we can all admit to being lonely sometimes, or feeling like we're not good enough but that's okay, it's part of being human, we need to have connection with others, without it, we could quite literally go insane.

The first four 'Human Needs' Tony's spoken of are often referred to as "personality needs" as they are centred on our individual quest for self-fulfilment and achievement in a worldly sense.

In Psychology, the final two needs are defined as "Needs of the Spirit" as they provide doorways to our deeper sense of true happiness and fulfilment in life – in both physical and non-physical realms.

"One thing that is true of every living thing on Earth is that in order to survive, in order to thrive, we must grow. Whether we are talking about a microorganism, a relationship or creative endeavour, that which ceases to grow ultimately stagnates and dies. The Human Need of Growth both relies on and feeds the first four Human Needs, breathing life into all areas of our existence. As with all Human Needs, the need for Growth can also be taken to out-of-balance extremes.

Growing and expanding can be so fulfilling in its own right that sometimes our quest to fulfil this need causes us to limit ourselves from being fully present in life as it is, or postpone applying our growth and knowledge in the world for fear of not being 'ready' or 'enough'. In the positive, fulfilling our need for Growth comes with an acceptance that **Growth is a journey, not a destination**, and that continual Growth also means allowing ourselves to be real, to be imperfect and to find authentic ways to share what we discover and learn with others."

So, we all need to be growing, whether that be physically from child to adult, emotionally from teenager to mature adult or spiritually from primal animal to spiritual being; we need to be growing and moving towards something greater and I believe this is where we can find attainment of the truths we're all searching for.

As a kid, when we move out of the stage when we're totally reliant on our parents, the stage at which we become self-aware; our conscious levels are so high, dreams and reality are mixed together in this weird state of existence, however our primal, physical needs aren't self-sustaining, you lack the maturity and knowledge to provide food, water or shelter for yourself.

Basically, although your conscious level is pushing on maximum, you're still not going to be around for very long because you can't sort out your physical requirements by yourself.

However, as we get older, because of the nature of the current narratives we live within, the conscious side of nature gets conditioned out of us, all the while our primal needs become self-catering, we learn to find our own food, to drink water and provide ourselves with shelter; however, while we are becoming self-aware, conscious beings, we lose touch of the inner-divinity that allows us to be these self-aware beings in the first place. This is the place where most people get stuck: living fully self-sustaining lives, without any conscious connection and this place is where most people miss out on the sixth Human Need.

"As we ascend to the sixth Human Need we move into the power of living our life's purpose and bringing real value to the lives of others. Our need for contribution rises naturally from the positive fulfilment of the other five needs, being expressed in such a way that brings a genuine sense of value to the word.

Contribution comes from a fundamental yearning to have our lives mean something, to make a difference, to give or bring something to the world that continues to benefit others when we are gone. Our need for Contribution can be fulfilled in a massive variety of ways – from launching a foundation or volunteering to support a cause we believe in, to simply pausing from our busy day to smile, hug or help someone in need. The challenge with this Human Need is that once we connect the power of being in genuine service in the world, we can quite quickly become overwhelmed with all of the places, people and animals that are in need of support.

Many people, who value the need for Contribution above all others, find it difficult to also contribute and give to themselves. One of the greatest expressions of this need comes when we allow ourselves to realize that Contribution comes not only from what we "do", but from who we are "being" on a moment to moment basis. When we are empowered to BE our Contribution in the simplest of ways, actions that arise from this place are aligned with who we are and carry great power."

Tony Robbins is sounding an awful lot like Ghandi in this moment, (which further proves that everybody who is saying a valid message is really just saying the same thing) and what he's saying is so true; we all have an urge to be counted for, we all ponder the big questions of life and we'd all like some sort of answer.

We can find these answers by going back to the place we spoke of earlier and instead of remaining stuck in the place where we are self-sustaining organisms that have no spiritual connection, we can change this dynamic and place ourselves in a position to meet all of our needs.

Because now we have all of our primal requirements catered for, we have a choice, we can now decide, to use this fulfilment of needs to create a platform to start growing our conscious side back towards the place it was at as a child, using things such as money and material objects as tools to elevate our consciousness, instead of having our primal needs and urges manipulated into a vicious cycle of discontentment which is where we all get trapped within the current story.

So, this is the place where we can stand as a self-aware conscious being, connected to our primal, physical self, fully mature and self-sustaining, while also connected to the deep, spiritual divinity we all possess, and when we can balance on a platform with all our physical, emotional and spiritual needs catered for,

That **is where contentment is found.**

Chapter 11

The Spiritually Scientific Conundrum

Now I don't want to of just showed you a profound statement about finding contentment in life, about detaching and over-coming the ego and then subsequently revert straight back to a comment on my own ego, but is that not exactly what we've been saying this whole time?

That yes, we are self-aware consciousness beings, but by over-coming our primal needs and urges, we can elevate our consciousness to a state where we realise we are also connected to the under-lying connectedness which is connected consciousness, which sits at the base of all phenomena and that by harnessing and tapping into this energy, we can grasp and conceptualise that we are simply a story in our heads?

Did I also just get ahead of myself? Perhaps, my ego suggests not.

However you may think proposing that all humans are 'good' if we balance our needs out is a little too intense on the old spiritual front, so let's look at it from the opposite end; a scientific view… (Well moderately science-y, but not too science-y, I'm not a scientist after all; although I have met world-renowned scientists, so does that balance the scale? But then again it's individual opinion as I made abundantly clear to ironically Mr. Grinter, who was my science teacher, who I spent many hours debating over life and the universe, before diverting into football to waste lesson time, much like I'm about to do now, as it appears we have sidetracked and by we, I mean me, as you are simply the poor human following the ramblings of a madman, so back to the story and come on you Spurs! How the hell did I get the go-ahead to write a book?)

This idea of 'needs' needing to be fulfilled is a common trait in two normally opposing teams: science and spiritually.

The reason I say this is because science and spirituality are two areas I've spent large amount of time delving deep into research and theories, however even spirituality and science have become victims of a fixed narrative and story being projected to us, that may be hindering and not helping the state of the way we see the world.

After running as far away as I could from politics at the start of my journey, realising that it didn't really serve any purpose, my next destination was the total other end of the spectrum; spirituality.

It was around this time that I met Russell and Brett and thanks to the two of them being so charming and supportive, I believed I had found the golden ticket, that spirituality was the total answer and solution to all of my questions and problems and that as long as I kept the old chakras all aligned, I would keep bumping into these amazing people who belonged in some sort of new-age utopia.

However, the further I got into the 'bulk' of what spirituality had to offer, the quicker I realised that perhaps Russ and Brett weren't the average mentors they appeared to be and were actually quite unique, their kindness and selflessness setting them apart from the rest, something I expected to find in every corner of 'spirituality'.

I'm aware that questioning whether everyone involved in 'spirituality' is there with everybody's interests and not just their own at heart is both controversial and maybe not 'politically correct', but I've already named all the planet-destroying corporations and exposed all the family-dynasties for their wrong-doings, so I might as well complete the set. (Besides, what are a bunch of yogis going to do? Beat me at downward dog? If you've got a problem with this, consult my lawyer, and since he or she doesn't exist, go find a quiet, serene place, close your eyes, connect to your breath and f*ck right off).

Look, in all seriousness I'm not commending yogis or the 'whole' spiritual scene, I just feel that we have to accept that in all areas of our society, there is an ever-increasing, economically-driven mentality and that simply disregarding the idea that this mentality could be present in the community of 'spiritual people' is naïve and dangerous.

I'm not even saying that we should all be travelling nomads with man-bun's, I myself see the contradiction and don't feel like we should categorise what 'spiritual' needs to look like, but I think we can all agree that we intuitively know who's the real deal. If someone sounds like they're better suited to be in a car insurance advert than on a yoga mat, then they probably don't hold the key to enlightenment.

I'm not even saying that we should be sceptical of people who charge for 'spiritual' services, I charge for workshops, events, talks and all kinds of shizzle that you could say contain 'spiritual' messages, but I feel there's a huge difference between charging to hear someone talk about their experiences and tell you that spirituality is a personal journey we all take (that's me, trying my hardest to not over or under sell myself, while juggling looking like a sceptic and a total self-aware asshole) and people who claim they have all the answers, that only they can give you salvation and that only they have worked out the path, to me, these people are just as bad as the politicians and TV presenters, in fact, they're worse, declaring they've seen the 'truth' that we shouldn't give these people our trust or money, instead trusting them. (There's a reason why these people care so much about their Instagram, and it hasn't got nothing to do with a spiritual connection to the inner-divinity we all possess).

Rant over, anyway what is interesting is the similarity between the ways science looks at the brain opposed to how spirituality views the blob in our heads and yet how opposed science and spirituality's theories are from each other.

It's like two teenagers engaging in the longest fight over who rides in the front seat in the history of man-kind, to me, ever since I started my journey and have been fortunate to speak to world renowned scientists and spiritual gurus and religious teachers alike, I've been astonished at how quick both sets of beliefs and teachings try to disprove the other, when to me, they're both saying the exact same things in different ways.

It's not just when talking about the brain where these two opposite sides having strikingly similar views, in fact, most scientific or spiritual beliefs can be directly linked, in this special time of human history science and spirituality are converging into a grand new vision.

In the past decades quantum science has demonstrated explicitly that our physical reality cannot be separated from our conscious awareness of it. In addition, quantum science discovered an all pervasive energy field that permeates the entire universe: the 'zero point' field as its dubbed by scientists (Who I'm sure call things like this 'The zero point field' to make it sound super-interesting and like it belongs in the folklore of superheroes and Hollywood sci-fi movies, maybe that's where they got the name from, that would be very ironic, but that's beside the point).

From this energy field, sub-atomic particles jump in and out of existence all the time. The material world does not seem to be as solid as we thought it was, it's a living, breathing creation that is constantly moving.

The zero point field is science's equivalent of Eastern spirituality's 'Akashi' field, also the equivalent to many religions 'Gods', the idea of an omnipresent, all penetrating ether field from which both the material and immaterial world comes into existence.

Recent scientific discoveries have inspired frontier scientists now to merge contemporary science with ancient Eastern esoteric wisdom. A group of frontier scientists who discovered that the Zero Point Field - an ocean of subatomic vibrations in the space between things - connects everything in the universe, (think of it like the Force in Star Wars), 'The Field' offers a radically new view of the way our world and our bodies work.

The human mind and body are not distinct and separate from their environment, but a packet of pulsating energy constantly interacting with this vast energy sea. This idea creates a picture of an interconnected universe and a new scientific theory which makes sense of 'supernatural 'phenomena, everything can happen, because through different realities, dimensions and states of awareness or consciousness, on some level, everything is connected.

This 'new' form of electromagnetic energy was already put to use by Nikola Tesla (that guy Bowie played in that film which was directed by the guy who did batman, which ironically also featured the guy who played batman and the guy who played Batman's butler *and* the guy who played wolverine, the fanboy in me can't contain the excitement, if you never saw The Prestige, this has been a weird bracket chat and if you have, then you have gained my respect) in the mid-1900's and has been discovered by the Russians as well referring to it as the torsion wave.

In the fifties Russian scientist Nikolai Kozyrev discovered that torsion waves are linked to consciousness and that our thoughts produce these waves as well, how incredible is that? The very waves that link our universe together are also created by the thoughts you have in your mind.

Torsion waves travel at super luminous speeds to the far corners of the universe and may be the explanation for many phenomena. It may also account for the non-locality phenomenon of quantum science. Ever wondered why Leonardo da Vinci stressed the importance of the Golden Mean, Phi in his art work?

The importance of Phi was preserved in the ancient art of sacred geometry by the Egyptians, the Greek and was also used secretly by Freemasons in the architecture of many cathedrals and churches.

Sacred geometry is now used in a new physics called 'Implosion Physics'. Implosion physics describes the atom as a standing wave pattern of sacred geometry patterns in the ether. Amazingly these geometrical patterns were already described by Plato 300 years BC as the building blocks of matter!

Could this suggest that actually all religions and ancient teachings were our ancestors way of trying to conceptualise that omnipresent energy we all know of, but due to the lack of understanding of the atomic world at the time, described it as a super-natural force and that now, at this point in our history, thanks to our advanced understanding of physical science and the physical world around us, we can now start to try to rationalise the same discovery in greater depth and potentially tap into this force ourselves, could we elevate our consciousness spiritually, or scientifically discover a method that can allow a connection to this energy and (if talking in 'religious theoretical terms) become that omnipresent energy? Could we become what our ancestors may have been describing as 'God'? And a greater question even still, can we already tap into this omnipresent energy, just through our own minds?

I appreciate at this point, your head might be hurting or you might be wondering why someone who has promised you answers, is now asking you a shed-load of rhetorical questions, well lets scale it back to basics, what all of these teachings are saying, regardless of what angle we're looking at is that 'consciousness is the first cause of creation', in some way.

Now what does that make you? A co-creator of your own reality!

In the movie 'The Matrix' there is a similar message suggesting that life is just a dream, could the Matrix be real? What if we are just collectively creating our reality, all living to a similar enough story, on a grand enough scale so that appears like this is the only way of existing?

Maybe you've heard about the Quantum brain? It is a new theory of the brain, stating that the brain does not produce consciousness but is merely a receiver of a universal consciousness that is every-where in the universe, how spiritual is that!

You couldn't get a more spiritual statement, 'we are not human beings having a spiritual experience, we are spiritual beings having a human experience' is like the go to quote for hippies and quantum science is now saying the same thing!

Could this prove that the fundamental reality is an illusion of separateness and that our separate egos are illusions? That the story we're conditioned into is actually one of over-arching division? That all boundaries; cities, nations, continents are divides we should over-come to achieve an over-arching oneness? That we all appear to be self-aware conscious beings but in reality are all connected?

Is the oneness of an all pervading conscious energy field in the universe the only real essence of our existence like the Eastern yogis in deep states of meditation have always claimed?

The journalist and author Sorcha Faal, told me this on the matter, when I met him out in New Jersey, "'Recent findings of Quantum Physics about our universe being made up of an interconnected unbroken wholeness, examples of Non-Locality phenomena and the Observer Effect, implying that consciousness underlies all reality, has striking parallels with our ancient Esoteric concepts that all reality is the manifestation of an infinite Singularity which some choose to call Source, and most others call God".

Now how far down the rabbit hole do you want to go?

The 2012 prophecies related to the ending of the Maya Long Count calendar predicted major global changes in human consciousness by 2012, remember, when everyone woke up that one day on 2012 a little bit nervous? Then there was that terrible disaster movie with the same name? Well, if you do your research you'll realise the Mayans never predicted the end of the world in the 'traditional' sense, but the final cycle in a rotation; leading to a re-birth. The 'apocalypse' to them, was actually the dawning of a brand new age, what if this 'age' is actually the start in the next step for us, as conscious self-aware beings, the age where we realise that science and spirituality are the flip side to the same coin and that this is age where we discover how to utilise that energy or God-like presence to elevate our next step in evolution?

Could it be that the ancient prophecies of a shift of the ages within our time period has already begun? Current revolutionary scientific discoveries now seem to corroborate Eastern spirituality's claim that the universe at heart is essentially one, but will these discoveries really lead to a spiritual and scientific revolution on this blue planet?

Me and Russell both agree that the next step in human evolution is a conscious one, a shift towards the 'end-goal' in our journey for enlightenment, for happiness, for the perfect story?

'Cosmic Consciousness', the spiritual belief, is an ultra-high state of illumination in the human mind that is beyond that of "self-awareness" and "ego-awareness." In the attainment of Cosmic Consciousness, the human mind has entered a state of knowledge instead of mere beliefs, a state of "I know," instead of "I believe".

That is the difference between science and spirituality, "I know" says the scientists, "I believe" says the gurus; how much more evidence do these guys need before they both realise how similar they are!

This state of mind is beyond that of the sense of reasoning, in that it has attained an awareness of the universe and its relation to being and recognition of the oneness in all things that is not easily shared with others who have not personally experienced this state of mind.

"The attainment of cosmic illumination will cause an individual to seek solitude from the multitude, and isolation from the noisy world of mental pollution"… is that not enlightenment? Is that not just another way for saying 'write your own story'?

"In the state of 'Cosmic Consciousness' an individual has developed a keen awareness of his own mental states and activities and that of others around him or her. This individual is aware of a very distinct "I" personality that empowers the individual with a powerful expression of the "I am" that is not swayed or moved by the external impressions of the trifling mental states of others. This individual stands on a "rock solid" foundation that is not easily understood by the common mind. Cosmic Consciousness is void of the "superficial" ego. (The ego is useful if integrated and working with the Soul and heart at an aware level.)"

There's currently a huge amount of research going into a molecule that is bringing science and spirituality together with a crash, being dubbed 'the spirit molecule'.

DMT or dimethyltryptamine is a simple compound found throughout nature which has profound effects on human consciousness.

Activist, Comedian and DMT advocate Joe Rogan says "These substances are tools that can be used to expand awareness in all areas of life and apply that expanded awareness for the betterment of people's lives, communities and families and all society. The good news is that there is a growing number of westerners and actually intellectuals, scientists, artists, movers and shakers, filmmakers and so on who realize that this stuff is all too interesting just to go on keeping it swept under the rug. The Inquisition was a long time ago, the birth of rationalism was a long time ago, at this point there is no good reason, apart from bad habit, to keep up these barriers. With the help of two concepts, which are traditionally opposed:

Science and spirituality, which we can use to humbly re-introduce psychedelics back in to the cultural dialogue."

My instant reaction was that as soon as you start using words such as 'psychedelic', the attachments of 'hippies' and 'nonsense' will also be attached, that's before we get onto the whole debate on whether we should be taken chemical compounds to enhance our experience.

Joe continued: "DMT - the spirit molecule, you know, it's a conundrum, it's a paradox. The spirit is the inner world; the molecule is the external world. So the psychedelics are entheogens, take us from the science to the spirit.

This is what the Jewish sage mystics have been describing in a coded language for literally thousands of years.

Through meditation, through fasting, chanting, any number of techniques their might be a burst of endogenous DM that is correlated with mystical and near-death experiences.

I had this theory that there is a big similarity between psychedelics and experiences that were possible with a lot of meditation. And that was one of the original findings that led me to start looking for a spirit molecule"

.Now it gets interesting, I can testify myself to having 'out-of-body' experiences and a connection to something beyond my normal consciousness thanks to a repeated practice of meditation.

There's something that, for me, makes sense about DMT. Many people call it the "spirit molecule", to me it makes more sense for it to be called the "reality molecule"

Philosophically, it makes sense that something that would be so fundamental to the way we perceive reality, would be, well, actually out there in reality.

Joe continues to talk about how DMT can be used to re-connect use to something deeper... "The Ayahuasca is a technique used in many parts of the world to use DMT, much harder for the power structures that we have now, it's much harder for them to put down because it has been a part of a legitimate religious and spiritual practice for thousands of years, certainly in the Amazon.

We can't just dismissal that as primitive mumbo-jumbo and superstition. We have to get grips with that on its own terms. I think there are a growing number of people who feel this desire to get back in touch with nature with plants, with animals and who know that through the shamanic path, there is way of doing this and that actually these tools, these psychoactive tools for plants like Ayahuasca is a very direct way of doing this. Now it may not be everybody's cup of tea and I think a lot of people are actually, with a reason, afraid of it.

DMT flash makes it clear that a disembodied consciousness is a possibility.

I ask you to suspend any opinions, either negative or positive about these compounds. Whatever you believe their value to be they continue to have profound effects wherever we find their use, whether it's contemporary Western culture or in the Amazon rainforest.

It was in the 50's that the Ayahuasca churches starting going public. You know there was a kind of transition from indigenous Indians to mestizo people in cities and then these churches - the Santo Daime church and then the UDV church later started doing ceremonies that would made the Ayahuasca accessible not just to Indians but to urban people in big cities who are as far from the shamans as we are.

Why is it that in the entire Western world, these substances that have been found to be so interesting by a hundreds of cultures for thousands of years are prohibited?

How did these cultures that consider them to be enlightened, democratic and scientific get to declaring plants "illegal"?

It can seem weird, but there's clearly something deep and revealing about the nature of these societies. Our society values enlighten problem solving and consciousness devalues all other states of consciousness.

Any other kind of consciousness that is not related, to the production or consumption of material goods is stigmatized in our society today.

Of course, we accept drunkenness. We allow people some brief respite from the material grind. A society that subscribes to that a model is a society that is going to condemn the states of consciousness that have nothing to do with the enlighten problem-solving mentality.

And if you go back to the 1960s, when there was a tremendous up search of exploration of psychedelics, I would say that the huge backlash that followed that had to do with the fear on the part of the powers that be. That if enough people went into those realms, had those experiences, the very fabric of the society we have today would be picked apart and most importantly, those in power at the top would not be in power at the top anymore."

Whether this part of the chapter has intrigued you or made you think I need to give FRANK a call, the point I'm making is regardless of what your views on this DMT substance are, we can't deny that Joe is spreading the same message as me, I'm calling for a personal revolution, he's calling for a DMT revolution, it's certainly food for thought, not, whether DMT is the answer, but how amazing is it that there is a natural substance that people have taken and come to the same conclusion that scientists and spiritual teachers have, certainly makes me think that maybe instead of focusing on the details and differences, we should start to notice the similarities between all these different narratives.

"The way I look at the 60s you can see as a kind of failed attempt at a mass, cultural voyage of initiation. People would, you know, try to go out to these other realities, but they didn't have a basis there weren't wisdom traditions, elders, there weren't like connections of shamanic lineages.

Social, political, scientific issues that came together pushed these drugs out of the scientific marketplace.

The public opinion in many cases had become that psychedelic research was dangerous.

The wide public was uninformed about the true nature of these compounds and what their importance may be in the understanding of perception itself. One of the tragedies to me is that the clinical research on these substances pretty much stopped around 1970."

Well, we certainly have covered what happened in 1970's in quite great detail, coincidence?

Joe ends with, "Because of the collapse of consciousness spiritual and scientific knowledge split apart.

Both these modes of knowing have to come together in order to science and technology from a traditional religious perspective is not an extra, it is part of the process by which humanity is going to evolve into its next stage.

How do we find like the right form for psychedelics in the future? Assuming that psychedelics are part of the human future at the moment there still, you know, generally repressed and suppressed and illegal.

If that were to change, how would we begin to construct a kind of a system that would allow for, for kind of rational and mature exploration of the psychedelics?

I think that the name of the game is to show science the pertinence of this somewhat outlandish realm.

It's not just crazy stuff. It shouldn't be considered as, let's say, not even worthy of interest or illegitimate I actually think because it's declared off bounds, it just makes it interesting to with start. But one doesn't want to throw the baby with the bath water and I think it's really important to stay faithful to science. What does it mean? Why is there a part of the brain that seems to before lack of a better word "a God-detector"? You know.

What's the evolutionary advantage to having some part of the brain that seems to, you know,

Now I am beginning to wonder whether consciousness may actually survive biological death. That maybe the model that we've been working under in psychiatry and behavioural pharmacology model, it's just wrong, it's backwards actually.

The consciousness is primarily in the universe and matter is a result of perception.

We were a dying species, we live on a dying planet, we're killing the planet so our disease is extremely serious and therefore we're desperate to find new information, ideas and so on that can transcend. We have to evolve, and I think our intellectual evolution may be predicated upon the psychedelic pioneers.

It's so easy to change the world; I mean that's the kind of thing that you can see on psychedelics. If you don't get trapped in the beauty of the psychedelic experience it."

Regardless, I think DMT is a forcible reminder that, even if we use it or just hear about the discoveries found from others, there's a lot more about reality, the universe, we, the biosphere, there's a lot more to it than we imagine.

It seems our reality is not the only reality; occasionally the cracks reveal themselves and may even want to be discovered. As humans, we are creatures that thirst for meaning and purpose.

We spend time, money and infinite energy searching for it, in schools, in churches, in business and in technology. Purpose is one of our greatest quests.

DMT, potentially in the future, could be, as Joe Rogan calls it "A molecule with a complex name and the simplest ability to unlock the door to another dimension, and perhaps, just perhaps, our future evolution."

Away from DMT, I love how there is now a deeper-understanding of the universe that is breaking down the walls of spirituality and science, all of these ideas regarding our brain, our realities, our consciousness and the way we experience life are strikingly similar for sure, however one thing that astounds me, is the way that we apply these revelations and potentially immortalise ourselves.

"Death is not an event in life: we do not live to experience death. If we take eternity to mean not an infinite temporal duration but the quality of timelessness, then does eternal life not belong to those who live in the present?" was a mind-boggling statement by philosopher Ludwig Wittgenstein, which basically means, if we are totally connected to the moment through whatever way we find fitting (all them techniques earlier) then really, we tap into this universal energy and we transcend the physical self and with it, the death and decay attached to it.

If we think about it, there is a constant dying and being born everywhere, even in the human body where old cells are expelled and replaced by new ones all the time. We are living in a world of becoming and not of being; fortunately so, because there would be no possibility of any progress if life were static and not dynamic, constantly changing, if nobody ever died then we could never progressively take what others learnt and build on them.

In spirituality, there is no death, no end but only a change, a new opportunity for wider and higher experiences.

Birth and death are like two gateways, the one at the entrance to the earth, the other at the entrance of higher worlds, both opening the road to wide fields of experience for the human soul.

Men believe that death is a going away whereas it is really a secret presence. They believe that it creates infinite distances whereas it abolishes all distance by giving back to the spirit what had been imprisoned in the flesh. To live is often to leave one another; to die is to come together again.

For those who have gone to the depths of love, death is a consecration and not a fall. Love can be the more intimate, more purified and full of deepest reverence. The heart plunges deeply into the mystery to seek those who have fled.

I personally love the idea that man is currently a 'being' in the intermediary state between animal and god, where he is able to understand both, having still the qualities of the animal and already the potentiality of a god in himself.

For all you sci-fi lovers, think of it like Doctor Who, one version, one incarnation of The Doctor can die, but then he regenerates and a new actor, who you're not sure if you like the look of or not takes his place, all of him changes, looks and personality, but yet he is still the same consciousness. I like to think Doctor Who could be a fantastic way to think about the true meaning of self, what if *we* are a consciousness, simply experiencing life as an 'individual' and then regenerating into a new 'individual', although our consciousness is the same.

What's even crazier is what if everybody knew that after death, we come back as a 'new' version of the same consciousness, what would that do to the dynamic of the human race?

Even crazier, what if the human race created religion, politics and everything else not to enlighten us, but to hide the real truth, all these conspiracy theories and rumours, what if they are all covering up the we are all energy and there is constant re-birth?

Because what if we are not ready to understand this truth and that 'enlightenment' is actually finding out this truth through self-evaluation and then still choosing to be loving and tolerant after finding this out, being able to understand the deeper questions of the universe with a loving eye.

Well, these are the crazy thoughts that whizz around my brain and in all fairness, my opinion on the matters change every day, so let's not get tied down to the details; I think anyone who is ready to find the truth will be able to find it inherently as we all possess the knowledge of the truth within ourselves, but I'm no profound spiritual guru... yet.

Either way, it all allows us to set standards for ourselves, to judge or condemn means not to have understood. Even if one cannot always approve this does not give the right to condemn. Lack of understanding is one of the reasons why we're constantly fighting each other. One of the most beautiful experiences during Christmas time is the endeavour to give each other as much joy and pleasure as possible, even if it is only in the form of a materialistic present. If this attitude of mutual helpfulness could prevail the whole year, life would be so much easier and pleasant for everybody, think about it, what is Christmas?

It's a shared belief, built on top of a religious teaching, where everybody is told you have to be nice to each-other. Where you refrain from swearing at the guy who spilt his coffee over you because 'it's Christmas', where you donate that money to the homeless guy, smile at strangers and bother to spend time calling your loved ones, all because "it's Christmas".

Why do we stop there? Why don't we replace that attitude from "It's Christmas" to "It's Life", why don't we all adopt that ideology we have around the coldest time of year; all year round, imagine what the world could be.

I think Christmas is a great example to prove that our lives are simply stories in our heads, the whole holiday wouldn't exist unless people agreed that upon this rotation of the sun around the earth, we're all going to spread love and joy, because in most parts of the world its lost it's 'Christian' meaning, but that's okay, because we shouldn't need to be 'Christian', or any specific religion to decide to spend a day spreading love, *we should all strive for that every day.*

I'm a strong believer that by changing the world we perceive internally, we create a different world outside of our eyes and by doing so, can change our perspective on some of life's greatest challenges.

I believe, for example, that if we understood perfectly the meaning of death we would not mourn. The great German mystic, Jacob Bohme, has said: "Freed from all suffering is he to whom time is like eternity and eternity like time."

Life and Death are our helpers, in a sense, also, how do you define 'life' and 'death'?

The moment in which a baby becomes 'alive', is an argument that science has battled with for years, with 'it's down to personal opinion' being the safest answer to give... so if 'birth' is a state up for questioning, why shouldn't death be?

Because I hate to be the bearer of bad news, but we are all going to die at some point. That's a realisation we don't really think about over here in the west, we feel bad when we hear somebody else dies, we get upset when our favourite celebrity dies, in fact, we even can accept that people we know and love will someday die, fore-warning ourselves that it's not going to be a great day, but we can never accept that the same fate lies waiting for us, we, or maybe just me, have always assumed we'll find a way around it at some point (probably after I've finished this book), but the brutal, physical reality isn't so.

My mentor and mate Brett tells a great story, he asks me, "What's the most important thing on a grave-stone?"... "I have no idea", I replied.

Brett explained that nearly everyone he talks to declares that the 'dates' are the most important thing, logical sense applied, the two dates on a grave detail the start and end of somebodies life and so matter the most. But if we shift our perspective and hear Brett out, Brett suggests the most important thing isn't the dates at all... it's the dash in-between.

That dash is you. That dash is your memories, your experiences, your loves and your life, all in a tiny little dash. The whole history of you, everything you did, everything you saw, everything you ever were, is stored within that tiny, little dash.

How safe would we be if we understood the real nature and purpose of life

and death?

Death would become to us not an enemy to be feared and run from, but a loving friend to whom we are dear.

We would take death quite naturally even if it does not come as a liberator after long physical illness and suffering but quite suddenly and unexpectedly or bereaving us of children when they are still young, as controversial as this sound, there is a bigger picture to see, regardless of how you see it.

Over here in Western civilisation, we are so scared of death, so scared of losing this life we have, however on my travels, especially out to the countries where the Eastern spiritual teachings are followed, I'm amazed at how beautiful they view death, as regeneration into something new; the apocalypse isn't 'the end' but 're-birth'.

In spirituality and religious teachings; birth and death are governed by the laws of Karma and Reincarnation and these laws are manifestations of Divine Love, the supreme law of all laws. We would be perfect and our lives would be perfect if we were able to follow this law implicitly, as we would simply 'be' all that we need to be in every moment; forever.

C. Jinarajadasa has said: "If only I could make our members feel that every beautiful experience in life is just like a window into an experience continuous in eternity, not merely the fragment of it which comes to us, I should feel that I have achieved something that I came to do...The thing here below, like a flower, is exquisite, but it is exquisite because it is a mirror of something so intensely dazzling and fascinating that the whole heart is drawn upwards to that Life in eternity." How mind-scrambling and beautiful is that?

If the fear of death could be abolished one of the darkest clouds which hovers over humanity would be dissipated. The difficulty is that everybody has to do this for themselves so that the process of dissipation is a very slow one but each individual who succeeds in overcoming this fear is contributing to the liberation of humanity from one of its nightmares, because his own fearlessness can be an encouraging example and become a stimulation for others to become fearless themselves.

As Shelley has said so wonderfully: "He is not dead, he does not sleep and he has awakened from the dream of life."

To me, the truth is for any person who tries to live according to the 'Law of Love' there are no obstacles which do not become means for inner growth, simply steps on the way to 'personal perfection'. Someone on this journey will become more and more religious, spiritual, scientific or whatever other way you wish to categorise it, in the widest sense of the words, because his knowledge of the truth becomes greater and greater.

As Bacon has said: "While a little knowledge inclines men to atheism, a larger knowledge brings them back to the truth."

Basically what he means that with no knowledge, we will follow the 'truth' blindly and be led backwards in our search for contentment, upon discovering the fact that the truth presented to us, is one with an agenda, we seek freedom and retribution, we decline from belief and believe in nothing, but upon gaining a greater knowledge, we finally find the truth we initially sought after, our own, real truth and that is where contentment is found.

Now that is a scientifically spiritual message if ever there was one.

Chapter 12

<u>The Way Out</u>

Now we're starting to get spiritual and hippie, which is where we're heading in the second part of the book!

Scary stuff right? Although it does intrigue me how the structure of our reality is so fragile. The next time you doubt the likelihood of a personal revolution actually being possible, remind yourself about the impossibility of right now in the first place and use that as motivation to remember that change is always possible.

So how do we change it? Well that's where we're heading in the second part of the book because right now there's no short or easy answer, but your obviously here for a reason and so you know that it isn't right, you know something new needs to take its place, but just know that as much as we need to spread this message, to get others to provide an alternative, it all starts with ourselves. Because, just for a moment, think, if every single person in the world had a 'personal revolution', who would there be left that we'd need to talk too?

Nobody, because we would've all changed!

It's so simple, it's so trivial and obvious and yet we're all so busy focusing on everybody else when in reality **our only way out is within and our one solution; is a personal revolution.**

So after reading this book you will be more aware and inspired to make changes in both your personal life and the bigger world around you, the first and one of the most important things you can do is to not be the person to except the world your living in, as Ghandi so famously said, 'be the change you want to see in the world'.

The thing that's happened lately is that because of the nature of our politics and media, we've become overly comfortable in our artificial, hyper-normalised environment (slugging around on our sofas watching x-factor) that we've stopped evolving and now we're just sort of coughing our way through existence, only experiencing a fraction of the incredible divinity we all possess. But why aren't we bothered? Surely we don't want this to be happening? And the truth is we don't, of course we don't, but most of us don't even realise it's going on;

1% is doing it, 5% of us are bothered and the other 94% are none the wiser!

Our idea of democracy, of materialism, of capitalism; is a game, one which the likes of Donald Trump, the big CEO's of corporations (that now have more power than small countries), bankers and criminals (spot the difference) have all been given all the cheat-codes and secrets, while we're all expected to start from scratch.

o let's not be surprised when we see corrupt media secrets being exposed, let's not be surprised when we see Trump being elected, *because we are maintaining the environment in which these people thrive and excel; in order to make them irrelevant and obsolete we need to create a new environment in which they will die out.*

Think of it like this; if you're going to fight a crocodile, don't fight it in the swamp where it has all the power and knows all the back-routes; fight it on land where it's less powerful, where you have a fighting chance.

This is where the current system fails, it's designed to separate and divide, the current system simply *must have* some people above others for it to work, it's how it's designed, the blueprints for this system tells us that's how it works... but that's not quite how humans work.

That's the underlying issue right there, by having a system that puts a few above the rest, it encourages the few to be selfish, it encourages the many to be jealous and spiteful; basically, it encourages all the wrong parts of our human nature; vanity, greed, self-loathing and tells us that these horrible traits are commendable and worth-having, these human traits are what will make you 'successful'. Compassion, unity, love, all get marked off as 'hippie Ideals' and are frowned upon.

Human nature isn't that all of us 'humans are bad, selfish and ignorant creatures'; humans are not naturally like this, no, what we humans inhibit is a very wide range of behaviours and tendencies, especially how subjective we are.

What I mean, is that we humans like to follow suit, copy one another, to fit in, it's one of our natural built in survival techniques, we're stronger together then we are apart, strength in numbers, etc.

That's all well and good, however the problem arose when this system that our ancestors created encouraged us to behave and act a certain way, the system in place meant that behaviours such as greed and being self-centred were the traits to have if you wanted to excel in the system and get in that 'top elites group'.

There was a study done, with a bunch of babies, only 1-3 years old, where a playroom was set up and every kid was given the same amount of toys. The kids were then left to do whatever they wanted, all the kids were different races, came from different wealth and religious backgrounds and guess what happened?

No, no baby extremists arose, no evil baby dictator took power and no sneaky baby rigged the playroom rules to benefit them.

What happened was all the kids shared one another's toys; they played with each other nicely and all genuinely got along. Now of course, due to different personalities, some didn't like each other as much as the rest, but these babies didn't start conflicts over that, they just simply ignored each other and got on doing the things they wanted to do. Now these kids weren't told. These kids weren't conditioned. These kids were genuine spiritually-free little people who when given a free choice and system that allowed and encouraged positive behaviour, followed suit and enjoyed their playtime. Now surely if a bunch of whining, pooping mini versions of us can pull it off, it can't be that hard?

What it also proves, is that if you create the right kind of system that engages us and encourages the positive parts of our humanity, the neocortex and limbic part, we overcome the reptilian mind and exceed using the others.

What it also proves is that deep down, we're all connected, if, as babies we choose to love another, if, as vulnerable little creatures with no grasp of the world we can automatically engage our brain centres for love, understanding and tolerance, then scientifically the *only* thing that can alter these natural behaviours is what we learn and how we're conditioned by our society as we get older, if our current system conditions that inner divinity out of us, it's got to go!

If you don't want to take the babies words for it, there's loads of examples, one of which is the Trew Era Cafe, a place that I hold dear to my heart, the cafe was set up by Russell and is a non-profit organisation set up in the middle of Hackney (in London; it's one of the most contrasting areas between wealth and poverty) that only hires ex drug-addicts as its workers, to get them back into work and give back to the community. That's in the middle of one of the most corrupt cities, proving if that can be done there, it can be done anywhere!

I love that cafe, there's such a beautiful feeling, a sense of hope, of unity, of change; optimistic, full of life, beautiful. It was also at the cafe where I originally met Russell and subsequently Brett, two people who've had a huge impact on my journey.

It was at this café where I heard an amazing story, all about crabs (I know, my expectations dropped on the word 'crabs' as well... but hear me out), the story painted the scenario of a crab inside of a bucket, due to its disproportioned body shape and huge claws, combined with the slippery and awkward material of the bucket; every-time the crab tried to climb out, it fell back down; although it desperately wants to get out, the cage (or bucket in this case) traps the prisoner (the crab) inside due to its structure not complimenting how the crab was designed.

The crab isn't happy in the bucket because the crab is not meant to be inside the bucket. This agitates the crab, makes it angry and aggressive and all round makes the crab look like not such a nice guy, so when another crab gets placed into the bucket along with the original crab, as soon as one crab tries to climb out the bucket, the other one automatically attacks the crab trying to escape, dragging the want-to-be-escapee back to the base of the bucket.

This happens because the structure both crabs are in, doesn't suit either crab and so it makes both crabs angry and aggressive so when one tries to escape, the crab automatically uses these traits to attack the other one, because the structure they're in creates the conflict and stress for the crabs. See where I'm heading with this?

Because those crabs are me and you and our friends, families and actually every other person of our society, **because we are existing inside a cage** (the bucket from the story) that doesn't suit our design or cater for our needs, it creates an ego and encourages our primal, reptilian brain to become dominant and so as soon as one of us tries to escape this bucket, maybe by going on a 'spiritual journey' or having a 'personal revolution'; maybe somebody wins the lottery or a friend becomes really successful, because we're living in the bucket, we turn into the crabs and try and claw each-other back to the bottom, we are working on a low frequency of hatred and fear, instead of a higher frequency of compassion and unconditional love.

However it's not all doom and gloom, because if you placed the same crabs on an open-beach with loads of shells and water, the crabs would co-exist and be quite happy in their own little bubble, because they're now existing in an environment that suits them, that encourages them to co-exist and get along, this is the exact same for us, because we are holding the current story in our heads in place as much as the politicians, media sources and corporations.

The way to overthrow Donald Trump, make Brexit a success and revolutionise the whole world isn't through aggression, hatred, fear and externally looking for an answer, the way to revolutionise the whole world is to internally looking for an answer, because the right thing to guide us, is right here inside us and nobody can divide us when we live a life of unconditional love.

There are hundreds of examples. The point I'm making is despite that we're told there's no other way it could work, despite our materialistic outlook most people have, it doesn't have to be like this; if we create a reality in our minds centred around love and compassion, our life will be transformed into one awesome adventure full of excitement and unity, instead of the competitive, 'dog-eat-dog' world most of us are experiencing today.

So how can we do this? Well we have to take responsibility and realise that we are in the driving seats of our lives. One of the simplest ways of taking responsibility practically is if there's something you don't want to do, don't do it.

Disobey; don't follow orders, its great fun! (Of course you should only disobey if no-one or the planet gets hurt, follow Ghandi's rules). What I mean is if you don't agree with eating meat, don't do it, if you don't want to go to university, because you'd rather go and travel; go and travel!

The point here is don't let anyone tell you what to do, be in control of your thoughts and actions, consciously. Don't let others dictate your life, live the life you want and love the life you live.

Step outside the system, don't worry about 'social norms' or what's 'acceptable' because these are boundaries you should set for yourself, not be told what is or isn't acceptable by others.

I appreciate it is hard, because I know first-hand by doing something different from the norm, the rest of society is conditioned to belittle and criticise you so that you'll fall back in line, ***don't.***

Stand strong, be brave and keep believing in what's true to you. No way when I first started on this journey myself did I think by the time I was 18 I would've released a book! But yet it happened, not because I'm special, or because I'm talented, simply because I believed in myself and listened to my own story.

The story that says you can't do it; you're not good enough, the same voice that says the only way things could work is the current way, is the story we have to re-write.

Beacause how fortunate! ***How lucky, that the only possible system that could ever work is the one benefitting the people telling you any other way isn't possible... what a fricking coincidence!***

Change is constant and necessary in everything. So now we need a new system, a new way to run things that benefits the many instead of the few; along with a new way to look at things, a new way to live our lives.

The reason we don't travel around in horse and carriage anymore is become someone invented the car, if we provide a better alternative; the old one will become obsolete.

It can change; if a new, better system was presented then everyone would want that one. Oh, and by the way, there are hundreds of ways we could be doing it differently; we don't even need to think of them, we don't need to dream up new, inspiring concepts because they're already there.

What we need is to use the better systems that are out there instead of the one we're going along with now. It doesn't even have to be complicated or confusing; let's not pretend that we don't live in an age where millions of us vote for Britain's Got Talent every Saturday on the TV.

People care about having power that they care about, they care about their say and they care about democracy when they're engaged and the truth is made clear.

Look at our referendum recently, this was the best example we've had in a long-time, showing that people are becoming frustrated and are feeling mugged off.

Now, this book isn't about design the blue-prints for a utopia, I don't have all the answers we need (when I do, that's the third book sorted), however I do know in order to be in a position to use the answers effectively, we first have to step away from how we currently do things and sort our heads out, so that we don't just create the same system again because we still have the same mentality.

I also know, somethings that we can all do to start this process; by the way, these aren't my ideas I envisioned while chewing on a crayon, these are the ideas from the experts I've spoken too, from all around the world, so its genuinely good, plausible stuff.

We're now going to look at the most obvious things we can do, outside of our own minds, on a global scale, to start shaping what this total 'revolution' may look like.

What travelling to other places in the world, speaking to experts and seeing new cultures and societies has taught me is that although some cultures and societies are equally and more flawed then this one, an alternative way of doing things is possible and possibly finding a better way of doing things is also possible.

Locally, we can do our bit by supporting local business' and having our personal awakenings all in equal measures, we've established that; but let's not sell ourselves short, this can be a global idea, the technology exists, the systems exist, the mentality and intelligence exists for global change, (if all information is presented in an unbiased way and clearly).

We no longer have to be dictated by a minority, or rely on a newspaper to give us the news, we don't have to follow religious teachings blindly or have a strict barrier when it comes to spirituality or science, we can simply live and encompass all these concepts.

We can change it now, firstly by overlooking the fear we're conditioned to have, secondly by believing change is possible and thirdly realise that change is happening right now and there's nothing the minority of rich elite can do. (They're frightened, believe me, on my journey, I've met and spoke to all sorts of political figures within the system, they're bricking it!)

They hate that young people like me are becoming aware, they hate that older people who were once quiet are now raising their voice, their backs are up and we're growing.

They will benefit from the change, they will also experience richer lives, this change isn't just for me, or you, but for all of us, a change to reawaken what's within all of us!

I attended a black lives matter march a year back and while I was there, I got lost in the moment. I was marching and chanting and calling for change (peacefully of course, good old Ghandi) and I felt like I was on the right side of history; everybody there knew that change was possible and that change was coming and that was rejuvenating to see.

It's like something is breaking through the mould. Old values are dying off gradually, the 50's mentality we've had for so long, the mentality Thatcher reinstated and the mentality that is the glue holding this structure together is weathering. It's no longer so much of super-glue, and more like a pric-stick.

What happened in the 60's is starting to manifest itself in small pockets of our society more and more, more than it ever has before. We're standing on the edge of a revolution.

Ready to sign up?

Chapter 13

<u>The Mind</u>

Welcome to the second act, it gets far less depressing and way more weird and hippie in this part, because over the upcoming chapters we're going to be looking at how we can change the mess we're in and how we can transform our world into one that benefits us and the ones around us, and it all comes from within.

But we're starting with the first thing we can do, something that in an ideal society we're all going to be doing: taking responsibility and loving unconditionally.

Because it's easy, it's so easy, to turn our heads away, to get drawn into worrying about pointless and minuscule things that we blow out of proportion to distract us from truths so horrible we'd rather ignore them than face reality. We've all done it, at one point or another and it's when we brave the storm and accept this, that we can face it and rise above it.

Think about it, the last time you got that horrible little guilt tremble in your belly; think about why did you feel guilty, what was it that made you feel that way?

Did you tell a lie to a loved one to cover your own back? Do something wrong at work and know you're going to be in trouble?

Maybe you decided to end a relationship that wasn't going anywhere and you knew that the right thing to do was call it quits even though it may feel terrible right now?

Once you've thought of the most recent time you felt guilty, take another few minutes and think of two times in your life that you can remember feeling really guilty, so much so that you still remember it today.

However, here's the catch, if we can take a step-back and see our problems from a third person sense of view we can learn how to go about dealing with them. These moments of our lives can't be changed, no matter how bad and horrible we feel, we'll never get to speak to that loved one that's passed again and we may not be able to reverse the damage we've caused someone, but we can declare that from right now, we'll use that guilt, that painful emotion, as a superpower to do better next time.

The past is gone, set in stone, done. It's just totally illogical to waste time trying to change something that can't be changed, it doesn't make sense, however nearly every single one of us sees our emotions take over and feel a million things about situations that are now no longer changeable. Now that's okay! I'm not now declaring, in the second chapter of this book, that we should all become emotionless, robotic beings (although if you've ever actually met a politician in the flesh, you realise some of us are a lot closer to achieving this than you'd first think), after all, it's these emotions that make us human, that really give us meaning, however, in order to make personal change, we have to learn to recognise our emotions and learn how to conquer these feelings so that we can develop, progress and create the life we want to live.

So, going back to our guilty conscious, now that we've recognised our guilt emotion by thinking and delving into times we've felt this emotion, we can conquer it, let it go, accept that the guilt you once had was human and natural, but now realise that we only feel guilty about a situation if we allow ourselves to, this doesn't mean we have to convince ourselves we were 'right' in whatever predicament we found ourselves in, but realise that by attaching guilt to a situation, we're only causing ourselves pain and stopping ourselves from moving on to bigger and brighter things. See the guilt as an indicator to learn from a mistake or moment of bad judgement and now carry what you've learnt with you from those moments into the bigger, brighter tomorrow.

This technique can be applied to any emotion: sadness, regret, even 'positive' emotions such as happiness or excitement. It's not to dampen or ruin our experience of life, but to instead enhance it, so that we can learn from our raw emotions, allowing us to understand ourselves better so that in the future we can in turn handle future bad times better, or **learn to enjoy and savour good times for the beautiful moments they really are**.

Think of it like this... Imagine you, in your really good times of joy or comfort and you, in your sad times of anger, regret, whatever they may be: all these times are actually a movie. You're in your own movie, your own story called life (ah, you see what I did there) and now imagine transcending outside the film, take a step back, and then another and another, until you've taken 10 whole steps, until you're now sitting in the audience watching this film, the film of your life.

See it from the outside watching in and now press play; from that moment of joy where the world seems amazing, or that cliff-hanger when you're not sure whether to kiss that date that's gone really well or that horrible moment when a huge event happens that turns the world upside down and think, if you were an audience member, or the director of that film and you were trying to make a story that entertains and pleases you, what would you have happen to the character now that the event has happened, where do you want the character to go next?

Would you tell them to savour and embrace this beautiful moment, to enjoy every second while it lasts? Yeah, I probably would too. But now what would you say if it was one of those bad moments? Would you say to that character that they should go, curl up in a ball and let those horrible feelings takeover and dictate everything they do from now on for the foreseeable future? No, neither would I. So, go on, what would you say to them? Write that down if you have to, keep it in a safe place for anytime you feel low.

I'd say that as bad as things seem right now, as much as it seems that life is just suffering, that we should just accept it, know it and get over it because there's always something to rage against, it doesn't have to be that way. Sure, nobody can go back and start over, but anyone can start today and make a new ending, it's moments like these, the toughest moments in life, where we can crumble, whittle and fall into the rut of mundane existence, letting our fears and worries pin us back every-time trouble comes knocking. **The challenges and how we deal with them; that is what defines us.**

Problems don't define us, it's our ability to overcome and transform. We can choose these moments to better ourselves, to learn, to rise. When you're at the point where you feel you have nothing to live or thrive for, be like a camera: use your negatives to develop, because we can use these moments of pain to learn, to

Our Story Called Life — Peter Abrams

enjoy, and focus on the joyful ones, to connect to the now and to the love in our life, so go, put one foot in front of the other.

Life is always happening for us, not to us. I'm not saying don't feel the pain, the hurt, I'm saying use it as a superpower. Use it effectively; use it from your heart, not from your head. I've suffered, like us all, lost people, lost moments in time I'd do anything to have back, but it's those moments, as bad as they are, that have made me the man I'm proud to be right now, it's made me reach a point where I want to dedicate my life to helping others, all because I know what it's like to feel pain and loss. This doesn't make me some sort of hero, I'm not batman, because I've felt pain and now use that to make sure no-one has to feel it alone again.. But as much as this pain is the most unbearable thing in the world, it's also one of the most necessary, we think we shouldn't have problems, but each time, it's an opportunity to grow, to sculpt ourselves, I did exactly that and if you can too, then game over, all the pain and suffering disappears, our problems are our gifts.

So, march forward, even when doubt, fear, and failure all come knocking at your door because this is your life, your emotions, your dreams, happiness, sadness, love, it's all down to you, you decide which ones to feel and linger in and embrace. So, let's agree to let this one go, write it off, move on, let's make tomorrow the first day of our new lives. We will be brave, fight for what we believe in and we will live our dreams, because you are the director of your own story, you choose where you go at each and every moment, so face problems, both internally, locally in your own life and externally and globally in the issues we face as a species with compassion and love, take the 10 steps back, outside the role of the lead-actor and into the role of the director, sit-back, sit-up, analyse, process, understand, breath, breath again, smile... and now act, because you control what happens from here, so go, direct and make a box office smash!

It may be temporary and materialistic, but it is brought about by the yearning for the beautiful divinity in all of us. Think about it, what do you love? Who do you love? Your partners, family and friends? What about your car, your house? Or how about your favourite holiday destination, the TV series you like most, your favourite sports team?

Now imagine if these things or people had never appeared in your life, you had never met your partner, you don't have your car or never went on that holiday; really sit for two minutes and imagine your life without the things you love... Did you get that little horrible feeling in your tummy, that 'oh no, I don't like that idea' feeling?, you probably did because these are the things that matter the most in our lives, and for all our moaning or pessimistic thoughts, we are all lucky to be here, to have the things we love, because it's the natural thing, it's really the only thing we as a species have got going for us, the ability to love ourselves, one another and the world we live in.

Now do the opposite, imagine all the things you can't stand, people you might despise, is it that guy driving a caravan, doing 50 on a motorway? How about that little rat of a dog next door that never stops barking? Or maybe it's something else; just think what really winds you up?

And now do the same, imagine them gone from your life, all those annoyances, all that stress, just gone from your life. Right, now how does that feel? Good isn't it? Do you feel lighter, freer, like there's nothing wrong with your life?

Well here's the amazing part, that life, where you're grateful that you've got what you love and all the people and things you don't like aren't part of your life, is real, it's your life you're living right now, just with a different attitude and mind-set. For those four minutes, when you imagined what life would be like, is exactly the same life you're experiencing right now, just with a different view point, a fresh perspective.

All the people, objects, places you've been and going too are exactly the same, only for those few minutes you were grateful for the ones you love and didn't care about the ones you didn't like because they 'weren't' there but, of course they were there, you just chose, in your mind, your reality, to not include them and how easy was that? In a few minutes, you transformed your reality to an epic adventure, you've just achieved the point of this book, congratulations!

But wait, don't put this book down yet, because you don't have to read a book and do all the exercises to get those feelings, to create that reality, because it's possible to live that life, every second, of every day, and over the rest of the book we're going to learn how to do it.

Imagine how amazing your outlook on life could be in 20, 200, or 2000 minutes of conditioning your mind?

So well done, whether you believed you could or couldn't do it, you just shifted your reality to one you want to live in, albeit for just two minutes, you changed your world, now it's about learning how you can create that reality you just lived in all the time and it all comes from your own visualisation and thought-power.

So, that's where this next task comes in; rewind all the way back to that rainy day at the train station earlier in the book. Now think about the last time you could've spoken to someone, whether you knew them or not, and chose not to, think why you chose not too (it may have been a very valid reason), and now after reading this chapter, think, should you have spoken to them?

Well we can't change the past, we can only be in the moment (more on that later), but here's what this task involves; for this task you have to try and have a whole conversation with at least one stranger for the next couple of days; trust me, it's amazing how friendly everyone is if you make some effort to talk and get to know them; ask them how their day is, it could be someone serving you a coffee or maybe someone waiting for the bus, no matter how you go about it, for the next couple of days, just try and have a conversation with at least one new person, go out and spread the love and let's fill the human race with a bit more humanity again!

All throughout your days, every day, remember all that is precious to you, what keeps you going.

For me personally, my faith as I've said is in people and my belief that we're all part of a divine beauty that we can connect to through our own consciousness is what keeps me going. Put simply, being nice to people, seeing what's created when me and someone else connect within a moment is what makes me happy and so I try to do that, I try to end any suffering I see in another human being in any way I can, every moment I can, so do the same, find your beliefs and commit to them, they're what make you who you are, they are the actions that create the story you live.

If you don't like it, change yourself, simple. If you can't change it, change the way you feel about it, change the story you're telling yourself in your head.

What are the triggers, what things do you do that make you feel alive? Pursue these things; this is where the bliss is found in life. As Tony Robbins, a front runner in motivational speaking says 'The change is like when you're at the gym, it's like building muscle, it's deciding to sculpt yourself into what you're capable of being as opposed to whatever circumstance life has given you the opportunity to just show up as.' Tony, out in Orlando, talks about the power of belief, he's yet another person who inspires millions and he believes that if we're going to see change in our life, it comes from us, within. Starting to sound familiar?

No matter who's saying it from what angle, whether it be religious, scientific, spiritual or any other category, there is another common theme found in all that our own thoughts can change the way we see the world. I love the saying

'We do not see things as they are; we see things as we are,' this is so true, if we see the world as

'The world is about to end, we're all going to die and most of the world is in suffering, we should all be grateful for what we've got' then the thought, narrative and story, that we're conditioned to experience will never give us any happiness or joy. However, if we re-condition our mind to see the joy and bliss in every moment, in everything we encounter, then we open ourselves up to huge revelations, one of which is;

We find contentment from being in the present moment.

And that's what we're going to be looking at in this part of the book, what are the different ways and techniques in which we can become present in the moment and elevate our consciousness to a higher frequency, so that we avoid going back into the old story and give ourselves the best chance to write the best story we can right now and in the future.

Because the past is a story we tell ourselves, the future is also a story we tell ourselves, all that really is actually happening is right now, in this moment and now this moment and now this moment and now… you get the idea. By being present in the moment we can re-connect to our consciousness easily as we are no longer looking anywhere else or searching for happiness anywhere else than in our lives, right now and it is right here, in the present, where life is lived and where everything we're searching for can be found.

Quite simply, there are three ways to change the world:

1. Change the way you view the world from within your mind.
2. Make a change to the physical world, and as long as it doesn't hurt anyone else or the planets then we're all entitled to do that.
3. Help someone else on their journey; help someone else to positively change the world, as long as it doesn't mean hurting another person or the planet.

Those three options we all have, in fact, it's all we have. The cliché saying "If you don't like something, change it and if you can't change it, change the way you think about it" rings true, the important thing to remember is the last bit of points 2 and 3. 'As long as it doesn't hurt other people or the planet' is probably a phrase you're going to be sick of reading by the end of this book, however it really is one of my main points I hope to convey. We basically have to act with love and compassion, and make sure we don't hurt others or the planet we're on, because if we don't, what's the point?

If we act through hate and anger, our message is lost, our journey becomes a bitter fight and the impact we have on anybody will be a guaranteed negative one, which causes harm instead of good. By all means, set out on your own journey to change your life, others' lives or even the world, but don't go about it and 'stand on a stall with a homophone' screaming at the world to listen to you, because the only people who will are going to be other venomous people, instead we have to act like sponges, we have to become our message.

Ghandi was once travelling on a train home from a long visit away, a reporter spotted him and went rushing up to him, this reporter thought he'd found his big story, his break, so he asked Ghandi, "Ghandi, if you could sum up what you teach in one message, what would the message be?"

It just so happened that on that day, Ghandi was undergoing a mark of silence (meaning that well, he had to be silent, obviously), which was pretty unlucky for the news chap, so to not let the news reporter down, Ghandi took a piece of paper and pen and wrote something down, he handed the paper to the man and boarded the train with a smile. The man took the paper and read what Ghandi had written.

"My life is my message".

How incredible is that? And how true; look at the likes of the Dali Lama and Eckhart Tolle, you don't see these heavy hitters on 'Good Morning Britain' telling you to listen to them, they simply are the message that they believe in and gain respect and acknowledgement over time.

They are sponges, they embody their message and become what they stand for, and by doing so, allow others to soak into them and learn from them as our lives intertwine and then pass by one another's. On one occasion when I was out in America, I was fortunate enough to be introduced to Noam Chomsky; for anyone who doesn't know who Noam is, he's a pretty big deal on the whole political and philosophy scene so try to remember him, he's bound to pop up now and again throughout the book, he said a similar thing to me,

"Don't try to live your life in hope that when you're old, you'll look back and think 'that was a great life', instead focus on living in every single second you get, focus on making it a great second to be alive, and then another, until every moment and wave you make is one with compassion and love at the front of all you do, if you can live, connected to yourself and the world around you in every moment of time you're alive, you'll live the happiest and richest life you'll ever live, regardless of your financial situation or the world around you".

The way these people conduct themselves is how we should all strive to be, not because they are better than us, or more worthy, just simply because they've trained their brain to be more awake to life around them, think about it like a hard maths problem, all humans have brains, but not everyone knows what 64 divided by 8 is... (If you got that and are now sitting there all proud of yourself, well done, you deserve that, congrats), so we have to train our brains to be able to contemplate these ideas and really connect with consciousness. This is how you have the biggest and deepest impact, whether you want to achieve a certain financial status or open your own business, help the unemployed or write a music album, this way of going about our lives is honestly so vital if we wish to make real change to ourselves and the world around us, so be 'spongy' not 'shouty' and as much as that sounds the tag-line for some new brand of shower gel, it's true, so act through compassion not fear, act with love not hate and do so by becoming your message, instead of preaching your message and that's how we can all, in our own ways, really change the world.

Now is the point where we start talking about consciousness, don't freak out, my way of describing 'consciousness' is just my way of coming to terms with the inevitable force that we all feel, you'd call it God if you're religious, or quantum physics if you like science and so when I say consciousness is the thing I'm going on about here, don't freak out, because at its purest, it isn't something that can be categorised by a certain group of words. What I mean, is that consciousness is really something that transcends language and words themselves, as crazy as that sounds, think about it, the word 'consciousness', the letters, the 'c's, the 'o's, all these things, are manmade creations. These things are our way of trying to describe and understand the things we see, in relation to our knowledge and understanding; for example, someone who only speaks French would be struggling greatly reading this right now..

When man first stepped out of his cave and first saw the sun, he didn't say "My gosh, look, there's the sun", he would've run around and shouted a bit, maybe doing a funny dance.

The same is true with babies, when a baby is first brought into the world, as the mother holds her child in her arms for the first time, the child doesn't turn around and declare "Get off me, I'm feeling claustrophobic after being in there for nine months".

Cavemen, babies? Where the hell is this going?

The point I'm making is the only way we experience life, experience anything is through our own reality, our own mind. I believe knowledge is understanding others, enlightenment is understanding ourselves and love is the easiest way for our consciousness' to express our knowledge while in search of our enlightenment.

The way the rest of the world sees these emotions and thoughts, is by how we act, how we talk, how we go about our lives. This means everything external (outside our own mind) is materialistic; anything external is just our way of trying to explain what we experience internally (from within our own reality).

This means that everything, from what we choose to buy, where we choose to go, even things such as language and love, are all materialistic in some way. This means that when we're trying to explain what 'consciousness' is (something that transcends materialistic things like words); it can be a little bit tricky!

Because of this, there are numerous ways people try and grasp just exactly what this 'greater thing' is that I like to describe to myself as consciousness.

However just because I describe this amazing thing we all know is there as 'consciousness' doesn't mean you have to, (I mean you do have to in this book, but outside of these pages call it whatever you want!), this is all about finding your own way of connecting to this higher frequency, some people believe it to be 'God' or 'Enlightenment', some people believe it to be 'energies of the universe' or 'the divine', some people just believe it to be 'common sense' or 'brain frequencies'.

The real truth is that it doesn't really matter how we all individually choose to connect to this, so long as we're trying to connect to it, conducting ourselves with love and compassion then it doesn't matter if we're doing it in the name of the Lord or the name of science, all these terms are just labels used to separate us, to cause friction between us when really as long as we're all trying to do the same thing then who cares how we're going about it, we should embrace our differences and appreciate that we're all trying to achieve that connection to something greater than ourselves and embrace each-other and support one another in trying to get to where we're all heading, God, Consciousness, Common sense, home, space, these words, labels aren't important, the message and love that we're connecting to is.

Because we've all heard of 'enlightenment', 'God', however we want to word it, it's always the same sort of idea too: awakening to the ultimate truth of life, usually achieved by relief from suffering. With the stresses of modern life — careers, love, family, Facebook — all that mental and physical pain, who wouldn't want to suffer a little less? Who wouldn't want enlightenment?

According to the Japanese Buddhist saint Kobo Daishi, enlightenment is obtainable within our own lifetimes. And you may even be able to prevent suffering in all lifetimes to come as well, so what are we waiting for?

However, most of us have heard the prerequisites for achieving enlightenment: intensive meditation (Damn, I can't even fall asleep at night, let alone meditate, not when there's another episode of The Walking Dead I can watch), detachment from physical and material things (But that's everything we've worked so hard for!), non-violence (But he/she deserves it, they really do, I promise!) and good will to all living beings (I don't want to go vegan, I love hamburgers!)

Well, no wonder more people don't go for enlightenment.

So, Kobo Daishi, what do we do now? I think if Kobo Daishi, the founder of Shingon-shu Esoteric Buddhism in Japan, were here now, he would tell us all to calm down and take a good look at ourselves. After all, life has changed a lot since his time.

Yes, enlightenment takes patience and a great deal of maturity to achieve, but it is not out of our realms of possibility, and I don't think he'd tell us to give up the material things we've worked so hard for, material things such as technology can help aid us in achieving this enlightenment. I doubt he'd even recommend becoming a spiritual hermit these days, (there's not a lot of caves that are available for 'hermitting' anymore, anyway.)

Instead, I think he'd politely tell us that what we really need to do to achieve enlightenment is to cultivate a better mind-set, a better story in our heads.

While the idea of enlightenment is a Buddhist concept, it's not unique to Buddhism and you don't have to be Buddhist to reach personal enlightenment. Think of Mother Theresa, and Mahatma Gandhi (religious pluralism) — both role models of enlightenment.

Rather than attempt the path to enlightenment a Buddhist monk or a spiritual leader takes, we can take our own individual path. Some of the most frustrating things people ask me are, "But what meditation do I do?", "What yoga is right?", "I have no idea what to do".

Of course you do! There are no strict rules on this journey of having a personal revolution! The only meditation, yoga, 'path' to take, is the one that feels right to you, it doesn't even have to be religious, but it can be, it doesn't have to be spiritual, but it can be.

It doesn't have to consist of any yoga, but it can. All these methods and techniques are just means of trying to reconnect you with yourself. There is no right or wrong answer, you can't get it wrong, some things may not work as well as others and that's okay, listen to your body, feel your body, learn to understand yourself, there's no right or wrong in enlightenment.

This process does, however, have to adhere to certain accepted principles of enlightenment, universal truths from our divine nature, many you're already familiar with such as for example mindfulness and compassion for others (basically do what we already know is right).

Here are some basic things that all enlightened individuals share, think of this as 'Enlightenment 101'.

They're peaceful. Sometimes it's hard to look at the world and even consider the possibility of world peace, especially since there has been fighting among people since the beginning of mankind. Imagine the arguments Adam and Eve must have had! And I surely wouldn't, at any time, want to encounter a miffed cave man carrying a club. But dreaming of peace is the first step to living it. The Japanese even went so far as to write it into their Constitution — no more wars.

They have compassion for those less fortunate. Enlightened people help the less fortunate, volunteer to make the world a better place, and encourage others to do the same.

Enlightened people find strength in the things they do have, rather than yearning for the things they have been denied. When bad things happen, they realise they are not alone. Bad things happen to everyone.

They know how to be critical without being judgmental. They do not use presumptuous statements or make negative comments based on unqualified evaluations rather than fact. When others like things, they do not berate others for liking them. They are not jealous. They're happy with what they have, appreciate it and believe in it. Furthermore, they're happy for others when something good happens to them, there is no ego attached.

Enlightened people don't badmouth, belittle, berate or disparage other people's successes. They realise there are many different points of view in the world, many of them different from their own and while they may not agree with them, they respect them. They realise there are not always clear rights and wrongs, especially within contexts others may not be aware of. Enlightened people would never blame others for their own lack of success.

Enlightened people do not show their anger forcefully but make their point quietly. Philosophers, inspirational speakers, horse whisperers, those kinds of people.

They do not want to harm others. Even if someone is breaking into their house, even if someone is threatening their lives. The enlightened person has no desire to hurt anyone mentally nor physically. They treat animals, all animals, with kindness.

The concept of revenge has no place in the hearts of the enlightened. Instead, they forgive. Revenge is a sign of weakness.

OK, now you're thinking: But I don't know anyone like that! Look closer. They are there. You can start via elimination: It's definitely not the guy walking around with a chip on his shoulder, for example.

Or look at the people you know who seem happier than everyone else. They deal with whatever comes their way with grace and poise. They're optimistic, but not overly, and they don't complain much. They seem to have no problems at all!

Maybe you feel more at ease around these people. They're kind. They're accepting. When they see more bad than good, they produce more good. They spend their time thinking and acting on good, positive things, not bad, harmful things. If they don't like something, they move on to something they do like. As my grandmother, a strong-willed, independent woman who was born in 1897, and who claimed to be the first woman jockey in the U.S., taught me: "Don't concentrate on the things you can't or aren't allowed to do, but the things you can."

When you're enlightened, you see the world in a different way than most. You're happier, have less stress and love your life as well as the lives of others. You bring out the best in others so that they become better people too.

So, detach the ego, control the primal urges, always be in the present moment and be a beacon of love…Personal enlightenment, I know it's a big ask. But I'm asking.

So now we've cleared that up, we're going to look at the ways a lot of people try and understand consciousness and hopefully try and get a better understanding of what consciousness is and how you can find the easiest way to connect to it, so to kick-start our personal transformation we're going to look at something that has transformed millions of lives throughout history; faith. We're looking at Faith in religion (the pure religion, not the organised one from earlier), just faith, dreams and beliefs in something bigger then ourselves.

Chapter 14

The Dream

One thing that many people believe in, the most believed thing in human history is religion in some form. Religion and spirituality have so many connections and ties that we're going to need a whole chapter to explain it all. Now I'm not going to sit here and list every religion, nor am I going to try and explain what/who God is and why you should or shouldn't believe.

Religion is a very personal subject for a lot of people and over time many people (far more intelligent and qualified than me) have tried to explain what 'religion' is, so I'm not going to insult your intelligence (or religion for that matter) and try and do that, instead I'm going to look at why believing in a religion, in any form, can help us to achieve our personal revolutions and find our inner peace.

For myself, I'm not religious per say, I don't practice a certain religion and I don't pray, however I do meditate and I do believe in higher powers in the universe than ourselves.

I find that the easiest way to convey what I believe, is to say I believe in what the religions teach in their purest form, what they give people in terms of guidance and support, without believing in the specifics; to me, I don't think it really matters which God from which book we look to, so long as we're trying to serve a higher purpose than our external, materialistic views. I think each religion is just one adaptation of trying to understand and put into words and guidelines what is inherent in all of us, meaning therefore I may not actually follow that specific religion; however, I whole-heartedly believe in what they teach (when in their purest form, without the corruption or commercial-spin we see put on them so regularly now).

I'm currently travelling and learning in depth about all the religions people believe in across the world, I'm also doing a degree in understanding people and societies, along with philosophy and religions (I'm interested in finding the correlations and connections that all religions, cultures and people share, to see if there is an underlying message all religions teach, trends all cultures adopt and things we all do on a personal level, however that's another book for another time, let's focus on ourselves first... I smell sequel!).

I've experienced Christian, Islamic, Jewish and Buddhist teachings and ceremonies to name but a few and have spoken to many religious figures within their communities and so while I may not practice a specific religion, I do have an open mind and have experienced all different walks of religions, all of which have shown me a different insight into how many people try to connect with something greater than themselves.

I like to think of consciousness like gravity, if you throw an apple in the air, you know it's going to fall, it's the same with consciousness, we all know it's there and with the right tuning we can access it at our whims desire. Religion in its purest form is where we can find ways, really the first way, in which people have tried to describe consciousness over time. The first thing to note is that all religions have a guide or rules to follow in order to achieve their desired goal. Examples of this would be in Islam, 'Muslims must pray 5 times a day', as it is one of the five pillars of Islam, in order to show devotion to Allah; or how Christians are encouraged to be baptised, to show their faith to the Lord.

The idea in these religions is that by practicing the teachings, by worshipping and by showing your faith, you will achieve a certain state of being/receive a reward (such as ultimately gaining your rightful place beside God in heaven). Does that sound familiar? Earlier we'd said that by connecting to the moment, living life compassionately and peacefully, you'll live in exactly the kind of world you want to be in, loving the life that you're experiencing, to see that religion and spirituality tend to cross over and share ideas pretty frequently. Both examples in both religions would suggest finding an inner peace of sorts, 'once you've reached that place, you'll be content'. In other words, if you go for it, commit to the cause, you'll get the rewards, sounds pretty good to me and something that's pretty logical thinking.

However, there are also numerous religions that believe having a personal revolution is the ONLY way to achieve what their religion states. Buddhism in particular believes that material life is 'suffering' and to end this suffering, we must look internally to achieve 'enlightenment'. People such as Ghandi and the Dali Lama have devoted their lives to teaching millions that we can fulfil our beliefs from within ourselves.

It's also ironic that the one religion that suggests all our answers can be found from within, is often regarded as the most 'peaceful' on earth. In fact, many Buddhists believe that world peace can only be achieved if we first establish peace within our minds. The idea is that anger and other negative states of mind are the cause of suffering and conflict. Buddhists believe people can live in peace and harmony only if we abandon negative emotions such as anger in our minds and cultivate positive emotions such as love and compassion. As with all Dharmic religions (Hinduism, Jainism, Buddhism and Sikhism), 'ahimsa' (avoidance of violence) is a central concept. Buddhists even have special monuments designed to promote peace. A peace pagoda is the monument to inspire peace, designed to provide a focus for people of all races and creeds, and to help unite them in their search for world peace. Someone who finds their inner peace through the most 'peaceful' religion in the world? Sounds good to me!

Buddhism isn't the only religion that teaches this ideology. Other religions such as Taoism and Hinduism believe that we are all on a set journey and that the way to accept this is to instead of trying to change it, ride the waves of life and enjoy every moment.

Amid all the chaos that religion is blamed for, it's very easy to pass off religion as an evil we should all frown upon, however let's not completely rule out the pivotal role that it can play for some of us. If we have as our dominant mind-set, 'I'm only going to believe stuff that I can see and prove', then we are just individuals and we may as well just go and try to sleep with everyone we can, we may as well go and try to make as much money and gather as many material possessions that we can, because in this mind-set, nothing exists unless we can feel it, touch it, weigh it and somehow make love to it, if we're solely only existing for ourselves why shouldn't we be selfish and self-absorbed?

If that is the dominant belief system in a society, where materialism, consumerism and capitalism all sort of dove-tail together, on that very premise, we manage to create the culture we find ourselves in nowadays, that's how we can have such a vast ecological crisis, this mind-set is an excuse for this outcome, it 'justifies' the poverty and wealth inequality because it excuses the fact that we need to care for one another, it excuses the fact that there's anything greater than our possessions and money and so it encourages this landscape, it gives people no reason or incentive to help each other because it suggests that when we look around and see possessions, things we have or wish we had, that is all there is to have and there's no drive to seek anything more; instead of maybe realising that we're nothing more than a pebble in infinite space, that we all have the potential to be spiritual beings, having a human being experience and that there's so much more of life we can connect to than just what's in front of us in the physical, possession-filled world.

I'm a strong believer that on an individual and cultural level, that if there's something we can do, we should do it, as soon as people realise that something's wrong or that there's a better way to do something or use the resources we have at our disposal to produce better results, as soon as we realise this, we should be moving towards that outcome, after all, they say 'wisdom is acting on knowledge', and also say that 'insanity is doing the same thing over and over again, while expecting different results', so when we see things like our fossil fuels running out and damaging our atmosphere to a point where it's the worst it's ever been, so bad that it can't return to its old regular state, we should instantaneously be looking at other alternatives, not completely ignoring the issue, it makes me very uneasy, and ask, who is ignoring this obvious problem affecting the majority of our species? And why can something that harms the majority of us as a species possibly be beneficial to a select few?

So, underneath it all, is there a way that someone can use a faith in a religion to achieve a personal revolution and potentially inner peace?

I love the quote 'be quick to see where religious people are right', because it's very easy to see where religion is being taken in the wrong way, it's all over the news, social media, pretty much everywhere and so it's easy to just see religion as something that is just being used to segregate and pose different people against one another but there is an underlying feeling of good I get when I've seen religion in a truly pure form, whether it be a Christian family singing carols at Christmas in Italy or a Muslim family all praying together in the mountains in Scotland, I get the feeling that a true faith transcends and rises above how religion is presented to us. That feeling when you see groups of people coming together to be part of something greater than themselves, that sense of togetherness, selflessness, trying to form a relationship with a deeper version of ourselves, accepting death and the possible transcendence of our human, primal self, are actually the most humane and beautiful ideas that I feel have just gone wrong and been twisted, but these ideas are always there, sure certain newspapers can install fear about a certain faith, or a certain drinks brand can cover up the message behind Christmas by turning the old fella who delivers presents into a red-suit wearing, consumerism love affair, but the true message and connection to what religion really stands for is still there, you can pile as much shit and bury a box with all the real information as deep as humanly possible, but it only takes an individual to dig past all the dirt and all the mud to find the box and realise the true message within, sure it can be hidden, but it's a message as old as our species and it sure can't be destroyed, we only have to want to find it.

Well I myself, like I said earlier, believe in what religion teaches and gives people, the underlying message that all faiths contain, without believing in the specific details enough to make me a believer of a specific one, my belief can be best described by David Bowie who said in 1974, (when asked about what faith does he believes in) 'life, I love life' he declared. Really, I think they all say the same thing.

But even Bowie had struggled with finding a faith he could connect with and not for the lack of trying, over his life he tried pretty much all of them, from Christianity to Satanism. It was only when finding out he was terminally ill that he returned to his earlier philosophy and admitted that although something greater does exist, instead of trying to contain it within our words of our human capacity, we should just accept it and enjoy our lives, knowing that we can be part of something greater than ourselves. "The one continuum that is throughout my writing is a real simple, spiritual search. Everything that I seem to have written, in some way or other, keeps refocusing on the idea that in the late 20th century, we are without our God. That what we're heading for is an era where we have to completely demobilize our religious organizations and reinvent God in some form … in our own new way of life to give ourselves another form of spiritual sustenance. 'Who is my God? How does he show himself? What is my higher stage, my higher being?'"

But, Bowie goes on to say, "looking for something outside of ourselves for sustenance, can only lead to depression, I think. We have to find that sustenance within ourselves." I love the idea that it's time we reinvented our core-belief system, coming from a man whose history is literally known for reinvention. But I also love the point being made, I think it's fair to say that most of us, now, are without a God, a belief in something greater then ourselves, we've placed ourselves at the centre of existence.

So as to whether people can use faith as a way of achieving inner peace, of course they can, but only if religion in its purest form, not a corrupted twist of a religion, far alienated from the truth, which is more and more common nowadays. Many sub-groups are emerging, all with their own interpretation and explanation of a religion, which would be fine, if these beliefs were not so twisted and funded by hatred and an actual lack of inner peace, in turn creating ideologies which we can see come to fruition to create abominations of religions such as ISIS of Islam, Britain First of Christianity or the guys down at the West borough Baptist church from the Catholic Church.

We need an informed education and media representation of religion as much as our political systems, probably even more so, as religions don't represent how our materialistic world is run (like politics is) but how we internally operate, how we go about our lives because how we act of course dictates how our political systems will turn out and so if the majority of society are going to use religion as their guide on how to live life and try to achieve inner-peace then we need a revolution in how religion is presented to us as much as everything else.

At this stage in our evolution, some of us can and have realised this, finding beauty and peace within ourselves but not everyone's ready to take that step. There's still a large majority that due to the current systems in place, can't be left on their own to realise this and it's these people that need the revolution in their minds, and until a time when they're ready to wise up and realise the bigger picture then a revolution is required and a faith in a religion in its purest form is a fantastic and trusted way to achieve that.

We've gotta have something to believe in.

Chapter 15

The Moment

So, as we quickly approach the ending of this story, I'd like to quickly talk about why being in the moment is such an important thing, why being here, right now, is one of the key ingredients for a successful personal revolution; and share my thoughts on the easiest ways for us to be here, right now, in the first place.

Eckhart Tolle is a man who strongly believes that contentment is found by being totally in the moment, this sounds like something incredibly spiritual and hard to master; however, we all do it naturally, in our everyday lives. Tolle says that we first connect to the moment when we become free of suffering; we do this when we over-come jealously, anger and temptation with compassion and love. He states that failure to do this happen when "We adopt a mental position, then we identify that mental position and it becomes invested with 'self'. Eckhart identifies that the 'self' is simply a construction and, I'm not saying I'm the new Eckhart Tolle, but that sounds a lot like saying our life is a story which we live inside of!

Anyway, Tolle declares that some memories, feelings, opinions, even our name, is just an illusion, an imaginary concept we hold in our consciousness. That indescribable energy, the hidden energy that connects us all to something more, the moment of creativity, of conception, it's real, behind all thoughts, things, animals, life itself is awareness… "Move into the awareness" says Tolle, if we truly want to be in the present moment.

One way, tried and tested, that has seen millions of people move in-between the awareness, is through meditation.

Firstly, let me clear the air, don't panic, meditation isn't some evil, devil-worshipping ritual, you also don't need to be a follower of a moon tribe to participate, I'm not, although I've got to say, I've met those people and they seem pretty buzzing for life!

Anyway, relax, as much as this chapter is focusing on meditation and yoga, I'm not going to pretend to be a guru, I'm no meditation master, but then again, I am a master at my meditating, because I've found a way to connect to something through doing so. What I'm saying is that despite what the classes or books may tell you, meditation, like religion is a very personal thing; what may work for me may do nothing for you, and vice versa. The truth is, everyone can guide each-other and advice how to go about it, to suggest and show what have universally been the most successful ways for the majority of people; however, ultimately whether meditation benefits your personal revolution depends on how much time you put into it, and you won't know until you try. Saying that, I myself have only been practicing for around four years and although that may seem like a long time for some people who have never tried, believe me it's not.

While out in Thailand, I spent some time with the monks over there, who quite literally, lived in the mountains; they certainly helped me to deepen my practice and showed me amazing ways to delve deeper into myself. Some of these monks didn't speak to me, not because they're vicious monks, but because they spend nearly all day meditating... And have been doing so for the last 30 years. The experience was incredible, the energy around the place was indescribable and it was honestly one of the most enlightening experiences I've ever had.

So now we're here, humble old me, with all my wisdom from the forever meditating monks. What we're going to do in this chapter, isn't look into the ancient history of meditation, delve deep into the rituals and practices and convert you to a full-fledged meditator. No, I'm going to try my best to be the 'gateway' I promised you at the start I'd be and try to introduce you to the concept of meditating. We'll have a quick lowdown and then maybe try a basic practice of our own. So, don't worry, no anxiety required, because meditation really isn't a scary thing at all, in fact it's rather quite natural, it's a beautiful process of using the power of your mind to shift your reality from the state of chaos it may be in now, into one epic adventure.

Have a look in front of you, look at the nearest object and go and pick it up. What does it feel like? What did you think while you picked it up (aside from 'what the hell am I doing'?); well whatever you picked up, you know that it's real, yes? You can see it, you can feel it, you have no doubt it exists, after all it's right there in your hand. But what about the molecules that come together to create the thing you're holding? Is it not now just molecules, formed in a certain way? And what about that weird fact you learnt in school, about how everything's floating in mid-air, because of the natural magnetic forces of the universe, only it's so small that we can't comprehend it? How bizarre is that? Certainly food for thought!

Nowadays it seems like seeing is believing, we all need proof, we need physical evidence, the idea that something beyond our senses can exist is simply too far-fetched for most people... So why can't we hear a dog whistle?

Our thoughts, our consciousness, these things are just as real, just as physical as the object you just picked up, only it's beyond our ability to register it, well to register it through our physical bodies. However, our minds are so incredible, we can register and connect to these things that our physical body cannot. How amazing is that?

Your physical body you walk around in can't touch your thoughts, it can't grab your consciousness, however with the right belief and desire, we can access it, we can feel it, grab it, all through our own minds, how incredible is that?

The point I'm making is that not everything is accessible through our five senses; there are an array of crazy and wonderful things, just beyond our normal state of operations. Like I said, in this chapter, we're going to look at meditation and how it can play a crucial role in giving us access to amazing connections and how it can open doors into new states of being that we never used to know were there!

However, it really doesn't matter if you've never even shut your eyes for five minutes unless you were trying to sleep or if you meditate for 10 hours a day; meditation doesn't have to be scary or daunting, after all it's a natural thing for all of us, but if it does scare you, don't worry, there is no right or wrong way, only the way which is best for you, you don't even need to think of it as meditation! Call it mindfulness, self-reflection or even just relaxing, the name isn't the important bit, the important bit is the fact this practice has existed for thousands of years, so I'm not making this up when I say it's one of the best ways to reconnect to yourself!

Background story time: a common mistake people believe about meditation is that it's strictly associated with Buddhism; however, the story of the Buddha's life tells us that he travelled around looking for spiritual teachers. He searched in the cities and in the wilderness. He learned from anyone who was willing to teach. He learned things like yoga, chanting, self-denial as a spiritual practice and several different forms of meditation.

Meditation has come down to us from ancient history. It probably emerged in the very early days of mankind. It's been suggested that primitive societies may have entered meditative states of consciousness while staring at campfires.

Meditation techniques are documented as existing in texts from India that are over 5,000 years old. This means that meditation was at least a few thousand years old in the Buddha's time.

Some form of meditation practice seems to be at least nominally present in all religious traditions and in all cultures, does the fact our very first ancestors practiced some form of meditation not just scream that meditation is a natural part of our existence, if we do it naturally without guidance when left to our own devices, it should be something we practice, not something that's looked down upon or something we're conditioned not to think about.

But while we're here I'll explain the Buddhist version of meditation. In some other religious traditions one could be meditating to become one with God or to invoke some sort of magical effect (and I'm not judging those ideas). In Buddhism the reasons are simpler.

Buddhist meditation only really has two goals. Stabilizing the mind and cleansing our perception of ignorance. So, while the Buddha didn't invent meditation, he did invent a set of practices that are centred on the goal of self-transformation. The goal in Buddhist meditation is to create, spread and experience less suffering and ignorance which isn't a bad route to go down at all, however it's important to remember we're not strictly tied to these rules if we want to engage with our consciousness!

Meditation is pretty universally agreed to be a resting state of the mind and being able to attain a state of consciousness that is totally different from the normal waking state. It is the means for fathoming all the levels of ourselves and finally experiencing the centre of consciousness within. Meditation is not a part of any religion; it is a science of sorts, which means that the process of meditation follows a particular order, has definite principles, and produces results that can be verified; it can be scientifically proven and is an ancient tradition which millions have participated in since the beginning of human civilisation.

In meditation, the mind is clear, relaxed, and inwardly focused. When you meditate, you are fully awake and alert, but your mind is not focused on the external world or on the events taking place around you. Meditation requires an inner state that is still and one-pointed so that the mind becomes silent. When the mind is silent and no longer distracts you, meditation deepens.

From childhood onwards, in my country and most countries world-wide and certainly in western society, we have been educated only to examine and verify things in the external world. No one has taught us how to look within, to find within, and to verify within. Therefore, we remain strangers to ourselves, instead of understanding and accepting who we are; we adopt and embody the labels society decides to label us, all the while trying to get to know others. This lack of self-understanding is one of the main reasons our relationships don't seem to work, and why confusion and disappointment so often prevail in our lives, why insecurities are common in all of us and why we often have to find happiness in materialistic objects externally instead of a deep inner-joy.

Very little of the mind is cultivated by our formal educational system. The part of the mind that dreams and sleeps—the vast realm of the unconscious which is the reservoir of all our experiences—remains unknown and undisciplined; it is not subject to any control. It is true that the whole of the body is in the mind, but the whole of the mind is not in the body. Except for the practice of meditation, there is no method to truly develop control over the totality of the mind.

The benefits of including meditation in as part of our education and upbringing could be huge for our culture. It could literally turn children with attitude and anger problems into loving and care-free individuals. This is evident in a school in America, at Robert W. Coleman Elementary in West Baltimore which is taking a new and holistic approach to disciplining students. Instead of punishing them or sending them to the principal's office, administrators send children to "the mindful moment room" where they are able to meditate and wind down.

The new policy has been in place for over a year, and in the time that the meditation room has been set up, there have actually been no suspensions throughout the entire year.

The goal of meditation is to go beyond the mind and experience our essential nature—which is described as peace, happiness, and bliss. But as anyone who has tried to meditate knows, the mind itself is the biggest obstacle standing between ourselves and this awareness. The mind is undisciplined and unruly, and it resists any attempts to discipline it or to guide it on a particular path. The mind has a mind of its own. That is why many people sit for meditation and experience only fantasies, daydreams, or hallucinations. They never attain the stillness that distinguishes the genuine experience of deep meditation.

We are taught how to move and behave in the outer world, but we are never taught how to be still and examine what is within ourselves. When we learn to do this through meditation, we attain the highest of all joys that can ever be experienced by a human being. All the other joys in the world are momentary, but the joy of meditation is immense and everlasting. This is not an exaggeration; it is a truth supported by the long line of sages, both those who renounced the world and attained truth, and those who continued living in the world yet remained unaffected by it, yep, some people from various backgrounds have actually meditated silently for years, literally years without breaking their silence, removing themselves from the world to connect to something greater than our materialistic plain.

Meditation is a practical means for calming yourself, for letting go of your biases and seeing what is, openly and clearly. It is a way of training the mind so that you are not distracted and caught up in its endless churning. Meditation teaches you to systematically explore your inner dimensions. It is a system of commitment, not commandment.

You are committing to yourself, to your path, and to the goal of knowing yourself. But at the same time, learning to be calm and still should not become a ceremony or religious ritual; it is a universal requirement of the human body, you don't need to be doing it in the name of anything or anyone but yourself.

Learning how to be still is the method of meditation. The process of cultivating stillness begins with the body. So, with that, let's begin with a description of a very, very simple way you can meditate to achieve a stillness and feeling of relaxation.

I've certainly seen a huge change in myself since, or alongside starting meditating regularly, I've found a new ability to be able to step back from all the rushing around in my life and look at it externally and I'm not perfect at it all the time, there are still times when I get frustrated at small things, or act on desires I probably shouldn't, however more and more frequently I find myself being able to remove myself from a situation and think about whether the next actions I want to take are really worth it, and meditating is the time I can reflect on those moments and reflect on everything going on around me, so whether you've never done it, have tried it and felt stupid or always do it, go ahead and give it a go.

Because our whole physical body is run without our permission, our gastric system, our cells, being destroyed and regenerated, we really are the pilots of our physical body, like a working machine. The specific design of ourselves is so detailed, so specific, many argue that it's proof there must be a creator, whether that's true or not is up for debate but what it does prove is that our consciousness can exist on different levels, on different frequencies. Different levels of being exist in me, in you, in all of us. I feel meditation has given me a new channel to access that, now don't get me wrong, it's not like you meditate and then all you can see is peace and serenity, your very mind doesn't become an oak cabin lodge, overlooking a sparkling lake, we are all human, we have and always will have human desires, want, lust, jealously, however meditative practice allows us to face these desires, to learn to not fear them or let them control you and mostly allows you to assess your actions and choose which ones to act upon.

So whatever your belief, it's important to remember how incredible you are, how unlikely you are to be able to function, there's obviously different levels of consciousness, our body wouldn't be able to function without it and if it exists, there must be a way to access it, to reflect upon it and to learn from it; meditation is certainly one way that thousands of people try to access it and being one of the most practical and easiest ways to be able to look beyond our material world, meditation is certainly something that should be taught in our education system and encouraged by our media, by looking at ourselves, by taking time out our mostly busy lives to just meditate can be the trick we need to realise that bliss is in the moment and there's so much life to be lived right now.

Really, Meditation is very simple. It really is simply attending, being there. You can begin by attending to your breath, and then if a thought comes, attend to it, notice it, be open to it—and it will pass, like a cloud. Then you can come back to the breath. Your normal response is to react to all your thoughts, and this keeps you ever busy in a sea of confusion. Meditation teaches you to attend to what is taking place within without reacting, and this makes all the difference. It brings you freedom from the mind and its meandering. And in this freedom, you begin to experience who you are, distinct from your mental turmoil. You experience inner joy and contentment, you experience relief and inner relaxation, and you find a respite from the tumult of your life. You have given yourself an inner vacation.

This inner vacation is not a retreat from the world but the foundation for finding inner peace. You must also learn to apply the principle of attending to your worldly activities, so that you can apply yourself in the world more effectively. Through practicing meditation, you can learn to be open to what comes before you in your daily life and give it your full attention.

Ordinarily, you react to the experiences that come before you in much the same way that you react to your thoughts. If someone says something negative to you, you become angry or depressed. If you lose something, you become emotionally upset. Your mood depends on what comes before you, and, as a result, your life is like a roller coaster ride. You react before you have fully experienced what you are reacting to. You immediately interpret what you see or hear according to your expectation, fears, prejudices, or resistances. You short-circuit the experience, and thus limit yourself to one or two conditioned responses instead of responding to a situation openly and creatively.

But if you apply the principle of meditation to experiences that come before you, you can fully attend to what is taking place. You can attend to your initial reaction without reacting to your reaction: "Oh, look how threatened I feel by that." Let yourself be open to experiencing your reaction and it will move through you and allow other spontaneous responses to also come forward, so that you can select the one that is most helpful in that particular situation.

In this way meditation is very therapeutic. It not only leads to inner balance and stability, it also exposes your inner complexes, your immaturities, your unproductive reflexes and habits. Instead of living in these complexes and habits and acting them out, they are brought to your awareness and you can give them your full attention. Only then will they clear.

Meditation means gently fathoming all the levels of your being, one level after another. Be honest with yourself. Don't care what others say about their experiences—keep your mind focused on your goal. It is your own mind that does not allow you to meditate. To work with your mind, you'll have to be patient; you'll have to work with yourself gradually, you can be a right pain in the backside sometimes, I know I sure can!

At first you may see progress in terms of physical relaxation and emotional calmness. Later you may notice other, more subtle changes. Some of the most important benefits of meditation make themselves known gradually over time and are not dramatic or easily observed. Persist in your practice and you will find that meditation is a means of freeing yourself from the worries that gnaw at you from the outside world. Then you are free to experience the joy of being fully present, here and now.

At the end of a meditation session, before everyone returns to our little mere selves, we finish off with chanting the OM sound. The most beautiful noise in existence and my first tattoo, I'll briefly explain what it's all about.

The sound of OM encompasses all of the human language, into one transcendent sound that is beyond our ability to understand, OM is a matrix of all sounds, when in its diversified form gives rise to all words used in language.

Linguistically, all audible sounds are produced in the space within the mouth beginning at the root of the tongue and ending at the lips. The throat sound is A, and M is the lip sound; and the sound U represents the rolling forward of speech articulation which starts at the root of the tongue, continuing until it ends in the lips.

Like I mentioned, it's not so much about getting it 'text-book right', but more a sense of trying to find the way in which you can best self-reflect and look within, when meditating, all of us are on the same journey, however our path to get there may be different and that's ok, we have advice to guide us, but all of us are unique, beautiful individuals and can use this guidance to find our best way of connecting to our consciousness.

It was through meditation (hence why the hefty chapter, don't worry, we're almost through it) that I had my first 'out of body experience'. That experience is what it kind of says on the preverbal tin, you experience life from outside your own body. It was a very long and intense (kind of contradictory to the point of meditation right?) session of meditation, I was in a state of total bliss at the time, I felt really connected to the moment, I was just existing, as a little human spec of life in the infinite and then something just happened and it was then when I really felt connected to consciousness. It was then that it all seemed clear, I realised who I was, what was what and how amazing this thing we call life is. I guess some people call that moment 'nirvana', some may call it 'finding God' or whatever you want to call it, but I knew once I found it, I had found a place where I could achieve my inner-peace.

I'm not going to try and explain through words how it felt, as words wouldn't do the experience justice, this is something that exists beyond words, all I can say is that in that moment, nothing was real, time didn't exist, material wasn't real, I felt like pure consciousness and it was there, while I was just happily either having my spiritual awakening or mental breakdown crisis, where nothing was real, where I felt an over-encompassing feeling of love. For myself, for people, for the planet, for life.

It's that moment of bliss that I'm talking about in this book, connecting completely to our consciousness. Looking back after the event, when I came back into myself, after breaking down into tears of joy, I reflected on what just happened, and for a large part, I was so attuned with myself that I couldn't even really remember, I certainly couldn't remember or recreate the feeling, I just knew how I got there and how it was the greatest thing I'd ever done and how I needed to get back, to turn my focus to reconnecting to my consciousness whenever and however I could (hence the book, duh). So, while self-reflecting I just couldn't believe that in a state where nothing seemed real, where all realities and rules had broken down, where all of existence was going Crash Bandicoot crazy around me, one thing, one emotion, one energy still remained, love. And I'm not trying to be wishy-washy here, because I promised all of you that this was going to be a light-hearted, fun read, not a young person's mental breakdown splurged across the pages, but I feel if I truly open up to you, then despite barricades like 'time' or 'pages', then we can connect on a level of consciousness, despite the fact you're reading this book while I'm probably burning the things to keep warm (because I sold my house and ditched an education to make this bloody thing you know!)

Because it's amazing, it really is, that when put into a total state of conscious freedom, our mind resorts to compassion, to love. That moment was the moment when I convinced myself that I truly believe, when all put in that position, we'll all reach the same conclusion, all this other stuff like greed or lust, is just our primal instincts being manipulated for some shampoo or something, we, as our divine selves, can all reach this state, we can all become love.

So, try out the old meditation, join one of the oldest weekly exercise clubs in the book, breath, focus and see if mediation can help you have your personal revolution, like religion it's an ancient way of doing so and it certainly helped me achieve mine!

However, if the idea of sitting still for hours upon hours, focusing on your breathing and energy doesn't seem that appealing to you because you can't seem to sit still because you're all frustrated with your job, or your partner or your life and now you're panicking because you've tried the old meditating and it hasn't worked but it worked for me and your mate and millions of others throughout history and now you're worried the most from life you're ever going to get is a little buzz from inside your belly because you see McDonald's are bringing back the monopoly game and this is going to be your year to find that dark blue one and win that free holiday that no-one in the history of the bloody thing has ever been known or seen to win, then fear not!

Just because faith or meditation isn't for you, doesn't mean you have to board the next plane to Vegas, we've still got loads of ways that you may find easier to connect to your consciousness, and up next we're looking at Yoga. (Basically meditating while moving!) I'm talking real, good-old yoga that connects you to your highest self, better get stretching!

"Yoga is a vast collection of spiritual techniques and practices aimed at integrating mind, body and spirit to achieve a state of enlightenment or oneness with the universe. What is normally thought of as "yoga" in the West is really Hatha Yoga, one of the many paths of yoga. The different paths of yoga emphasise different approaches and techniques, but ultimately lead to the same goal of unification and enlightenment.

Don't let the media, cultural-exhausted version of yoga allow you to immediately dismiss the practice, I was a culprit of doing so in my early days on my path to connecting to my consciousness. Don't get me wrong, yoga certainly does have its money-makers, its brands and its scams; you have to be careful not to fall for it, of course. But everything has its dodgy versions and manipulated spins, from religion to the pirate films we've all watched once or twice, where the quality is quite good, until someone in front of the camera stands up to go to the toilet in the most important bit and you just watch their little silhouette head bounce along the screen.

Yoga in its purest form, like meditation, has been an ancient practice for centuries. To become a teacher, an expert in yoga, takes hours of training, and after that there's advanced training, it's a lot of bending and moving, so I thought instead of me embarrassing myself trying to explain this ancient tradition, I'd get someone who has done over 500 hours of training to explain...

"Yoga's history has many places of obscurity and uncertainty due to its oral transmission of sacred texts and the secretive nature of its teachings. The early writings on yoga were transcribed on fragile palm leaves that were easily damaged, destroyed or lost. The development of yoga can be traced back to over 5,000 years ago, but some researchers think that yoga may be up to 10,000 years old.

The beginnings of Yoga were developed by the Indus-Sarasvati civilization in Northern India over 5,000 years ago

In the late 1800s and early 1900s, yoga masters began to travel to the West, attracting attention and followers. This began at the 1893 Parliament of Religions in Chicago, when Swami Vivekananda wowed the attendees with his lectures on yoga and the universality of the world's religions. In the 1920s and 30s, Hatha Yoga was strongly promoted in India, while the importation of yoga to the West still continued at a trickle until Indra Devi opened her yoga studio in Hollywood in 1947. Since then, many more western and Indian teachers have become pioneers, popularizing hatha yoga and gaining millions of followers. Hatha Yoga now has many different schools or styles, all emphasizing the many different aspects of the practice." - Timothy Burgin.

See, now wasn't that nicer than me babbling on about Downward dog? Good stuff Timothy, good stuff.

So now we know the basic backdrop of the yoga scene, I'll give you a low-down of how I was introduced to the practice. Me and my friend Brett, went to an event called 'Yoga connects' (check them out, they're really cool guys) where Brett was doing a meditation workshop, me, being very new to everything hopped along nicely and embraced the atmosphere. It was fantastic, people from all cultures, all backgrounds, all coming together in peace, right up my street. Then came my first yoga practice, I felt I had to, seeing as I was at a festival called Yoga connects. So, I thought 'f*ck it', I mean how bad could it be? I hit the gym regularly, in pretty good shape, can bench press pretty high, what could go wrong?

My Yoga teacher was Natasha Kerry, (she's trained for so many hours that it's actually stupid to try and count them, she's introduced thousands of people into the practice, including Russell) basically she's perfect if you want to learn from the best, she's also the worst if you've never done any before. Natasha practices Yin yoga, which is basically, yoga done slower for longer. You move slower, but that isn't a 'get out of jail card' because you hold it for an amount of time that to me seems like the time it takes to make it feel like that part of your body has fallen off; it hurt, a lot.

The experience was humbling; there was me, a fit, strong, sports player, shaking and sweating unbearably while these petite little humans triple my age were doing it... and enjoying doing so!

It was intriguing, mesmerising in a way, I had to learn more. I've practiced yoga a lot more since then, on the beaches of Thailand, and on the hills of the Yorkshire countryside to the mountains in Europe; haven't got that much better, personally, Yoga is more of a challenge for me, meditation was something that came naturally and although I'm also learning and growing while I meditate, it feels like something that sits comfortably with me, yoga is not that, it's a battle between my mind and body, it's unexplored terrain and that's just as exciting. Just because one form of re-connecting to your consciousness doesn't sit as naturally with you as another, doesn't mean you have to dismiss it. All these techniques are proven, they're naturally something within us, it just may take more time to awaken ourselves to one, more than another, which is also good.

I view yoga as my time to learn and embrace a challenge, I may not get the same buzz out of Yoga as I do meditation yet, but then again it's because I haven't done it for as long, I'm still training and learning the basics, it's great to test ourselves and step out of our comfort zone, to live on the edge. After all, as William Faulkner told us "to reach new horizons, you have to lose sight of the shore". Or was that Captain Jack Sparrow?

The field of Yoga is so vast, probably larger than that of meditation, given all the off-shoots available now, ranging from the traditional practices to the more modern spins of 'hot yoga', which means doing yoga in a hot place to evoke sweating for weight loss - all the way to a New York company called 'Bold and Naked' which well, if you want to look into it, go for it!

One of the main things I picked up from Yoga was how much it affects your time away from the mat. A lot like this book, it seems that only 10% of the progress is felt during the practice, the other 90% is where the real effects are felt.

So as is evident, the range of possibilities within yoga are enormous, because of such, the likelihood of people re-connecting to themselves through yoga is quite possible, if one version of the practice doesn't work for you, you can always try another one, some will work better than others, it's all about experimenting and finding the one that suits you best (kind of like a mini-version of what we're trying to do here). So check yoga out, you don't have to wear the gear, (although I don't recommend wearing jean shorts like I did the first time) and see if yoga can be one way that helps you along your journey to re-connecting to your consciousness and having your personal revolution.

So, as you can see, both meditation and yoga are techniques that can take us beyond our initial awareness; however, I'm a strong believer that there is no solid definition of what 'meditating' and practicing 'yoga' actually mean.

Is someone at a concert, chanting the anthem of their favourite band at the top of their lungs not in the moment? How about Nigel the West Ham fan who belts out twelve rounds of 'I'm forever blowing bubbles' on a Saturday afternoon, is he not in the moment? What about a person who is writing, or painting, playing sport or making love to somebody? Are we not in the present moment then?

To me, I believe there are thousands of ways in which we can move between the thoughts and be present, totally connected to the moment, utilising the power of now and I think these are all techniques which manifest as appealing to us depending on our interests; some musicians will be more present in the moment, playing guitar, than sitting with their eyes closed, my mate Jacob certainly becomes present when busting out some chords, the same feeling I achieve through my spiritual practice.

When you are in conflict or in doubt, when you are afraid or lose hope or even lose a loved one or person you miss, move beyond the pain and you'll see there is awareness present. An awareness that has and always will be there, in loneliness and suffering and darkness and suffering, silently there is an awareness waiting to connect with you. This awareness is a field of consciousness from which all life came, the absolute energy that creates all and is beyond all and within all and it is within you, in this moment, so connect with it.

What I've realised is, if we're truly going to detach the ego and labels, **we have to accept there is no 'right way', simply the right way for us**.

We don't need to be draped in mala beads and bracelets to meditate, we could do this on a stage; in front of a drum kit, we don't need to spend thousands of pounds on yoga pants and fancy mats to do 'yoga', we can stretch in the morning or be totally emotionally present while making love with somebody, there is no definite explanation and like with our argument on spirituality and science earlier, we don't need to explain and label it, we simply have to not worry about labels and connect in the moment, however we find it easiest to do that and if we can do that, not only can we be present, but we can *really connect with our inherent spark of awesomeness*.

If there is light in the soul,

There will be beauty in the person,

If there is beauty in the person,

There will be harmony in the house,

If there is harmony in the house,

There will be order in the nation,

If there is order in the nation

There will be peace in the world

Chapter 16

The Miracle

So, we've just looked at the various ways in which we can be present in the moment and why being present in that moment is so important in our personal revolution, however, have you ever really considered the unlikelihood of this moment?

Have you ever really thought about this very moment? Probably not, I doubt that you in your busy life ever pondered what would happen the moment you picked up my book and read the sentence "Have you ever really thought about this moment?" (Which you've now read twice as I'm an expert procrastinator of getting to the point), but did you see how fast that moment went?

How did you feel, what were you thinking, can you even remember? (it wasn't that long ago!), but how fast did it fly by, that moment back then was, at that point in time, the oldest you've ever been and the youngest you'll ever be again, for the rest of your life.

Scary statement to think about, the oldest you have ever been, the longest amount of time you've ever experienced since birth and in the same, paradoxical moment, the closest towards your birth you'll ever be again and even crazier than that, we are all always in that moment, that very specific calculation of all stimuli from all of our lives, culminating in the precise second in which eternal existence can transcend the strains of morality and humanity, but most of us have never pondered the rarity of right now, how lucky we all are, so that's what we shall do now.

Because together, me and you can try and work out the impossibility of this moment, although I'm terrible at maths so I'll do what I always did in school, give you the question, flatter my eyes and then steal your answer! So firstly, let's work out the chances of you being born as you…

- Probability of boy meeting girl: 1 in 20,000.
- Now let's say the chances of them actually talking to one another is one in 10.
- The chances of that turning into another meeting is about one in 10 also.
- The chances of that turning into a long-term relationship is also one in 10.
- The chances of that lasting long enough to result in offspring is one in 2.
- The probability of your parents' chance meeting resulting in marriage and kids is about 1 in 2000

So, the combined probability is already around 1 in 40 million

Now things start getting interesting. Why? Because we're about to deal with eggs and sperm, which come in large numbers (a slightly different tone from the rest of this book!). Each sperm and each egg is genetically unique because of the process of meiosis; you are the result of the fusion of one particular egg with one particular sperm. A fertile woman has 100,000 viable eggs on average. A man will produce about 12 trillion sperm over the course of his reproductive lifetime.

Let's say a third of those (4 trillion) are relevant to our calculation, since the sperm created after your mum hits the menopause don't count (pass me a bucket). So the probability of that one sperm with half your name on it hitting that one egg with the other half of your name on it is $1/(100,000)(4 \text{ trillion}) = 1/(10^5)(4 \times 10^{12}) = 1$ in 4×10^{17}, or one in 400 quadrillion.

But because the existence of you here now on planet earth presupposes another supremely unlikely and utterly undeniable chain of events. Namely, that every one of your ancestors lived to reproductive age we must also go further presuming 150,000 generations going back to man's origin.

- That would be one in 2,150,000, which is about 1 in 1,045,000– a number so staggeringly large that my head hurts just writing it down.

But let's think about this some more. Remember the sperm-meeting-egg argument for the creation of you, since each gamete is unique?

Well, the right sperm also had to meet the right egg to create your grandparents. Otherwise they'd be different people, and so would their children, who would then have had children who were similar to you but not quite you.

This is also true of your grandparents' parents, and their grandparents, and so on till the beginning of human time. If even once the wrong sperm met the wrong egg, you would not be sitting here engrossed and totally grossed out about the chances of you and thoughts of your mum hitting menopause (why am I repeating this statement?). If anything was different, you wouldn't be you, you would be your cousin Jack, and you never really liked him anyway.

That means in every step of your lineage, the probability of the right sperm meeting the right egg such that the exact right ancestor would be created that would end up creating you is one in 1200 trillion, which we'll round down to 1000 trillion, or one quadrillion.

So now we must account for that for 150,000 generations by raising 400 quadrillion to the 150,000th power: That's a ten followed by 2,640,000 zeroes, which fills 11 volumes of a 250-page book with zeroes (so just be grateful I managed to stick any forms of words down!).

- For the sake of completeness and for all you maths boffins out there that's:
$(10^{2,640,000})(10^{45,000})(2000)(20,000) = 4 \times 10^{2,685,007} \approx 10^{2,685,000}$

Probability of your existing at all: 1 in an infinite probability

So, there we go; if at this point your brain isn't hurting, then you should be seriously considering that you are either a born-genius or a complete idiot, because those numbers are crazy!

In fact, the chance of you being born creates a number so big, that mathematicians jump onto the rival team and use a *word* to describe a number, meaning your chance of being born has broken maths and language, (which tops the 'Karcrashian' who broke the internet, so well done you).

You are impossible… just think about that, you are an infinite improbability, you are totally unique, totally special and nobody else can bring to this world what you can, do you realise what that means? The truth hidden in plain sight…

THE MIRACLE IS YOU.

Chapter 17

The underlying connectedness of a connected consciousness

So now that we've worked out that our reality is our own personal reality and it's whatever we want it to be and that one of the best ways to achieve a high frequency of consciousness is to be in the moment and that we can do this through many different routes, leading to us realising that the only way to find happiness is to learn how to connect to consciousness so that we can be a beautiful mentality that allows us to choose what to take on board and choose what to disregard, how should we start?

Well let's focus on this aim: to create the life we want, while being tolerant and accepting that other people will have other ways of life and that's okay, as long as we're not hurting each other or the planet, then we can all be happy for ourselves and each-other. Imagine if we all did that? How simple and beautiful all our lives would be!

What's even crazier is that people are already in that scenario, places and communities are operating with that intention and it's growing; that is why the news stories are getting worse, the politics is getting crazier and everything is getting so ridiculous, because people are waking up and so more extreme measures have to be taken to keep the illusion in place, to keep the veil on the situation, but the veil is being lifted, one personal revolution at a time and now it's time for yours.

Travelling around the world, one of the pre-judgements I'd been conditioned to believe was that everywhere else is worse off than where I am, that most of the world is terrible and that we should be lucky for what we've got. It couldn't be further from the truth; there are places, like currently Syria and Aleppo that clearly need our help, the situations they find themselves in is in-humane, they have no primal, animalistic needs catered for, they are suffering at one end of the spectrum. The plot-twist that we are the other end of that spectrum.

Over here, we are spiritually suffering, disconnected from life, because what travelling all over the world taught me more than anything is that actually, most of the world is quite content with how they are. Sure, they don't have the material possessions we have, nor the financial wealth but here's the twist: they're not craving that, they don't live inside a story where that is the 'end-goal' and actually, many of them take pity on us, the fact that these things is the 'end-goal' for so many of us. Just because the news says the world is a bad place, it doesn't make it true, because actually, most of the world is good, they're happy and doing okay, it's the places at both end of the spectrums that need help and revolution.

We need people on the streets; we need people out in countries that need help, saving children's lives and making a difference. However, we also need people back here, changing the way charities and corporations are run, subsequently saving more lives globally, because when we change the political systems to one which focuses on aiding these countries before bombing them and then shipping out volunteers to help them afterwards, the world will quickly see an eradication in the extreme-poverty currently around.

But this is the extreme cases, most people aren't focused on simply surviving or chasing an endless game, most people I've met are focussed on something greater; connection.

Think about when we're with one another, friends, families, lovers, enemies, mutual associates, whoever; the possibilities in that moment are endless, it's the beauty of human interaction. In those moments when we're connected, anything can happen, any words can be said, any stares can be absorbed, enemies can become friends, associates can become trusted allies and friends can become lovers. Because we're meant to love one another you know?

It's not something that may or may not happen for you, it's made for all of us, Noam Chomsky an activist, philosopher and all round good guy (in all of this talk for change, he's a pretty big fish to remember so you're going to need to remember his name) said "life's empty without love" and I'd have to say I agree. However it's not just Noam or I advocating that compassion for others is so important in fulfilling our true potential, it's a timeless message, scattered throughout our existence and the message is always the same. Whether it be from Jesus telling you to love thy neighbour in the bible, the Buddha telling us to connect to love, icons like Luther King or Ghandi telling us love will defeat tyrants, or our nan's telling us to stop throwing potatoes at our little brother's heads because 'it's not the right thing to do' (or was that just me?), because that message, it isn't my opinion or my belief, it's an inherent universal truth. No matter who is saying the message, the message is the same, maybe presented or worded differently, but anybody who is on a high enough level of consciousness will be of the understanding that love is key, love, or if love is too hippie of a word for you, compassion, tolerance, understanding, whatever label you want to attach to it, that undeniable feeling when your around family and friends, the moment you fall for someone, moments of connectedness and unity, that feeling we feel is love and that is what should be guiding us when we need guidance, that feeling of common love is what will help us evolve and connect into a better way of living our lives personally and also globally.

On the note of 'global', in this country, it doesn't get much more global then Facebook, the founder, Mark Zuckerberg held a conference in America, I was lucky enough to watch this conference and one of the greatest things Mark said, was his really interesting statement on history.

"History is the story of how we've learned to come together in ever greater numbers," Zuckerberg writes, "from tribes to cities to nations. At each step, we built social infrastructure like communities, media and governments to empower us to achieve things we couldn't on our own."

"Progress now requires humanity coming together not just as cities or nations, but also as a global community," he argues, and "Facebook stands for bringing us closer together and building a global community."

Zuckerberg sounds like he's talking on the same wave-length as we are, he wants to use Facebook as the platform on which to build a global civil society, creating a service that encourages communities and cooperation and political participation on a transnational scale. He frames national governments as merely one piece of "social infrastructure," and suggests that the world might need something to push beyond their limits. He wants Facebook to help humanity take its "next step."

But to do that, he'll need to make some changes to Facebook, we don't want to jump on board the 'Facebook to overthrow the current narrative' train and then find out there's an annual membership of £100,000 a year, or that all of a sudden, virtual status of Zuckerberg start popping up after every click. If Mark wants to connect the world, that's great, but let's make sure we use Facebook to consciously connect, instead of corporately.

The theory Mark speaks of is one which I've researched in great depth, which can also be found in the book Sapiens, which Zuckerberg has recommended on, well, Facebook.

'Sapiens', which is written by the Israeli historian Yuval Harari begins by establishing our species' lowly beginnings. "The most important thing to know about prehistoric humans is that they were insignificant animals with no more impact on their environment than gorillas, fireflies or jellyfish," Harari writes.

So what changed? Well Humans learned how to cooperate, and nothing else did. But cooperation, Harari emphasizes, is no easy task, you can't just start cooperating, hence why we don't see thousands of bees flying around, having realised that if they all flew around together, nobody would try and squish them and they'd all find nectar a lot easier. Now I'm not saying that all sentient life don't have the capacity, after all, due to that reptilian brain, we have that tribal instinct, we see families of dolphins and packs of wolves, however it's never on a grand scale, only on a primal scale... so what has created this unification of humans on such a large scale, to the point where we now forget we were once little, weak animals all together?

The basic way humans form and sustain groups is by using language to tell common stories about their community... a shared story we all agree on, but Harari cites research suggesting that "the maximum 'natural' size of a group bonded by 'gossip' is about 150 individuals, like the chimpanzees."

So how did Homo- sapiens manage to cross this critical threshold, eventually founding cities comprising tens of thousands of inhabitants and empires ruling hundreds of millions? How did we become connected on such a conscious level, one which to a less advanced species would appear as a telepathic like link between all of us? When seeing each-other we instantly know if somebody like us or not, we can judge if someone is happy or sad, we can read people as if we are sharing the same database, separated by two individual minds?

Well let's come back to that, but both I and Zuckerberg agree it's time for humanity to take its "next step," and he thinks Facebook can play a crucial role in it.

Today we are close to taking our next step. Our greatest opportunities are now global -- like spreading prosperity and freedom, promoting peace and understanding, lifting people out of poverty, and accelerating discovery. Our greatest challenges also need global responses -- like ending terrorism, fighting climate change, and preventing pandemics. Progress now requires humanity coming together not just as cities or nations, but also as a global community, this is especially important right now.

Zuckerberg says "Facebook stands for bringing us closer together and building a global community. When we began, this idea was not controversial. Every year, the world got more connected and this was seen as a positive trend. Yet now, across the world there are people left behind by globalization, and movements for withdrawing from global connection. There are questions about whether we can make a global community that works for everyone, and whether the path ahead is to connect more or reverse course."

This is a time when many of us around the world are reflecting on how we can have the most positive impact. I am reminded of my favourite saying about technology: "We always overestimate what we can do in two years, and we underestimate what we can do in ten years." We may not have the power to create the world we want immediately, but we can all start working on the long term today. In times like these, the most important thing we can do is develop the social infrastructure to give people the power to build a global community that works for all of us.

As I understand it, Zuckerberg argues that the story of human history is the story of ever-more cooperation on an ever-greater scale. We went, he writes, "from tribes to cities to nations." The next step is to become a "global community."

This is why the personal revolution I advocate will lead to a connection on a global scale, a story we won't fall out of touch with, because the same forces making the global community possible also imperil it. Our myths and stories which bought us together have been poisoned and conditioned to not serve us.

We don't just lack the institutions necessary to make global cooperation possible in the current narrative. We are watching the institutions that make national cooperation possible fail and living to that story, one which, will ultimately lead to a destruction of humanity instead of unity.

Facebook, to Zuckerberg's dismay, is playing a part in that failure. "Giving everyone a voice has historically been a very positive force for public discourse because it increases the diversity of ideas shared," he writes. "But the past year has also shown it may fragment our shared sense of reality."

This is inimical to the driving force of human progress. It is a shared sense of reality that permits widespread cooperation. If Facebook, globalization, and other trends are leading to fragmented realities, then they are impeding that crucial cooperation — they are standing in the way of humanity's next step and so to overcome this issue, we have to look internally and realise that if we all take separate looks inwards, we will find the very things that make us all the same.

Merely making the world "more open and connected" turns out to be insufficient, and in some contexts, dangerous. An open and connected world can become an angry, fractured world. For the global community Zuckerberg sees as humanity's next step to manifest, all that openness and connectivity need to be guided towards common understandings and cooperation, connection and compassion.

In our society, we have personal relationships with friends and family, and then we have institutional relationships with the governments that set the rules. A healthy society also has many layers of communities between us and government that take care of our needs. When we refer to our "social fabric", we usually mean the many mediating groups that bring us together and reinforce our values.

However, there has been a striking decline in the important social infrastructure of local communities over the past few decades. Since the 1970s, membership in some local groups has declined by as much as one-quarter, cutting across all segments of the population.

Whether Zuckerberg aspires to make Facebook a quasi-governmental entity, or whether he hopes to use it to launch himself into leadership of an actual government, what he's outlining here is a vision that would make Facebook the primary platform mediating those "many layers of communities between us and government" — but on a global scale.

There's no perfect analogue for what Zuckerberg is proposing, but it's closest to the role that major religions have played throughout history. Facebook is to become an organizing space where you meet people, engage with your neighbours and your world, organize to make changes in your community, relax with people like yourself, and receive information that helps you participate in government. And like religions — but unlike virtually any other organizing force in human history — Facebook is truly, intrinsically, global and for the first time, totally possible to not afflict an agenda.

But if Facebook is to play that role, then like a religion, Facebook will have to develop views on what it means to live well and responsibly. And in this document, Zuckerberg begins to do that.

"Going forward, we will measure Facebook's progress with groups based on meaningful groups, not groups overall," he writes. He promises that Facebook will begin pulling away from "passive consumption" and towards "strengthening social connections." He doesn't give much guidance on what this will mean, but the signal is clear: Facebook wants to start making more distinctions between worthy ways of spending time on the platform — ways that create real social bonds and cooperation — and less worthy ones.

Zuckerberg worries about fake news, but professes even more concern that the media is overly sensationalized, that it "rewards simplicity and discourages nuance," and he promises that Facebook is working to surface more "good in-depth content" as well as "additional perspectives and information."

Then he goes further than that, suggesting that Facebook will become crucial not just to learning about politics, but participating in it. He says that in the 2016 US election, Facebook's voter registration program "was larger than those of both major parties combined," and suggests that Facebook could "enable hundreds of millions of more people to vote in elections than do today, in every democratic country around the world." Remember the point I made all them chapters ago about how we all phone in to vote for the winner of Britain's Got Talent every weekend? Well what if we could start voting for people, policies and solutions to problems by a simple click on a Facebook-like platform.

Will Zuckerberg succeed in all, or any, of this? I have no idea. Scepticism is surely in order. Leaning hard into these ambitions might prove dangerous to Facebook's advertising business, or create room for a competitor that gives people what they want, rather than what they should want. The harder Facebook pushes to curate media content, or to generate political participation, the greater the threat certain governments will perceive from its presence.

This also all seems crazy to imagine these opportunities stemming from a place where the majority of people using Facebook share pictures of their cats and dinners, but let's remember as with any tool for change, it's down to us to choose it in the right way and Facebook is, at a first glance, a new world where we live, not physically but are represented virtually, consciously, what if we can use this world to change the world we live in right now?

Zuckerberg wants Facebook to be the platform for much broader swaths of human life than governments typically drive, and he is thinking far beyond the borders of any single country or narrative such as money or 'wealth'.

But to do that, we have to use tools such as Facebook beyond being a neutral platform and tie it to an idea of where humanity can and should go next. Religions do this in its purest form. Political parties do this in their purest form. National governments would do this in their purest form and now Facebook is doing it, too. What Zuckerberg is offering here isn't a business plan so much as it's a philosophy or an ideology. But philosophies and ideologies are harder and more dangerous to follow than business plans.

Abraham Lincoln — a leader who governed in a time of division that makes this era seem a model of comity and calm says "The dogmas of the quiet past are inadequate to the stormy present. The occasion is piled high with difficulty, and we must rise with the occasion. As our case is new, so we must think anew, act anew." We're on the verge of a political, media, social and human revolution and potential evolution, so how do we make sure we evolve instead of devolve? In a world where the average life-span is 67 years, where:

- 131.4 million People are born per year
- 55.3 million people die each year
- 360,000 births happen per day
- 151,600 people die each day
- 15,000 births each hour
- 6,316 people die each hour
- 250 births each minute
- 105 people die each minute
- Four births each second of every day
- Nearly two people die each second

How irrelevant and fragile do you feel right now?

Because after I discovered those facts I really thought, I'm so irrelevant and unimportant, I'm a blip of a blip of a blip that is the human race within the story of the universe, so how the hell can I feel ever happy with where I am, if all my actions are really quite irrelevant in infinite space?

Here's the secret: they, like you, are not irrelevant.

For every country I've every travelled, every city I've ever seen and every person I've ever spoke to, I've never met somebody who wasn't relevant, because they like you and me, are part of an ever-changing, ever-fluctuating, universe. Nothing is ever constant, consistency is just the illusion of the human mind, nothing is ever the exact same, no finger-print, no face, no life is ever identical. The universe

Our Story Called Life   Peter Abrams

is constantly moving and changing, revolutionising and evolving and you are part of that, so what universe are you going to create?

Because your actions, your frequencies and vibrations give out energy and create the reality you perceive, but there's a whole other level to this, because your reality, the ripples you send out, create the stream, create the over-arching universe for everybody. Every action big, or small, creates a ripple effect, creates a vibration of energy and frequency of consciousness which is felt by another person, who will then send their own ripple out to the rest of the world and so on and so the ripple effect of your actions will be felt beyond your wildest imagination.

Every-time you talk to someone, the message and vibration you give off will be felt by an average of between 5-10 indirectly from your actions, positive or negative. If your rude to the bus driver, the bus driver will be rude to somebody else, if you steal from somebody, that person will still back from somebody else, the actions and frequency you live on, impact the whole world, reality and universe around you.

This is why you have as much impact on people's live as Donald trump and Vladimir Putin. Crazy, I know and although you may not reach as many people's lives as they do, the impact you have is actually greater. The bus driver can listen to Trump on the radio, and this may impact his attitude towards the next person on the bus, but if that person is kind, funny and genuine, the bus driver will become pleasant and happy towards the next fifteen people getting on, if, after hearing Trump, the next rider is rude and obnoxious, the reality the driver is living within will become hateful and poisonous and he will replicate this rudeness towards the next thirty people because hatred and fear travel the fastest, understanding a little slower, while love requires a step-back.

It is down to me and you and everybody else on this planet to realise the underlying link between all of us. Because sure, some of us are linked by Facebook, or common interests, some of us are linked through cities or countries or societies, but they are just labels that have been attached to us.

Male, Female, Black, White, Straight, Gay, Rich, Poor, Happy, Sad… all of these things are external attachments given to us, attached to us, but none of these things make us who we are. The vibration of energy and the frequency of consciousness that makes us the same has never been the fear of the unknown, it's never been the lack of understanding of the world around us, because the thing that can break labels down, the thing that can tear down social standards and overthrow governments, that can create tidal waves of change and a reality of contentment, can be found by looking inside and understanding that regardless of what label we want to attach to it; god, science, spirituality, all of these things are saying the same thing, we have to live with love.

It was while I was out in Thailand for the first time, in a little place isolated between Lamai and Chaiweng on the Island on Koh Samui that I realised this truth.

I was out there seeing a mentor and friend, travelling around temples, meeting monks, deepening meditation, just your generic spiritual pilgrimage of sorts, think cliché Leonardo Dicaprio in 'The Beach' sort of scenario.

I'd gone on my own, one of my first travels alone and I'm grateful I'd chosen to go as an individual as it was while I was flying, walking, biking and hiking around the globe as a singular entity that I realised how connected we all are, I realised that we are never alone, we are never truly on our own and it was on the trip that I had the realisation in what I believed in.

I'd look at religion, I'd seen science and I'd jumped head first into spirituality but travelling out to Thailand, meeting the many different faces from as many different races going to and from just as many different places made me realise that actually all the above possible belief systems or ideologies were more or less saying the same thing and that I didn't believe in a God or a rule of physics... *My belief is in people.*

I'd met some truly beautiful people on that journey, as I'm lucky enough to do every day, corporate business members looking for something deeper, some hermits who had run away from problems elsewhere, people looking for salvation, for answers, for connection, all total strangers and total random encounters, however this love, the unconditional, no agenda-attached love I felt for these people (and received back from them) blew me away, they motivated me and inspired me that people are the real beauty of our stories, it's people I put my faith in.

But it was with three people; Brett, Catherine and Charlie, that made me realise what 'unconditional love for life' really meant.

Brett Moran I met through Russell's café, I'd found his book there, after meeting up a few times in London, we started attending festivals, talks and seminars together, Brett took me under his wing and guided me beyond any level of selflessness imaginable. Brett jokes how he sees me as a mini-version of himself; before he got into the sh*t he did when he was my age, he said he hoped to find me a better path. A few months ago, me and Brett spent a whole day riding on his motorbike around the mountains in Thailand, before sitting on balcony over-looking the dense forestation to the east, contrasted by the lights and noise from the city in the west. It was mesmerising, stunning, perfect. We spoke for hours about, consciousness, spirituality and life and in that conversation; I felt mine and Brett's story had come full circle, Brett had reached a place in his story where he was happy and had led to me finding a place where I was happy in mine, both of our stories sharing this chapter, summarised perfectly by this connection on this balcony.

As we sat and spoke, below us on the green appeared two little puppies and two little children, all four of them just running and wrestling, being totally present; me and Brett stopped our ranting and just froze, in fact, I'm sure the whole world froze in that moment, life was still; life was perfect.

In that moment I got it; as much as Brett is superficially my 'mentor', the truth is that really, we're two individual souls, connected by something deeper; a shared love for life, we recognise that divinity in each-other and on that day (apart from when I filmed him sleeping to get revenge for when he stitched me up on Facebook), I felt totally connected, I felt at one... so Namaste bro!

Charlie, on the other hand, makes my life anything but peaceful, she scares the sh*t out of me with the things she shows me, she constantly makes me question if anything is even real and has been the reason why I've stayed up many nights, wondering about the workings of the universe and if I've actually learned anything; with Charlie, it seems any answer I give her, leads to a million more questions!

But Charlie is the most free-spirited and elevating person I've ever been around, this lady practically holds the universe (or universes, it's all rather complicated) in her eyes. Kind, warm and totally care-free, Charlie inspires me, challenges me and reminds me that there is always more to learn and to discover.

Where Brett made me realise a love for life, a love for peace; Charlie made me realise that loving the crazy, loving the unknown and loving the adventure is equally important!

Finally there was Catherine, I met both Charlie and Catherine through Brett and I remember on first meeting Catherine, the whole room seemed dull compared to her. She honestly radiated this light, this warmth, this energy.

Me and Catherine clicked straight away and have had an amazing connection ever since, however in Thailand something special happened.

My Thailand adventure started by accidently bumping into Catherine at the airport in England, totally by chance, in all the people, in all the terminals, in all the times we could've been in all the places, we literally bumped into each other!

However once in Thailand we shared a special connection, whether it be me hiding under her umbrella to shelter from the torrential rain, scaling 'The Big Buddha', or chilling on some beanbags, I recognised a total, unconditional love for somebody else, with no agenda, I simply loved Catherine because Catherine simply loved life.

There was one special moment, where we sat on the edge of an infinity pool, over-looking the bold, blue empty sea and sky horizon and spoke about loving life, again, it was perfect. Shortly after, Charlie joined us, all three of us, staring out into the open world... I remember telling them that this moment would be one I would remember forever, and I will.

Catherine, the final piece in my trio of peace-makers, taught me to love the beauty in everything, showed me happiness is wherever we choose to see it and that no matter what anybody says; *a smile is the greatest super-power in the world.*

Brett is still my mentor until this day and is still a huge influence in my life; I can't wait to see what other trouble we get into, Charlie still blows my mind regularly and Catherine is still reminding me that everything is going to be alright!

I see Charlie as my elevation, Catherine as my grounding and Brett as my samurai-style teacher (like the turtle from Kung Fu Panda), watching from a distance, but always near.

I won't ever be able to thank these three people for what they've given me, however I also understand that the best way I can pay these amazing souls back is by what I give to others and despite them all being selfless little hippies, they all deserve this little mention in this part of the book, because they made me realise an inherent truth which is so important for all of us, we have the answers we need, we always have and we always will, Brett, Charlie and Catherine never knew my answers I needed, but by loving me unconditionally, supporting and guiding me, they were able to hold the mirror up that allowed me to see myself.

It's so important on this journey that you surround yourself with people who will elevate, ground and guide you; having people who love you is what allows the writing in your story to flow, it allows us to grow.

We are the authors of our story called life, however remember there is nothing wrong with having some friends proof read it as you write, we are always stronger together then we are apart and having a connection with others is what gives our story depth.

And I still do, when people ask me what do I believe in, what religion do I follow, what are my views on science or spirituality, I smile and say I believe in people, I believe in myself, in them, in you, in everyone; that deep down we're after the same thing, searching for the same feelings, looking to answer the same questions, looking to have the same revelations and realisations, I don't believe we need to label, categorise or cage in this indescribable attainment of what exactly it is, because I believe this indescribable thing is what religious people would call God, or what a scientist would call the laws of physics, or what spiritual gurus might call energy or consciousness; I don't think it matters on what way we choose to look at it, let alone argue over which way we should all be looking at it, because there's a deeper level to the question, a deeper level to the answer, all these things we've discussed; religion, science, spirituality, *I believe at a base level are the same thing,* each one just another man's way of trying to achieve the same thing that you're doing in your way, let's not worry about trying to disprove someone else's beliefs or prove why ours is the only possible way; *because what if they're all right?*

I sat every morning from 5am-7am on an open little wooden platform with a straw roof, isolated on top of a singular rock, a few metres above the ocean surface; I watched numerous sun-rises and sun-sets, while on that Island.

I saw tropical rain storms make the world, even the few feet in front of me, become a blurry, invisible mist; I saw birds and butterflies fly by, life in abundance, a deep appreciation for the world, on that one spot I felt bliss, revolution, connection, I also felt fear, danger and worry, I witnessed lighting storms, strikes breaking the waves around the platform, thunder rattling and shaking the very foundations I sat on and I realised where I was; the most perfect spot in the world.

Looking out all you could see was sea and sky, no land, no boats, no people, just Mother Nature and the horizon. The only other thing that could catch your attention was a small circular rock, with the breakages and patterns of the wear of the rock that made this little boulder-like formation look like one side of the earth, so detailed, it appeared this rock even had the carvings of lakes and rocks, I'm still not sure if that rock was deliberately carves to represent the earth, or maybe it's a wonder of the universe that's undiscovered but I realised In front of me was the perfect visualisation of life (So I nicked the idea for my book cover).

No life, All life, the perfect contrast; the sea and sky in perfect unison in both destruction and creation, the yin to the yang, the science to the religion, the infinite and temporal, the birth and the death of the world, the universe; in front of my very eyes, tunnelled into my soul and connected to my consciousness, this was the place my personal revolution took place and my life changed.

Because it was on that spot I realised that they are all ***right.*** Religion is right, science is right, spirituality is right, because they are all *a different way of saying the same damn thing*, they might as well *be* the same damn thing.

Imagine it like looking at a yellow, orange and red Ferrari, you could spend all day arguing that the only colour a Ferrari should ever be is red, just as easily as the other guy could spend all day arguing why going for 'edgy' yellow makes his stand out more, therefore superior, all the while the weirdo who chooses to get his Ferrari painted orange will sit and argue all day why his stands out more because he thought it'd be cool to drive around in a massive satsuma, BUT; they are all still fricking Ferraris. Regardless of what paint or exterior they make appear as, they are still the same thing, the same interior and the same purpose.

This is the exact same for us; regardless of what exterior presentation we show, or what beliefs we have; on the inside we're all the same, all flesh and bone, all blood and heart, all soul and consciousness and we all have the same purpose; to elevate our consciousness *to live a content life in the name of connection, compassion, peace and love.* If you can make that connection by praying to your God, then do that. If you can make that connection by believing in science and the laws of the universe, then do that. If you can make that connection by believing in energy and the chakras, then do that.

Because we are all self-aware conscious beings, connected to the underlying connectedness which is a connected consciousness that sits at the bed of all phenomena, we are all half primal, animalistic creatures and half beautiful, divine entities, we're all heading to the same place and so that's why I believe in people, because I've met enough people, living crazy adventures, writing crazy stories of their lives to know whole-heartedly, if I've only learnt one thing from life, It's this:

People are worth believing in, worth fighting for, worth helping and worth loving.

That's why so many of us have got it wrong, it's why some many people are discontent and disillusioned with life, because we're conditioned into a reality that makes us believe that if we can be externally 'powerful', 'successful', 'world-changers' on our own, then we will achieve some sort of inner-peace and be content every day of our lives; however that couldn't be further from the truth, because it's only when we look internally and become happy, content and achieve an inner-peace that we will become truly powerful, truly successful and truly change the world; the total reverse to how most people currently go about their life.

Because, as crazy as this sounds, the perfect world, utopia, a total enlightenment and consciously connected existence already exists; the universe and realty in which every day is filled with happiness, contentedness and connection isn't somewhere in the future that's coming, it isn't somewhere in the past that's been and gone, it isn't even somewhere beyond like a heaven or nirvana that we can ascend too, it is somewhere we go, something we achieve, when we realise that the perfect world; the perfect utopia, the prefect moment, *is right now.*

You are already in your utopia, you are already in your perfect world, life is already indescribably perfect, if you choose to see it that way.

Like we've discussed, you may find the easiest way to see life as perfect through a belief in a God, or through the vision of science, the teachings or spirituality, or however else you've managed it, but what's the underlying message of life in all these avenues, the underlying message of this book, of Ghandi's teachings of everything ever, quite frankly, is that life is perfect, you are perfect and that you are exactly where you need to be right now, this moment is perfect if we live a life of pure love, peace and connection.

Ah, now doesn't that take the pressure off? How good does that feel? Like stretching your back in the morning just after you wake up when everything is great because you haven't realised its Monday yet!

You can breathe, relax, meditate, party, smile; ***you're going to be alright.***

Because if we just think laterally for a moment, how are we ever going to achieve this indescribable awesomeness if we're constantly looking back, constantly looking forward, always looking up or down, left or right?

Because we will never actually be anywhere.

If you live your whole life looking back then you will only ever live to the stories that have already happened, this is a place a lot of people get caught up, repeating bad habits, continuing damaging patterns, stuck in the narrative and story they've been conditioned into, not one they're conditioned for themselves, however not being present because your always thinking ahead can also be just as damaging.

If you only ever live in the future, then you too will never actually be anywhere because the future your envisioning may never actually happen, I'm not saying don't dream, because dream big and then dream even bigger, visualise and imagine the perfect world, fake it till you make it and totally become your message, but the key point within those guidelines is to live within every moment, to realise the utopia you are in within every single second of existence on your way to those dreams, because if you're living in the ideal version of your life, then those dreams you've envisioned and dreamt of will become true and you'll exist in the perfect life for you.

That is a personal revolution, that is finding the way out within, **that is writing your own story called life; enlightening your consciousness to a state of unity, peace, connection and love in every moment because life is amazing** and is in every single second we get of this crazy adventure, once we see it that way, it no longer becomes a search for happiness but a state of bliss, our world now perfect and then using this elevated consciousness to go and spread love and connection to every other world and life we encounter so that we as a connected consciousness elevate ourselves to pure connection.

Love is the key and three varieties of it in particular: - Firstly, the love of the stranger; the capacity to see the other as like oneself and worthy of the same mercy and charity.

Secondly, the love of the unborn: the concern for those who do not yet exist and whom one will never know but whose lives one is shaping in the selfish present.

Thirdly, the love of the truth: the strength to resist illusion and lies and square up to uncomfortable facts of all kinds.

We can see a disastrous scenario only too well right now. The fate of civilisation lies ultimately not in the law courts, at the ballot box or in the corridors of governments. It lies in our ability to master the most short-term, selfish and violent of our impulses active in the dense folds of organic matter between our ears; it lies in learning how fiercely to compensate for the flawed system we've been presented with and create a better one, all together as a united, human race, overflowing with humanity, sending nothing but a vibration of love.

That is certainly the journey I've taken and personally believe we all take, if we re-frame the wording of the messages above into more poetic form, we can say:

We are born into a story which does not serve us, we retract and find emptiness, no longer following any story, but upon having a personal revolution, we write our own story and that is where contentment is found.

I feel part of the reason that a global conscious revolution is coming and happening now, is because we've sort of run out of things to discover in front of us. It seems and at least appears that we have a grasp on the basic physics that make up our world and so we are now looking internally for answers both on a scientific and spiritual level, as we've learnt the external physical world can't satisfy all of our humanly needs.

We've worked out why apples fall from trees, why there's a huge ball of fire in the sky and why grass grows, what I'm saying is that the things that happen in front of us, we've deduced and attached words and theories as to why and how, the big questions of previous generations need not be answered and the fact that we now have tools such as the internet to debate and preserve these theories means that we don't need to be constantly questioning the same questions, we can learn the answers to previously unsolved mysteries from our ancestors discoveries and then spend time working on new ones.

In the physical world, the political and social revolutions of the past and the first of this book all stemmed from us being externally led by distractions such as money, status and power. All of this culminated in the combining of the political, economic and media landscapes into one 'bubble' of a society and system where our consciousness was being oppressed.

Now, we're on the edge of seeing all of our ways to elevate our consciousness; science, religion, spirituality, all combine into one 'universal truth' which could re-connect the whole world to the beautiful essence of our nature, internally awakening the inherent awesomeness within you that I addressed at the start of the book.

Because we're all connected, whether that be through beliefs, the moment, shared labels, thoughts, memories, physical similarities or emotions, we are all connected to each other and the world, that's the whole point of this second part of the book, the idea that all the current issues and narratives in the world, political, media, social, economic, all of these are secondary narratives when looking at the bigger scheme of things and realising that we can find the best solutions and alternatives to all these narratives by focusing on that shared connection we have.

This brings be back to the ever-present David Bowie, who in an interview in 2002, had this to say about the meaning of life: "We may in fact not have a purpose. Are we big enough or mature enough to accept that there's no 'plan', there's no 'going somewhere,' there's no gift of immortality at the end of this if we evolve far enough? ... Well, maybe we can't live like that. Maybe we have to exist and live on the idea that we have one day at a time to live—and can we do that? Because if we could do that, we may be serving some really great thing."

I believe whole-heartedly in that idea, that we create our own plan, our own 'going somewhere', our own gift and our own immortality by being here, as a beacon of love, one day at a time. Whether we connect to this idea through a religious belief, a scientific belief, meditation, yoga, parent-hood, monogamous relationships, playing football or by writing a book, matters not, so long as we are connected to it through unconditional love; we can destroy the high culture that we've been presented and tear down everything that has been created and given to us and regenerate ourselves into new.

The whole first half of this book was testament to the statement "God is Dead", in this sense "God" meaning that indescribable force we've spent this half of the book describing in various ways, the whole of the last century, people became so aggrandised with our own sense of self after having the enlightenment that man himself can shape the world, however what we failed to realise was that we can only shape the primal, physical world through our own desires and fears, we can only be 'successful' externally, chasing money, fame and wealth, however there's a deeper, more human level that we've abandoned. All of this lead to us placing ourselves as the centre of our reality; believing that we are the most important thing in the universe.

The selfless acts mothers will commit for their child, the crazy things we do for someone we truly love, the strength and motivation it gives even the most depleted of us, its all testament that we, as physical beings are but a shadow of importance in regard to the love we embody and embrace.

This abandonment of love, led to Einstein's discoveries that time and space, weren't as we thought they were, to Freud's discoveries that there is a human, inside the human; that voice in our head, all these things, culminated in the idea that everything we knew before must be 'wrong', everything, we never contemplated that maybe the way we saw things before, could actually be a less-detailed and more vague way of people who were less rationalised thinkers then ourselves describing the very same thing we have no conceptualised in greater knowledge.

So when we started the 21st century, we started with this clean-slate, declaring that we are now the gods of our lives.

Remember that the greatest invention, the grandest master-piece we were able to create, putting ourselves, as the physical, primal beings we were, was work out that the material world around us could be utilised, atoms could be split and we could alter-physics as we know it, but because of the primal, ape-like mentality we possessed, out of touch with love, the greatest thing we we're able to create from this knowledge, what all of our combined efforts resulted in: ***was a bomb.***

I think that by contributing our physical selves as the reasoning for our morality, our universe, our existence, was the reasoning why we craved a deeper-level of connection to something more in the 60's, which resulted in the few of us who didn't crave that re-connection to take control and build on this 'capitalist', 'money-led' mentality, where we placed 'us' as the most important thing in existence, which in turn leads us back to the very first few chapter in this book of how we got to here in the first place, ***bringing this story full circle.***

However through this we can connect with the indescribable phenomena's of the universe and through connecting with it, we now have the ability to live inside a story and create a perception where we can simply live a life of contentment knowing that, at least at this point of our evolution, or in this state, plane of existence or point in our spiritual journeys; we will never be able to truly understand 'it', but actually, to live a life of love, peace and contentment, we don't need to, we simply have to connect to it through whichever way, spiritual or scientific that we find easiest to rationalise and *live*.

We can do all that, then we realise that life is; in every moment of eternity, connected to the underlying connectedness which is a connectedness consciousness; perfect and we never need to see it in any other way.

As Bowie said; that's something really quite special; how Dandy indeed.

Chapter 18

The Revolution: Part II

While talking all spiritual and grand about the meaning of life, the question of "what would this revolution look like?" is still present.

In this chapter, I'm not going to be designing the blueprints for a revolution; but we're going to work out the things *any* good revolution would have.

Well any revolution, by grammatical definition is "a forcible overthrow of a government or social order, in favour of a new system."

So our revolution will be defined and achieved by a mass-supported attack on the power of corporations and the rules in place that allow them to dominate everything else. It will have a massive decentralisation of power, private or state, with the power then returning to us, the people at the level of community. It is then the appliance of a deeper-connected thought process, whether that is science, spiritual or religious, it doesn't matter and we don't all need to have the same one, but whatever it is, it needs to be placed to the heart of our social structures.

We're not quite Omni-present beings yet and so we're still going to eat food, so we need to re-evaluate the global trade agreements to make them favourable to local, organised farming and food production, opposed to one which is just focusing on profit, killing needless animals and the planet all because the current agreements are financially beneficial to a few of us.

We've spent half a book dedicating our focus to understanding that economics is at the heart of our nations-agendas and philosophy and even if you could argue that this ideology served a purpose in the past, it certainly doesn't anymore and so it's time we dissolved it and rebuilt it.

We can do this firstly by handing power over from the hands of singular individuals who run banks and corporations and disperse this power out into cooperatively run business-models.

Remember, the people who tell you these ideas can't work, in government, on Fox news, on Trump's twitter, or wherever else, are the people who have a vested interest in things staying the same.

The other truth, is that there is no heroic revolutionary figure in whom we can invest hope, except for ourselves, as individuals together, working as a collective.

There's no lack of alternatives, there just aren't many people in current powerful positions that want to show you that things can change, capitalism isn't irreplaceable and absolute but the earth's resources are. Obviously we know that capitalism has to go, everyone does, even the elites that benefit from it the most.

They know that the majority of people will benefit from a revolution in how we do things, which means they've resulted in creating a 'bubble-world' where they've used money, media and all the other tactics from the first half of the book to make you disillusioned, they've set up a story in our heads to make us controllable within the current mind-set we possess, they're prepared for protests, activism and moaning, they're not prepared for us changing the story in our heads and causing a revolution they can't anticipate.

But we have to be careful. Because blind, radical call for change, just leads to chaos. People's anger and frustrations which have been building for so long, is in danger of boiling over and creating a very dangerous world. It is *so important*, even more important than having a political revolution, that we have a personal revolution.

Because otherwise nothing's really going to change; sure, the faces will change and some of the rules will change, but as we stated at the start, we the people create the society we live in, so if we the people don't solve our internal issues so that we can change the external issues, we'll just end up back where we started, just under a different layout and style because our mind-set and mentality towards life and each-other will be the same, thus creating the same end result and that's the very thing that needs to be revolutionised, *that's the underlying issue.*

Otherwise we get people declaring a new way of thinking, who then forcibly impose their own ideals. (Someone who says something along the lines of 'My idea is really, really great, trust me it is, we don't have enough time to explain why it is, or how it is, but if you did know, then you'd totally be all over this, however, we're in a rush so we might have to commit a bit of murder to anyone who opposes').

This is why Noam Chomsky is sure that a utopia can't exist with our current ideology; it encourages short-cuts, which is when killing all the other people who don't fit into the new world order stops sounding like a ridiculous statement and starts becoming the news stories we hear.

This is why revolutions require a spiritual essence; it doesn't matter why violence is being committed, it doesn't matter who is causing the violence; *violence is wrong*.

This is a universal truth found within any sort of spiritual teaching. The idea that violence is never acceptable is an almost impossible idea for us capitalist consumers; capital punishment is wrong, torture is wrong, armed struggle and revenge is wrong. The only way to be able to accept these ideas is by transcending the individual and material expressions of violence.

Non-violent Christians and non-violent Muslims have to come together to end the violent terrorism we see going on.

This means that the rounding up and disposing of Donald Trump, Rupert Murdoch, the Rothschild's and the rest of them is counter-revolutionary. Politics doesn't have a place for these people outside the current system, it would encourage us to do whatever we wanted, however spiritual and deeper practices do have a place for them and if we truly want a global shift, one of the biggest tests we'll have is how we deal with the people who were in charge, once we've other-thrown them.

It's our collective future we're building and as we stated earlier in the book, a society can be judged by how it treats its poorest members, once we live in a spiritually-driven society, the bankers and politicians will become the poorest, how we will be defined as a society by generations after us, will come down to how we deal with them and it **must be with love**.

Buckminster's theorem states "We have to make the world work for 100% of humanity in the shortest possible time through spontaneous cooperation, without ecological offense or disadvantage of anyone". Remember that we are not in competition with perfection. We are not competing with fair justice or righteousness; we are intervening in a shockingly desperate time of a corrupt system on the edge of collapse.

So, let's change ourselves, help others to change and then watch as the rest of the world around us changes from a dirty, run-down machine, into a full-functioning platform on which we can all thrive. This shift is going to happen eventually for all of us, one way or another, sure, you can exist and wait to see if this shift happens within your lifetime, or you can wake and have it happen right now; instantaneously within our own personal lives and reality (the spiritual bit) and then gradually globally (the political bit).

So let's disobey the current system, let's organise locally and unite together, work towards our own personal revolutions and be tolerant and accepting of others; offering help and guidance if asked for, without imposing any ideal or belief.

Let's question everything we're presented with, no matter where that message comes from, but no longer through fear, or hatred; but now from love and compassion, let's live to our own truths, our universal truths and listen to the real voice inside our head, not the one telling the stories from somebody else.

That's it. If we all did that then we would have what we're aiming for. Yes it's idealistic, yes it may not be practical right at this moment, but let's set that as the standard to live to: as *our* standard to live by, let's try and achieve that and before you know it, the revolution has begun.

We need a good system that doesn't restrain us and a good mentality so that when we're free, we play to the best part of our nature and not the worst. That change, that revolution I'm on about, it doesn't start with me, or with a famous person off the TV, it doesn't start from the wise guy down the road or the woman who puts all that crap on Facebook, it starts with *you*.

So let's review the situation; we know that the world needs to change; we're on the brink of going past the point from which we can return. We know that certainly the majority of people, (I'd argue all people), would benefit from a revolution and we know the basics that will have to change; corporations' power and influence needs to be eradicated, we need to stop irresponsible destruction of the environment and we need to solve the economic equality being maintained by the current political, media and social narrative.

We know how to remove them too, personally revolutionise our perception on life so that we stop fulfilling the expectations set for us and live to our own expectations. Trade policies, monopolies, unrepresentative democratic institutions all need to be dissolved and reformed into something new; revolutions that transfer power from one rich elite to another (The state to Trump) are pointless… revolutions that hand the power back to us (the one I'm on about) are worth having.

We know, relatively, what can replace them too; localised, self-governing alternate systems that operates on the level of community and local business, where power is equally maintained.

We won't know what the post-revolution world will look like for definite, there might be some inequality, conflict or issues still to address, but these will be miniscule compared to the situation we're currently in and a lot easier to manage and sort out.

Russell says an awesome little quote about voting, one which he got ridiculed before in the past, but everybody missed the point, when talking about not voting due to there being nobody worth voting for he said,

"It's not 'Don't Vote, watch porn'... It's 'Don't Vote, build your own system'!"

We need a system where we negotiate with our ego to let the collective power that is not allied to any individual govern. Detach our ego, hand over our power, believe in the connected consciousness; guided by trusted, divine principles to be the authority.

We don't even need to get rid of the whole 'representative democracy' we're so crazy about, so long as the one we have does two things:

- Make sure the people's will is represented
- Be totally answerable to the electoral system we use to elect them in the first place.

Our common welfare should come first; personal recovery depends on our unity.

Basically, the majority's interests should come before any individuals, so that an individual can never dictate and gain unwarranted power.

No individual should have authority. The group has authority, the groups conscience is expressed through voting; imagine for example, I want this book to replace the bible in this post-revolutionary world, I'll declare my statement "I want this book to replace the bible" and then we vote.

If you press the green button you agree, if you press the red; you disagree, then, if for whatever reason there are less green then red, then it doesn't happen and that's that.

If, (logically) there are more green then red, then that's also that.

If only a few people voted and the outcome was one the people who didn't vote wouldn't have voted for, then they should've voted, but can oppose this by creating their own statement.

You may be thinking this is already the system in place, but it's not, in this idea, we come up with the ideas and solutions, we don't choose a party to support who do the work for us, we take responsibility and use technology and current platforms to all, collectively decide what happens, the people who carry out these actions aren't 'leaders', they are representatives, people who have no power, simply a duty to fulfil.

It doesn't matter what gender, sexual preference, colour, religion or class we are, if you want to join, you can. Everyone is entitled to set up communities or groups that they want, so long as it doesn't hurt anyone else or the planet we're on, have a racially, religiously or sexually exclusive group if you want, but don't let it affect the over-arching aims of society.

Our primary purpose will need to be the protection of the ecological welfare of the planet and aim to create a harmonious and fair democracy, likely only possible through manageable-sized communities that run voluntarily and democratically.

We'll have regulations in place that will prevent people from profiting off a system designed with spirituality in mind. We'll all still have egos and our reptile brains to deal with, so we have to make sure we have a guide to lead us back to our better nature; our compassion, our creativity and our unconditional love.

Everything needs to be independent and democratically run; this prevents sleazy capitalists acquiring power and authority through financial means.

Me and you and Donald Trump and everyone else have to individually connect to the divinity within all of us so that collectively we can create a society worthy of beautiful beings. In an alternate system, one day Trump's ego might throw a tantrum, or perhaps, I'll declare my book is the new bible, but thanks to our new system, we can avert our internal struggles from impacting everybody else, our problems remain our problems that others can help us address, instead of suffer along with as well.

The systems that allow us to vote for talent shows can be used to create truly-represented decision; we no longer need buffoons on our TV screens telling us what to do, separated by Mickey Mouse advertisement and pointless ecological destruction.

We can revolutionise corporations and disband their power, we can provide an alternative for the services they provide and then use the excess things we have left to feed and resource the people in extreme poverty around the world.

This will all start small, but grow quickly because we will have a limitless resource and be providing an alternative, opposed to a dying system. There is no limit to how global this can reach, if we behave lovingly, collectively and humanly. The world is changing and we are awakening, these old stories cannot be maintained if we don't believe in them, we have no choice but change and all these external revolutions will all come from within.

It's now time to learn how to re-connect to our beautiful side, the part that has been discouraged for so long, to come bursting back into life and with it, so will fulfilling, beautiful lives; fair lives, a new age revolution, internally, because thanks to the cyber-utopians of the 90's, thanks to the 60's psychedelia's and the 80's protestors, the 70's artists, in fact, thanks to every man and women that ever stood their ground, to every child that grew up to question the world around him/her instead of just existing inside the world presented to them, thanks to the bravery, compassion, hope and love of all the people that never lost their connection to love, we now stand on the edge of a revolution, with something to believe in, where we can be our own heroes, our own candidates, our own visionaries and leaders and live a perfect life, totally free, totally unique and totally content, in the name of unity, peace and love... and it all starts with our very own personal revolution, a reconnection to love and elevating of consciousness.

So now we've cleared up the past, the stories we've been living and now are standing on the platform to elevate our consciousness, call it idealistic, call it unrealistic, but after what we've discussed, how we got to this point, it's certainly no less realistic then the crazy scenario that created the circumstances that have got us to this point. It may be idealistic, it may be 'best-case scenario' but why don't we have that as our end-goal? Why don't we dream bigger, love harder and live faster?

Because everything can be criticised and scrutinised, every idea isn't fail-proof and no system is truly incorruptible but our lives really are stories, so why don't we make it the best one we can? We are the heroes of our lives, we are the rulers of our fate and we are the creators of our reality so why don't we make it unrealistic?

All 'realistic' means is an idea that can be achieved and expected and since we create our own stories and realities, there is no limit to what we can achieve if we reconnect to our consciousness.

That right there my friend, is the personal revolution.

It's about being the best you can be, regardless of how you achieve that, through a belief in religion, prayer, meditation, music, sport; the path is down to you, but that's not the important bit, what it's really about is choosing to embrace life; to open yourself up to all life has to offer, not constricting yourself through labels or categorising but to simply live life; remembering to laugh; because it's always funny, remembering to smile; because it's always beautiful, never to be cruel or act through fear or hatred because at the end of the day; love conquers all.

It's about believing in yourself and believing in others, it's about believing in us, it's believing in companionship, in unity, in connectedness.

The personal revolution is about creating the best of our story called life; so make it idealistic, make it unrealistic, because nothing and everything is real so dream bigger than reality because we are destiny, we are eternity, we are consciousness.

Live for compassion, live for peace, live for love, live life. It's time to become the author of our own destiny and NOW it's time for you to write your own, story called life.

Chapter 19

The Fantastic Voyage

Recap: We've now worked out that the way to change the world is to change ourselves and subsequently what sort of world would be created if we all changed ourselves, good job guys, we're doing well.

So now we're going back to the 'woo woo' and I'm asking you; how the hell did we get here?

The reasoning on how we became us, much like religion, is a personal belief for many people, I've made quite abundantly clear that I believe that we're all part of the connected consciousness, at the bed of all the phenomena and that instead of trying to worry or work out about where we've come from, we should just life our lives knowing the internal truths we all possess, however, recently I'm becoming increasingly interested in finding these ideas out.

My interest stems from my best friend Shannon's baby called Elsie, (for some reason Shannon wouldn't call her beautiful little baby girl Peter, which I accepted, but when I found out she'd opted for Elsie over Petria, I was furious) who was born last year and I remember distinctly the moment I first held her and I could see 'it'.

The light being switched on, the moment she came 'online', when consciousness sparked into life and created a connection indescribable to translate the beauty and love bestowed into one tiny, little human.

Since then Elsie (or Petria, as I'm trying to brainwash into her little consciousness) has spent many hours being questioned by me on where did her consciousness come from, how did it get there and what happened in the moment it did, however, all she's managed to confirm to me so far is that if you hold a baby at the wrong time, perfectly good hoodies get stained for life with some sort of regurgitation of their last eaten food.

Seeing Elsie discover the world, where everything is new and exciting, is fascinating; trying to work out the environment in which she exists, without a narrative or story being afflicted onto her, no expectation or judgement, just totally discovery of the life around her, is amazing to witness.

However even more fascinating than that is the connection Shannon and Elsie have, it's like an inherent understanding of one another and for somebody I've known my whole life, seeing Shannon create new life and now sit there, holding Elsie, was confirmation to me that we're all connected on some conscious level, we simply have to be.

Whether this connection is the work of a God-like entity, the scientific evolution of homo-sapiens, or the spiritual manifestation of the divine, is what I'm asking Elsie the next time I see her, so I'll let you know what she comes back with in the sequel.

However that moment which saw Elsie come into this existence, had the same probability of happening as you did, as I did and as everybody else did and so now we're moving away from cute baby stories and going back to some brain-scrambling maths, because the impossibility of this moment has not yet been calculated.

Because the infinite numbered chance we worked out earlier, was only for the moment you was born, something that actually, was out of your control.

However what we're trying to calculate is this very moment right now, something that you've had the most influential role in creating, so let's get on with some adding up.

Now we know what the chances are of you being born as you are, it's now time to work out what the chances of you getting to this moment are and in doing so, you will realise we are all connected in one; in this chapter I'm going to prove to you why our life is a story.

To start simple, I want you to think about how you got this book, where did you buy it, in a book-store, online, from me?

However you got a hold of the copy of this book your reading now, so much had to happen to create the moment you attained the story you're now reading, let's try and work out the amount of people involved that resulted with you getting this book.

For starters, I had to write the damn thing, so that already doubles the count to two people: I had to write it, you had to buy it.

However I didn't write it and then hand it straight to you, I had to get it published, which means we already sky-rocket the numbers up, as every single person who was tasked with making the book publishable (you poor, poor people) now has influenced you getting the book, let's say for easy maths, about fifty people.

However, we're not done with the publishers yet, because they had to be created in the first place, so the original creators of the publishers and all the subsequent workers who built the company in such a way that allowed for the moment we agreed on a deal to happen, means the number of people now involved in getting that book to you is closer to around 50 thousand!

On top of this, I have to give credit to everyone who influenced me, which really is everyone, as this book is the direct result of my whole life's journey put down into a more poetic layout and so really, the number of people whose influence created this very book is everybody I've ever met, which already puts our counter in the millions.

Once again, it still grows, because if you bought this from a bookshop, the same calculations are required, you have to consider everyone who bothered to get up to work that day, one of which would sell you the book, the people who run the bookshop and keep it open, all previous workers and the people who made the bookshop in the first place.

If you bought it online, it's even more complicated, because we have to consider the person who made the website you bought the book off of, the paying service which you paid for the book, the people who made and work for the paying service which you paid for the book, the people who made the internet have to get a shout-out, because without them you wouldn't be online at all, along with every subsequent discovery and advancement in the internet and all the people involved with that; also the people who influenced them and the people who influenced those people, along with everyone who signed up to the internet so that it grew in the way it did, which results in the amount of people who have influenced the moment you bought this book, as the ***entire world's population.***

My head hurts again, however the point I'm making is that if given enough thought, we can realise that every moment isn't just happening.

Everything is connected in some way; everyone has had an impact in creating the world in some way.

We could spend a whole book looking at the finite details, but for the purpose of my point, nothing that you do is irrelevant, everything that happens is a direct result of an infinite number of actions and lives, which have directly and indirectly created the moment you bought the book.

And that's just thinking of their impact on your life; we haven't even considered the amount of people who impacted their life which resulted in them impacting your life.

So our brains don't fry, let's make it personal.

I want you to think of someone who you've chosen to have in your life, a friend, a child, a partner who created that child, a lover and I want you think about the moment you first met, where was it, how did it happen, who was there?

Because that moment you and that person met, wasn't just chance, again, it was a direct result of all your previous actions; you could never of met your partner if you hadn't broken up with your ex, you could never of become friends with your best-mate unless you'd gone to that interview to get that job you met at… you get the idea.

Think about all the life decisions you made which resulted in you and that person meeting; the number of things that had to happen are astoundingly, insanely big. However we're not done, because now you need to consider this; your whole life lead up to the very moment you met.

Every single decision you ever made in some way has helped create the moment you met them, your whole childhood, learning to talk, learning to walk, all these trivial things we forget about, our school years, everything we learnt in those school years which we sued to sit exams to get into a college or a university, where we used those years to learn more, drink more, party more and then sit more exams which results we used to get into a job, where we work to make money, which we've spent our whole lives choosing what to spend that money on; basically, everything you've ever done in your whole life up until that point, created the exact moment which you and that chosen person met.

So the amount of things that has to happen to you, to make you meet that person is quite literally your whole life, however we're not even done yet.

Because now the number of connections that have happened in your whole life has to be *doubled*; because the exact same thing had to happen to the person you chose, in order for you both to arrive in the moment you met!

We're still not done, because now you have to times the amount of connections that have happened in both of your lives, by the infinite improbability of you both being born as you (the number from earlier) to give us…

An infinite improbability times by infinite impossibilities

So think about how lucky you both are to have each-other in your lives!

The worst part of this all? *We're still not done.*

Because thus far, we've only added in the chances of you both being born, by the connections that had to happen which resulted in you meeting; now we need to add in the amount of connections that have happened *since* you met.

Every moment of laughter, every argument which you chose to forgive, every time you've been in each-others company; every word, every blink, every single breath that you've taken together has continued that relationship with them, for every time you think about them, talk about them; for every single second that your alive with them in your life, is another moment of connection which creates the story of your relationship with them.

And that's just one person. Think about how many friends you have, how many partners you've had; every single person you've ever met is a direct result of your life up until that point and then a continuation of everything in your life that has happened with them in your life.

The point I'm making is this: ***Every single thing that has ever happened in your life, in some way, is a result of everything else that has ever happened in every single person's life that has ever been born... since the dawn of time.***

Take a quick break; you've earned it, because after we come back...

Sh*ts about to get even more crazy.

Chapter 20

Our Story Called Life

In this final chapter, I'm going to end the book by proving to you why our lives are stories and why life is always perfect until we see it in any other way (after all, I always liked a big, fancy ending; nothing worse than an anti-climax!).

In the last chapter, we bought the story of this book on the story of life (another paradox), full circle, realising that life really is perfect, once we have a personal revolution, so I hope this book has helped start you on the road to changing, to having your own revolution and seeing the bigger picture, I hope you're now on your journey and ready to take your own steps forward.

You may not change by tomorrow, but if you're closer to it now then you were yesterday, you're heading in the right direction. I hope reading this has informed you of things you weren't aware of, motivated you to go and make a difference and if nothing else made you think about the current life you're living and how awesome it really could be, or how awesome it already is, even if you may not feel that way right now.

Because I believe that its people like you, who want to change the world for the better, are the ones who will, I believe that if your go on your journey as I'm on mine with love and compassion, then we will be the changes we wish to see happen in the world.

Like we've said, people who genuinely have love in their heart, will all say the same thing, because what they're saying is the inherit truth we all know, they all may have their own opinions or spins on the truth, but it's still the same underlying message, just how all religions have the same underlying message, just how all types of yoga have the same goal, just how all meditation is trying to achieve the same state of mind, all these different way of connecting to consciousness or changing your life have the same underlying message because it's the truth, it's the truth that I know deep-down and the truth you know deep-down and the truth we all know deep-down because it's that inner-knowledge in all of us; **it's our inherent awesomeness.**

That inner-divinity that flashes when we hear and see other people connecting to something greater and maybe on day they'll eventually come to an end, but someone else will take up the truth and embody it, because it transcends the political puppets, it transcends people stuck in the day-to-day boring routine and it transcends the greedy consumers trying to cash in on the poor souls trapped in boring lives.

It will always be there, it's what's real and it's accessible to all of us, we don't have to be famous or on the telly to embody this truth, it's within in all of us, yes, it's in some famous people and a lot of these people are famous because of how much they've dedicated their life to it, however that truth is there for all of us to access and to start helping others achieve it and nobody deserves to connect to that higher-source, to achieve what they want from life and get all their wishes and desires than *you* do.

Because what are you waiting for? What's really stopping you, apart from the current story inside your head? Because while you're waiting your wasting time, we can deal with fear, we don't need to wait one more minute because we have to go and aim for the top, to chase and believe in every dream we have, we have to give it our all and not be afraid if it doesn't quite work the first time. There's not a good enough excuse, there's no better moment to choose then right now, because you're only living once.

You, reading this last chapter right now, nobody in this universe deserves that second of peace, that minute of laughter, that state of bliss, that connection to consciousness than you do, because this is your universe, this is your world, this is your life and I promise you that by acting with love and compassion in your heart, you will achieve what you wish, you're amazing, unique and the fact you're here, reading this means you either know me and have bought this book out of pity to make me feel better (and if that is you, then you are even more beautiful and I tip my hat to you, thank you mum, thank you for buying 38 copies of this) or because you're trying to change your life or others' lives and that is ***amazing.***

The chances of you, of you being born are so unlikely that the fact your alive is incredible in itself, throw in the fact you are literally made of stardust (good old Ziggy) and that you're looking for something deeper, it all means that no matter what you think or feel about yourself, that you *simply* are amazing, you are beautiful and I'm grateful that we've connected, even if it's just through these pages, because you honestly deserve nothing less, so be fearless, love yourself and love life, ***you're going to smash it!***

And so to finish, I'd like to remind you on some of the things we've learnt throughout this journey....

Our life is fragile, it's short, we're not going anywhere or heading towards anything, our life in black and white has 'no purpose'... It's up to us to give life colour, to give life meaning, and we can find that beauty within each and every moment if we look within and realise the beauty that life has to offer in every instance.

Politically, by disobeying the current system peacefully and instead choosing to operate in ways which seem more suited to our human nature, we can create a global change in which a shift in procedure can occur, once we've all had an internal shift in consciousness, we will be functioning on a higher level, a higher frequency of existence then that of the current political and media narrative and so it will become obsolete and not be our main focus but simply the on goings of people working of a lower level of living, now that we will be surrounded by love and contentment.

Our global problems can be solved by all looking within ourselves and learning to both understand and love one another, even if we have different opinions or interests in how to live our life, if we all sort out ourselves, the problem would resolve themselves.

Remember we can shift our world, our reality into anything we want, at any giving moment, once we have our personal revolutions, our world will change and allow us to develop an ideal existence for ourselves and encourage others to do the same with compassion and all of that is possible *right now*!

The true connection to our consciousness or 'higher-self' is what we're all striving for, each of us find it easiest to achieve this in different ways, however experiencing all avenues allows us to find out which one works best for us.

Our pasts are stories we choose to tell ourselves, our futures stories that we try to anticipate, the only thing that is real is 'now' and it's 'now' where true connection and beauty is found.

The three ways we can make a change to our realities is to reflect and change ourselves, to do something to affect the world around us and to help someone else affect the world around us, if we can do all these three things then change can and will happen.

We're only given two definite dates in our lives, our birthdate and death date. However these dates aren't what is relevant; it's the dash in-between these dates because this is where life is really lived, so make it amazing.

And when given a choice, most of us choose *carrot.*

So how should we bring this whole story to an end?

Well I'd like to talk about something we touched on briefly in the last chapter, the thing that makes us who we are, the thing that bring us together and the thing that makes us human; **connection**.

Because despite the current story some of us live too, we aren't the only creatures to inherit the earth, Dinosaurs were equally dominant but then wiped out as quickly as a nuclear explosion would wipe us out. It's obvious that being the dominant species through primal, animalistic force simply because you are the majority will never be long-lasting in the big scheme of the universe, a mass connection to a low-frequency of consciousness, that stimulates only the reptilian mind, will only result is discontentment as a species and as individuals.

So what is the secret that has connected us to one another, to evolve beyond any species, to make us spiritual beings on the verge of immortality with the power to destroy the very foundations we've created by the push of a button, what is the secret to that under-lying connectedness of the connectedness consciousness that we call God, Science, Spirituality, that gives us an identity, a reality to exist within and a life to have meaning?

The secret is the common-stories in our heads.

We've evolved into conscious, spiritual beings, closer towards 'enlightenment' then gorillas due to the fact we've developed and tapped into the divine side of our nature, large numbers of strangers can co-operate and co-create successfully by believing in common myths. By living to the same stories inside our heads, we can all unite and then use our power as a majority to evolve and elevate our consciousness forward, to connect with something deeper because we are all connected together by common principles that make us human.

Does this mean that the journey of life, of our species, of sentient life, is a journey from a singular, primal organism, into a united, connected consciousness at the bed of all phenomena?

Well that's what many religions, science theories and spiritual teachings would suggest. Whether it be the belief in reincarnation, enlightenment or the attraction of positive and negative ions, the collision of atoms which created life in the very first place, or perhaps even the creation of Adam and Eve, which every story you look at, all stories have the common theme of a uniting or connection between two or more things, always progressing towards a total unity of everything.

The key word here is "*common.*" For the purpose of human cooperation, evolution and revolution, the issue isn't whether people believe true things, or good things, but whether enough of them believe the same things.

Human beings — through stories, through religion, and eventually through governments, laws, and political ideologies, technologies, culture and everything we've covered in this book, all these things stem from us and the story we tell ourselves— we create common understandings of reality that provide the basis for massive, evolutionarily unprecedented levels of cooperation and connection and that's why humans dominate the earth, we all live to a similar story inside our heads.

This is why a political, media, social or human revolution will all come from a personal revolution; once we change that common story we live to inside our heads from economic wealth to spiritual wealth, from fear and desire to compassion and forgiveness and from hatred to love, then we can, on a global scale, live as self-aware conscious beings all connected to the under-lying connectedness which is a connected consciousness, globally living together through the very principles that make us human; love, peace and connection and individually elevated consciously and grounded in the present moment, understanding life is always perfect until we get distracted to see it any other way.

Let me now explain to you, in one grand final moment of enlightenment, why life is always perfect and why our lives really are stories.

Firstly, let me remind you that we've just worked out that we all are physically created, but the reason we all are sentient, spiritually advanced beings, is because we have all lived to a common story, meaning that the reason we are human beings is because we all have the same story inside our head, give or take a few details.

The whole first part of this book was examining the story we've all been living too in recent years and why this story needs to change; the second part of the book was looking at ways we can change the story, along with what we should change it into, so, to finish, I'd like to tell you why you can do that right now, why right now is the only time you can actually ever do it.

Here's the truth; your whole life is one story, my whole life has been another story, every single life there has ever been, every man, every woman, every single animal and every living organism has been part of a world which we've taken into our consciousness and created a perception, a story of our lives, which has seen us become beings who are on the verge of understanding and conceptualising the truth and meaning of life, all because we live to a story inside of our heads, as a collective, united, human race.

We are the direct result of a million moments and a billion decisions; we are the culmination of *all* that has ever happened before us and we are the foundation for everything that *will* ever happen after us.

That's not even all of it, because we are also the result of all the other moments that never happened; remember we are not experience life, we are writing it and so when working out the chances of this moment, not only do we have to consider all the moments that have happened, the things we have experienced and lived through, *but also every single moment that could've happened but didn't*, every moment we didn't experience and there are an infinite amount of these moments.

The girl you nearly asked out but didn't and then never saw again; the guy you decided to walk past instead of stopping to say hello; the job you quit or the chance you took, but even more finitely then that, every single action, no matter how irrelevant, even the moments you looked left instead of right, the moment you held your breath that second longer, or blinked twice, the moment you paused an extra second on *this* word because it's in italics or re-read the last sentence... all of these create a story which could've had a billion, tiny, little different details.

Fact: for every decision we make, there is around a quadrillion decisions we could've made but didn't.

I want you to really think about that. Every single thing that ever happens in your life will amount to an infinite number, but on top of that, for every decision you make within that infinite number of your life; every single moment of that infinite number had a quadrillion number of things that could've happened instead but didn't.

- If even one of those quadrillion things that didn't happen had happened instead of the thing that did happen, your life, and your story would be in some way different.
- If your story was slightly different, every single decision that happened in this new story, would have, in every moment a new number of quadrillion

- This same thought-process applies to every single person that ever lived, as every single decision that every person that has ever lived has ever made has created, in some way, the current world we live in, along with every single decision every single person didn't make.
- If any single person had even made one single different decision to the one they did make, in the whole history of existence; we would be living in a slightly different world, a slightly different universe and a slightly different story.

Einstein says it best when he says "There are two ways to view life; one as though nothing is a miracle, or secondly, as though everything is".

Think of our world, our universe, our stories, like a beach; every-time you take a single step on the beach, it can never be the exact same again, if even one grain of sand is moved, then the beach is now a different beach as to what it was and so, in relation to our earlier realisation, metaphorically we really are just a grain of sand... but what an important grain we are.

Because for every time we take just one step along the beach, we are forever changing the story of the human race. If an all-seeing, all ominous entity could look through every single moment of history, part of that history would be every single thing, thought and decision you've ever had (to me this sounds awfully like the ever-present God in many religions).

So this means that when working out the chances of this moment that…

- This moment you are experiencing right now, it isn't just the result of everything that has ever happened in existence to you, but also everything that has ever happened to everybody that has ever lived.
- That then has to be added to the result of every single decision you didn't make, along with every following decision that would've created, alongside the same thing happening to everybody else who's ever lived.
- Finally to complete this brain-melt-down, on top of all the decisions you did and didn't make, as well as every decision everybody else did or didn't make (and the infinite possibilities that could've made and then the possibilities all those would've made), we have to times all of that by the infinite unlikelihood of your birth from the last chapter and then times that by the number of every single organism that ever lived *also* then times by the amount of organisms that could've lived but didn't.

Which means this moment is the culmination of everything that ever OR never happened; to everyone who ever OR never lived.

That is why life is perfect, why life is a story; how the f*ck can it not be?

The whole of existence; every moment of laughter, every tear, every smile, every breath, every heart-beat has created an infinite impossibility which has collided with infinite improbabilities to create this very moment, how can it not be anything but *perfect*?

Whether that be as a result of God's creation, scientific laws or spiritual truths is really secondary in importance, because the truth is we can actually understand life on a deeper level, we don't need to understand why we are here, we don't need to understand who put us here, or what we are meant to do according to politicians, presidents or other people, we don't need to prove why we're right, we don't need to be martyrs or revolutionaries, all we really have to do, to find the meaning of life is realise that if we take all labels and words away from how we're perceiving life; that life is always indescribably perfect.

How can we be anything but happy, content and perfect, how can we be anything less than spiritual beings of total unconditional compassion, how can we not be all connected to the underlying connectedness of a connected consciousness which all phenomena stems from?

All the stories that have ever happened has created a blank page for you, the whole of creation and all of existence has created this moment of your life...

where you have something only you can give to the world.

We are now at the point in our history, where we now seek a new connection, a re-connection to that indescribable phenomena we all can feel, the questions which we are asking are perhaps a little harder to uncover as the answers may not so much about describing, categorising and labelling the discoveries we find, but simply feeling, embracing and connecting with it.

Whether we use a 'scientific', 'religious' or 'spiritual' way of thoug-processing to come to terms with this doesn't really matter, as, when you strip all the labels back, they are all the same thing.

We don't need to be worrying about trying to understand it in its entirety, trying to cage and label it, or spend our whole lives trying to disprove someone else's version of it, but instead marvel at the fact that we, as scientists, religious men and women, politicians, journalists, civilians, celebrities; males, transsexuals, females, blacks, whites, homosexual, heterosexuals; spiritual gurus, animal-lovers, planet-lovers, friends, partners, lovers a-like can realise the only label that's ever-mattered:

Human.

I'd like to end by saying the point of this book, the point of what I'm saying, to me, the whole point and meaning of life is that...

Life can be powerful and yet be so fragile, life can be structured and yet so chaotic, life is forever and yet it's only ever right now, life can be finding the meaning behind the existence of the universe; life can also be enjoying the trees outside your window.

Life is whatever we want it to be, so live with compassion, live with peace in your mind; because the thing that makes you the beautiful, unique organism you are, the thing that separates you as a spiritual, self-aware being with a neocortex to feel, to thrive and to live with love: *is the story inside your head*.

You are infinite, you are immortal, you are timeless, you are nothing, you are everything, you're an author and most importantly you are you…

Quite simply; one life, one love, live.

And so to the conscious spark of inherent awesomeness within you, go now and make a perfect journey of our personal revolution and then use this to write the perfect story…

Our story called life

Final Words

Life

    The universe is ominous, reality is forever, and existence is eternal; humanity is temporary, everything externally, even words and thoughts, are just perceptions of manifestations... but despite all that, that something so great, that transcends all and is unimaginable, that something that we all know is there and have tried to understand since the dawn of time, despite its ominous, and indescribable power; that higher power, that consciousness we're all aware of, that divinity within all of us, that expression of reality experiencing itself; that causes one cell to become two, that spins quarks and planets. That total transcendence we can get by living in the moment; despite its cosmic power and transcending energies, all of life's problems and all of life's beauties, the one super-power we have, the one tool we have always and will always have for change; the one indescribable compulsion that language, self and being rest upon, that spark to come together, that has omnificent and omnipresent characteristics, we all actually know;

The only thing that gives existence meaning and describes that indescribable energy can actually be described by one simple, familiar feeling:

And we all know it's...

Love.

Told you you'd be alright! (I'll see you in the sequel)

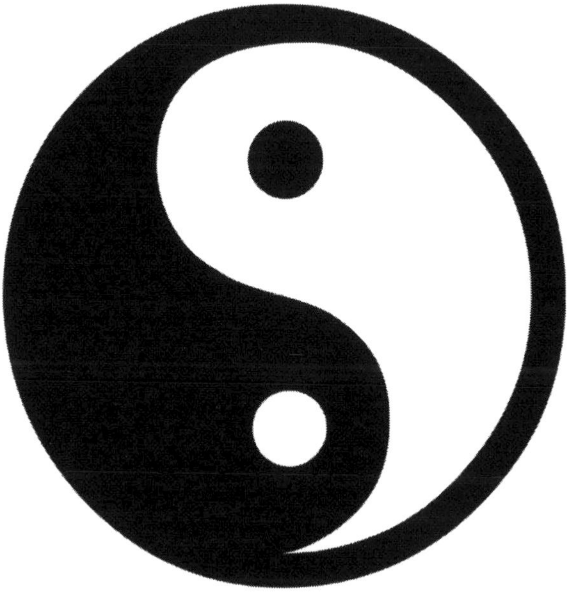